A SPRINGTIME TO REMEMBER

LUCY COLEMAN

Boldwood

First published in Great Britain in 2019 by Boldwood Books Ltd.

A CIP catalogue record for this book is available from the British Library.

Paperback ISBN 978-1-83889-052-0

Ebook ISBN 978-1-83889-050-6

Kindle ISBN 978-1-83889-051-3

Audio CD ISBN 978-1-83889-053-7

MP3 CD ISBN 978-1-83889-430-6

Digital audio download ISBN 978-1-83889-049-0

Boldwood Books Ltd
23 Bowerdean Street
London SW6 3TN
www.boldwoodbooks.com

AUTHOR'S NOTE

The Palace of Versailles is legendary and awe-inspiring. After numerous visits over the years, I hope – with all sincerity – that my descriptions throughout have done it justice.

So too, in sharing some of its history; but this story, including the characters I have created, is the product of my imagination.

I would like to pay tribute to those who have been involved in its long and colourful history. It's a place I think about often, in between visits, and I have no idea why I feel such a deep connection to it. But I do.

It was on one such visit, on 12 June 2018, that Lexie and Ronan first spoke to me.

A few months later, during a rather stormy English winter, I found myself transported back there. It is, indeed, a place to inspire both the heart and the mind.

PART I

MARCH 2018

1

WHEN FAIRY TALES COME TRUE

'Once upon a time there was a little girl who had a very big dream.'

'How big?' Little Maisie stares up at me questioningly. Surrounded by a mantle of shadows in the darkened room, only the tiny shaft of light seeping in from the landing allows me to see her baby-blue eyes. She's determined not to give in to sleep, but it's obvious she's fighting a losing battle.

Maisie blinks in rapid succession and already her breathing is beginning to slow.

'Hu-u-u-uge.' The sound of my soft whisper fills the air. 'And she promised herself she would never, ever, let anyone deter her from trying her hardest to make everything she wished for come true.'

I glance down at my darling niece and catch a fleeting glimpse of a smile before sleep finally whisks her away. Hesitant to make a move for fear of disturbing her, I decide to sit for a while, fascinated by that perfect little heart-shaped face. It tugs on my heart strings as I realise how much I'm going to miss her this spring.

As I'm about to ease myself up very gingerly off the bed, to my complete surprise her little voice suddenly rises up out of the darkness.

'When you come back you will tell me all about your adventure, won't you, Auntie Lexie?'

I reach across to smooth a few strands of hair away from her warm little cheek.

'Of course, I will. And it will be a story of palaces and kings and magical gardens that stretch out as far as the eye can see. Now go to sleep, beautiful girl, and keep a tight hold of Mr Panda, because he will keep you safe until I get home.' She snuggles her rather threadbare companion even closer.

Stooping to plant a kiss on her forehead, I notice she's fallen back to sleep. It's hard not to feel sad, because when I return, she'll probably have grown another inch and I will have missed so much. Even a few months can see so many changes in a five-year-old and she's growing up way too quickly. Maisie is an old head on young shoulders, and takes after me, rather than my sister, Shellie. Much to Shellie's annoyance.

I creep out to find my older sister in the kitchen, sitting at the breakfast bar leisurely reading her Kindle.

'That was quick, but Maisie was exhausted. Swimming always has that effect on her. She's going to miss you, you know.'

Shellie holds up her empty coffee mug and shakes it at me. I nod, sinking down onto the stool next to her as she jumps up and heads in the direction of the coffee machine.

'I know she's only a phone call away, but it won't be the same. She's my little buddy. You made a special one there, sis.'

Shellie laughs. 'Well, I might not have attained the lofty

heights of ambition and fame that my baby sister and my older brother have, but this is the life I wanted, so I'm happy.'

I studiously ignore the reference to our estranged brother, Jake. Success often comes at a price and, in his case, it went to his head. I guess family doesn't mean much if your ego tells you that you've outgrown the people who love you.

Reining in that little surge of anger his name always invokes, I watch Shellie as she moves around the kitchen. With baby number two due in seven months' time she's in her element. I know she's impatient, ticking off each precious day on her calendar at the thought of giving Maisie a sibling. Shellie is a mini version of Mum, whereas Jake and I take after our late father, Paul.

Chrissy, our mum, has always been the rock of the family because Dad was often away travelling, or home working late in his study. They were a team, though, and she was a bigger part of his success than most people realise. And because they were both happy in their respective roles, I can't remember them ever having a cross word.

Dad was someone who grabbed every opportunity and was determined to live his dream. Was he a little self-centred? Well, yes, I suppose he was, because as soon as he was away, it was as if we didn't really exist for him. But on his return, Dad would thrill us with stories that captured our imaginations and fired our enthusiasm.

Dad was lauded as one of the top wildlife photographers of his generation, and he lived for the thrill of capturing that perfect shot. With a long list of magazine articles and natural history programmes to his credit, he was always in demand. The fact that he died while doing something he loved seemed fitting in a tragic sort of way.

I remember the day of the fateful call and the phone

falling from Mum's ear as she struggled to take in the devastating news. Dad had a massive heart attack while filming on location in Tarangire National Park, in Tanzania. If only it had happened in the UK, maybe we could have...

'You haven't heard a word I've been saying, have you, Lexie?'

Shellie appears in front of me, proffering a mug of steaming coffee and one of her delicious, homemade chocolate and beetroot brownies.

'Sorry. My head is all over the place right now. So many last-minute things to do before I fly out tomorrow.'

She eases herself up onto the stool alongside me, frowning.

'No regrets? I mean, you're always heading off somewhere or other, but this is the longest stint in one go. I know there's a lot at stake for you personally on this one.'

I burst out laughing. 'A lot? You could say that. I'm sinking every penny I've saved into this, and it's my one-time shot.'

Absent-mindedly, she scoops the long blonde hair back from her face, yanking a scrunchy from around her wrist to pull it into a ponytail. I've always envied her hair, another gift bestowed by Mum, and my short, feathery look is about all I can do to tame my wavy mane. Taking after Dad doesn't come without its drawbacks.

'You aren't regretting this project?'

I shake my head. 'No. I don't want to be *just* a TV presenter any more.'

She smiles. 'Your chance, at last, to be a producer, too. You just like being in charge.'

The smile becomes more of a smirk – she knows me so well and yet her comment puts me on the defensive.

'Well, you know that I love gardening programmes. You can blame that on Grandma. All the time I spent with her in the garden as a child. And teaming up with cameraman Elliot Nielson is a dream come true. Elliot has great connections and has filmed at Versailles before. Fingers crossed, between us we can do the business.'

In fact, Elliot is setting out to make a big name for himself and his work already commands a lot of respect within the industry. But this project is a huge risk for him too, because, while in theory we have interest in this mini-series of documentaries we're going to be working on together, there's no signed contract yet. The reality of the situation is that no TV network will commit until we have something to show them, which means using our own money, and putting everything on the line.

'So, when exactly are you due back from Versailles?'

'The fourth of June, at the latest, as I'm hosting a new slot on the *Morning Sunshine* show. Elliot won't be working exclusively on our project while we're away as he has some paid work that he'll be doing in between filming. It was a big factor in him being able to commit to it, so I'm happy to work around him. What's left of my nest egg will keep me going until I get home, hopefully. The bonus is that this is finally the chance I've been waiting for, to spend time doing some family research.'

Shellie's forehead lifts as she pulls one of her renowned *is that wise?* faces.

'I guessed as much, but have you actually spelt that out to Mum?'

'What, that I want to dig around and find out more about Grandma's time in France? Well, I sort of assumed she'd take that for granted. I'm a journalist, after all, and I'll be in Versailles with time on my hands.'

'Good luck with that, then, as 1961 was a long time ago.' She rolls her eyes, clearly thinking any spare time I have could be better utilised.

'I loved Grandma Viv's stories about her childhood – she was a natural storyteller. You missed a lot not joining us in the garden, you know.'

Shelley bats her eyelashes at me. 'That's why your hands were always so filthy as a child and, besides, you were her undisputed favourite. She knew it was never my thing, anyway.'

'Well, I think you missed out. But as for her French adventure, well, it was strange because she wouldn't talk about it. I mean, what did Granddad think? They met, she was offered a once-in-a-lifetime opportunity to head off to France on a year's work experience and when she returned home, they were married. But she never once, as far as I can tell, mentioned her year away.

'Even in the letters she sent to Granddad she was secretive, and I have no idea why I had to talk Mum into letting me borrow the memory box. It's not like there's anything in there to hide, as the letters were simply little updates between them. But I am curious about what isn't there, aren't you? I mean, a year apart is a long time and I wonder what Granddad really felt about coming second to her other grand passion in life.'

Shellie looks at me, a hint of a frown working its way over her brow. 'This is precisely why I worry about you sometimes. When you get an idea in your head you simply won't give up. Grandma Viv had her own little adventure before settling down and if Granddad respected that, so should you.'

There are times when I find it hard to believe the two of us share any genes. How can Shellie shrug it off so easily when it's always been such a secret?

'But it's a part of our family history. Aren't you in the least bit curious? I wish she'd been around for much longer but at least some of her feisty spirit lives on in us. And now I want to discover the woman she was before she became our grandma. I don't see anything wrong with that. Her passion for horticulture never left her, but she turned her back on what could have been a very promising career for the love of one man. Don't you think that's an interesting story?'

'See! You're thinking of making a documentary out of it already! You and Jake are just like Dad. That drive is all well and good, but don't you ever long to switch off that mind of yours? Or simply let something be, because some things aren't meant to be aired to the world?' Exasperation is making the pitch in Shellie's voice rise up a level.

'Don't you want a husband and a Maisie of your own, one day? She'd love a cousin at some point in the not-too-distant future and if that ends up being from Jake, then I doubt they'll ever meet. I'm pinning my hopes on you, Lexie.'

The look she gives me feels like a reprimand.

'I love being an auntie because it's the best of both worlds. I get to enjoy and spoil her, then hand her back.' I give Shellie a grin.

'So, you're not missing the gorgeous Will, then?'

All my boyfriends seem to come and go, but that's life. The initial buzz just fades away with time, or it always has so far, anyway.

'No. It was fun, though, for a while. But seriously, Will works hard but parties even harder and I have more important things on which to expend my energy.'

The look my sister gives me is full of disapproval.

'Tick tock, Lexie. You're thirty next year and that's a big deal whether you want to acknowledge it, or not. I just worry that you're sinking everything into this project and what if it's not quite what you hope it's going to be?'

Just like Mum. 'Stop worrying about me. I don't need a man in my life right now. I've never found one quite like your Drew. Maybe one day I will, but, in the meantime, I'm not going to wish my life away. If the right one pops up and grabs my attention, then fine. But this project *is* my baby and I'm going to nurture it every step of the way like the fussiest of mothers.'

Shellie throws her hands in the air.

'You're a lost cause. What is it with this family? Am I the only one who inherited anything at all from our mother?'

I lean in to throw my arms around her.

'Don't think I don't appreciate that you always have my best interests at heart. Or that you give it to me straight when you're worried. But this is my dream and I'm fed up of people holding me back. I mean... I'm not saying that's what you're doing, but after the thing with Jake... Being sacked by one's own brother was beyond humiliating. He never even asked for my side of the story, and when your own flesh and blood gets rid of you without a second thought, well, everyone around you tends to think the worst.'

She sighs, looking into my eyes, and I know deep down she understands.

'It closed a lot of doors, but you've made it, Lexie. People recognise your face everywhere you go and you are a daytime TV star. What more could you possibly do to prove yourself? At some point you need to relax a little.'

'Standing still isn't an option, Shellie. I want to show everyone that I have what it takes to be a producer. And besides, this won't be all work. I'm going to immerse myself in the French way of life and you know that old saying, a change is as good as a rest. Versailles, here I come!'

Standing here in front of this pretty little cottage, its pale grey paintwork with the tiniest hint of blue reflecting that rustic, French vibe, I take a moment to gaze up at the façade of my home for the next few months. It's every bit as quaint as it looked in the photos on the agency website and I couldn't be more delighted.

It's one of six mews cottages clustered around a beautiful, and very old, cobbled courtyard. With two cottages on each of the three sides facing the entrance, it's a gated community in miniature, hidden away behind a row of four-storey buildings with shops and offices at ground-floor level, and apartments above. The buildings act as a welcome sound barrier, given the proximity of the bustling Avenue De Paris, the central artery of three main thoroughfares leading to the iconic Palace of Versailles.

The entrance to this very secluded hideaway is two enormous, ornate metal gates sandwiched between a charming little café and a boulangerie. It couldn't be more perfect, or more enchanting, and is an oasis of tranquillity just metres away from the busy chaos of the streets.

Number Six, La Cour Céleste abuts the high wall that runs behind the rear of the properties on the main road and, whilst rather modest in size, these wonderful little cottages have the feel of robustly built and characterful stone houses in miniature. Each property has a golden emblem set above the front door, based on a celestial theme. Number six has a star; the others feature the sun, a moon, a planet, an angel and a King's crown. The latter, no doubt, a reference to the Sun King himself, Louis XIV.

There are no delusions of grandeur because of the simplicity of style, but at three storeys high and with the trademark grey slate, Mansard-style roof – often referred to as a French roof – the four sloping sides do make it rather whimsical. Three elaborate dormer windows with the traditional lead dressings make the scale pleasing to the eye. It's not just a roof, it's a statement and one repeated throughout the city of Versailles.

The ground-floor frontage of number six comprises an integral garage, next to which is a storage facility accessed by double wooden doors. A few feet the other side of that is the entrance. A standard rectangular building face-on, inside it only extends back the depth of one room, albeit generously sized.

The lintels and reveals around the garage, doors, and windows have been fashioned from huge pieces of stone and are beautifully preserved. The whitewashed stonework contrasts nicely with the soft colours of the paintwork and the attention to detail adds to the overall charm.

None of the other properties have a garage, I'm surprised to see, but mainly because there are four raised flower beds housing manicured shrubs and a couple of medium-sized trees. Three of the properties have weathered metal chairs and bistro tables in front of them and, together with the greenery, it feels neighbourly and well loved.

I'm tempted to check out the garage first, grateful I went for a smaller, economy hire car, which I hope will fit easily inside. Street parking is notoriously difficult so close to the palace. The taxi had to double park while I popped into the boulangerie to collect the key and the entrance code for the gate.

Instead, I turn the key in the front door and lug the two suitcases inside. After more than a year of planning, it's all suddenly happening and it's hard to take it in. I'm buzzing with optimism and I can't wait to get started. But first things first.

I realise I can only carry one suitcase up the stairs at a time. Just as well I sent the taxi driver away, as two of us wouldn't have fitted into this tight space, anyway. But what it lacks in size, it makes up for in cuteness.

Easing the first suitcase around the sharp turn in the stairs, I hold in my elbows as I push through into the open-plan living area. With beautiful old sash windows to the front and rear elevations of the room, it's wonderfully light and, while the kitchen area in the far left-hand corner is compact, it's perfectly adequate.

Placing my heavy load down on the floor, I stroll across the room to gaze down onto the courtyard. It feels peaceful and rather decadent. With all the windows closed there's hardly any sound from the traffic at all, with only the noisy wail of a siren in the distance disturbing the peace.

Glancing around at the other properties, I have no way of knowing whether any of the other five cottages are occupied, or not. Maybe they're private holiday homes rather than rentals. They have all been sympathetically maintained as beautifully as this one and in keeping with their character. Registering the aged parquet flooring beneath my feet, I turn around to take in every little detail of the room.

With a double sash window above the garage and a single above the front door, the amount of light helps to make the space feel a lot bigger than it is; the only drawback is that when I stare out I'm looking directly at the two cottages on the opposite side of the courtyard.

'Note to self,' I say out loud, as I retrace my footsteps to retrieve the second suitcase. 'No walking around naked.'

In the centre of the room there are two three-seater sofas facing each other, to the right of which is a charming alcove with an inset, bespoke cupboard. It follows the general rustic style of the cottage and has been hand-painted, many times probably, over the years. A TV screen sits on top of the lower half of the cupboard and above it are several shelves crammed with old books.

With a case in each hand, I head towards the rear-facing windows. They look out over a higgledy-piggledy collection of roofs and beyond, in the distance, a forest of tall trees looking naked without their leaves. Very possibly they could even stand within the luxurious *parc*, or grounds of the palace itself.

Part way along the wall to my left, the kitchen area comprises one double base sink unit sandwiched between an upright fridge-freezer and an oven and hob, in front of which is a generously sized table and four chairs. A range of wall units, in an off-white shaker-style, wrap around the corner section and tie in well with the design of the alcove cupboard on the opposite side of the room.

The staircase spirals upwards, disappearing into a shaft of brilliant white light. The metal steps are much wider than they looked in the photographs on the website, which is a relief, although I climb them rather gingerly, my hands full. Looking upwards, I see above my head a vaulted ceiling with a large Velux window. Despite the chill in the air, the sun is making a bold appearance and streaming through; little particles of dust kicked up by my feet are like a shower of tiny confetti.

Surprisingly, it's not quite as cramped as I'd feared, and the light from above filtering into the small, square landing makes a huge difference. It's usually wasted space anyway, I muse as I'm faced with the choice of two doors.

The one to my left is partly open and I nudge it back with my foot. It turns out to be a reasonably sized, elongated bathroom with a rather grand reclaimed slipper bath, a toilet and hand basin; there's also a half cupboard set into a recess next to a dormer window.

When I stoop to open the doors to the cupboard, I'm surprised to see there's a washing machine inside. Well, I guess I won't want for anything while I'm here, but a shower would have been handy. Guess I'm going to have to factor in a little more bathroom time every morning, as you can't possibly slip into such a grand old bath with anything other than a little pampering in mind.

I head back out onto the small landing area to check out the door directly in front of me. As I step through, the wall to the bathroom runs along the left-hand side creating a small inner corridor, but as the room opens out it's at least double the size of the bathroom. My eyes go straight to the apex of the roof where the beautifully exposed timbers ooze charm.

I was expecting restricted headroom as is often the case

with attic rooms, so this is a bonus and it actually feels light and bright. On the far wall there is a king-sized bed flanked by two shabby chic bedside tables. To my left, where the wall of the bathroom returns, there is a hand-painted desk and chair: a perfect niche for a study area. The two larger dormer windows to the front give plenty of natural light over the desk and mean it's easy to access the other side of the bed.

Opposite the windows is an enormous built-in wardrobe, which is a great use of the eaves space where the angle of the roof slopes rather steeply.

The paintwork in here is a very soft blue and the walls plain white to match the bedding. It's simple and it works. Slipping off my shoes and leaving them next to the suitcases, I head back into the bathroom, the old oak floorboards creaking slightly beneath my feet as I walk.

What I already love about this place is that it isn't full of things; there are no ornaments cluttering up the space and yet it feels so welcoming. Simple, country charm at its very best with a hint of elegance and it's all mine for the next three months.

Throwing my arms around my body, I hug myself tightly, letting excitement wash over me. This is the culmination of a dream I've had for a very long time and, for all my bravado and gritty determination to succeed, I needed a place to stay that felt special. Like a home from home. The moment I saw the photos of this place online it was calling out to me and now I'm here it feels so right.

I find myself wondering if Grandma Viv stayed in a little place like this back in 1961. Wouldn't it be wonderful if I could find where she lived during that year and trace her journey? I smile to myself as thoughts of her begin to fill my head.

As I lean across the bath to swing open the window, aside

from a very low hum of traffic in the background, all I can hear are two birds in one of the trees in the courtyard. They are singing their hearts out and taking it in turns, as if in conversation. The birdsong soars and dips quite magically and it makes my heart skip a beat. It's full of hope, excitement and promise. This is my destiny, I'm sure of it. Being here, in Versailles, fulfilling a long-held dream, I can already feel the history of this city pulling at me from all directions. Is this what Grandma Viv felt when she first arrived here? And why did she never speak about it?

* * *

'Hey, Lexie, how're you doing? I'm here at last. Are you all settled in?'

It's Elliot and it is a bit of a relief to know he's arrived safely, too.

'Yes. It's a brilliant little place and a gentle stroll up to the palace.'

'Great. Sounds perfect. How's the hire car?'

I can hear a teasing smile coming through in his question.

'My brand-new soft-top is a great little drive actually. I've already taken her around the block and thank goodness I didn't get anything bigger, as the garage is tiny. How's your apartment?'

Elliot does a lot of work for a French company whose offices are in Paris. It's only the fact that he has contacts from a video shoot he did inside the Palace of Versailles two years ago that persuaded them to get on board with our own project. They are so notoriously reluctant to let cameras in that I'm still keeping everything crossed nothing goes wrong and no one changes their mind.

'It's splendid. I'm probably ten minutes away from you. It's a new complex off the Avenue de Sceaux. It has a huge TV and surround sound, so I'm happy.' Suddenly, there's a loud, ear-shattering sneeze.

'Sorry, this damn cold is a real pain,' he adds.

I laugh.

'Well, let's hope the sunshine clears it up quickly. At least it's warmer here than in the UK and nowhere near as damp. We can't have you sneezing while filming. No news from anyone?' I ask tentatively.

'News?'

'I mean anything from your contact at the palace.'

'No. I wasn't expecting to hear anything. They're awaiting our draft schedule for approval prior to our first meeting though, so you and I need to sit down and thrash that out as quickly as possible. I've been in contact with Cameron and confirmed the dates that he's available, too.'

Screwing up my eyes triumphantly, I silently fist-pump the air. Cameron Davis is our sound man and, although I don't know him very well, he's worked with Elliot several times in the past. It's all looking so promising, but I won't believe it until I'm standing on the terrace at the rear of the Palace of Versailles and gazing out over the famous Grand Canal – a folly only King Louis XIV would have been bold enough to commission.

'Right, dinner is on me tonight,' he adds.

I can hardly hear him over the excitement buzzing in my head. There are so many reasons this could be life-changing. Firstly, if this project takes off, I transition from simply being a presenter to becoming a producer making programmes about topics I find truly inspiring. Secondly, I get to savour the delights of Versailles in springtime. And last, but not least, I might discover what Grandma Viv did while she was here.

As she always said, life should be lived to the full. My father's success tended to overshadow everything in our family, although as the years passed it became very apparent that Jake intended to make his mark in a big way. But Grandma Viv was the one who kept drumming into us girls that we should chase our dreams, too. Fearing, I think, that with two very strong, and at times warring, males in the house our successes wouldn't get a chance to shine.

'Success comes when it comes, but only after an enormous amount of hard work and application,' she explained. 'If it comes easily, then it usually doesn't last very long. In my experience women often have a harder battle to prove themselves, but then times have changed for the most part,' she reflected once, rather wistfully I thought at the time. It made me wonder if she had fought and lost a battle of her own at some point.

'When your chance comes just grab it, Lexie.' I remember her words so clearly. It was the summer of my final exams before I was hopefully starting college, and I was filled with anxiety and self-doubt.

'Like you did, Grandma?' I asked her, eager to hear more about her own experiences.

She smiled at me then.

'I don't regret one single second of my life. The good, or the bad. I was true to myself, Lexie, and that's the key to happiness. Sometimes we're not sure what it is we want, but the most important thing of all is not to have any regrets. Promise me you won't settle for anything less than a life spent in pursuit of your dreams, because you and I are very similar. I had my adventure and it allowed me to come home and find true happiness with your granddad. Without that, my life might have been full of *what ifs* and they don't make for a happy life.'

Well, I'm doing the best I can, Grandma, and I'm determined to take your advice.

3

THE TEAM IS COMPLETE

Elliot stands up as I approach the table for our working dinner.

'This is rather nice,' I comment as he leans in to kiss my cheek. 'How's the cold?'

'Better, thanks. It's left me with an annoying cough though, but I'm sneeze-free now, thank goodness.'

A waiter appears at my side to seat me at the cosy little table for two, before Elliot even has time to step forward to pull out my chair.

Turning my head to give the incredibly handsome young Frenchman a warm smile, I settle myself down. 'Merci.'

Elliot can see I'm a little puzzled at the choice of such a smart restaurant, and I'm glad I made a bit of an effort, choosing a simple, but pretty, dress to wear. He's wearing a pale blue shirt, and navy trousers, looking very man about town. But then he is very handsome, very talented and very engaged to the vivacious Mia.

'We deserve this,' he informs me. 'I wanted to kick off our time here with a bit of a celebration. This project was a great idea of yours, Lexie. I think our new business venture is going to snowball once we succeed in selling this first series. Ah, and here comes the waiter with a rather nice bottle of red wine I've ordered, ready for the toast.'

'Lovely,' I reply, trying hard to contain the growing smile on my face. If Elliot has a good feeling about this, then I'm not kidding myself in thinking we really have a shot.

Elliot nods to the waiter for me to have the honour of tasting the wine and he pours a little of the ruby-red liquid into my glass. I rather self-consciously pick it up and gently swirl it around before drawing it up to my nose. Savouring the richness of warm blackberries and a curious hint of – honestly – chocolate; that first sip is comforting, welcoming and rich.

'Perfect, thank you.'

The waiter gives me a little smile of approval before pouring an inch of wine into each glass. Then he turns on his heel and sashays away as if he's walking on air. I could sit and watch him all night; walking like that is an art form.

'Ahem,' Elliot clears his throat, drawing my gaze back in his direction.

'That's an expensive bottle of wine. You must let me pay for this meal, Elliot. It was your contact who managed to get our foot in the door and without that connection this would probably have been a project that never went anywhere,' I admit.

'Next time – the start of our second project, eh? It's all about timing, Lexie. Your idea came at precisely the right moment. The popularity of the lavish drama *Versailles* by Canal Plus just showed there is a fascination with all things related to the palace that never wanes. The Palace of Versailles and its history is iconic, but people are also curious about what goes on there today. Honestly, the timing couldn't be more perfect. So, here's to us and to a very fruitful journey ahead.'

We touch our raised glasses and he smiles at me over the top of them.

'And Mia will forgive me for whisking you away for the entire spring?' I ask tentatively.

He nods, taking a moment to turn his head and cough. 'She knew I had to spend some serious time in Paris anyway, so it's not a problem. She said she was glad to see the back of me and my germs.' We both laugh.

'How easy will it be to coordinate everyone's calendars and work around the availability of the interviewees?'

Elliot pulls out a small file from his leather satchel, placing it on the table.

'Let's order first, as the waiter is hovering, and we can discuss the draft schedule in between courses. Le Paradis is famous for its classic côte de boeuf, which they serve on a thick wooden slab. It's hearty, but goodness me it's good – trust me.'

Elliot is so well travelled in his line of work and at times I feel rather parochial in his company. Being a TV presenter, all I usually see is the inside of a studio and while to some it may appear to be a glamorous lifestyle, it really isn't. Sure, I get to attend the odd award ceremony but even those are few and far between. By comparison, he's used to restaurants as smart as this and seeing sights around the world I can only dream about. Maybe if our joint project is a success, then who knows what the future might bring? As Grandma Viv said, the only limit on how far a person can take their dream is the limit they set themselves.

* * *

After another long and busy day, I now have the task of pulling together the draft schedule, based on my conversation with Elliot last night. We need to have the first official version thrashed out ready to email across in advance of our meeting at the palace tomorrow. The sound of tinkling chimes sends me scurrying for my phone where I see it's Shellie calling, and a welcome face comes into view.

'Hi, Maisie. How are you, my darling girl?'

'Good, thank you, Auntie Lexie. Missing you. I wanted to see where you are staying. Mummy said I could.'

'Let me walk you around the cottage. Hang on, I'll take you over to the window to show you the little courtyard at the front.'

I stride across and turn my phone to slowly pan from left to right.

'Oh, Auntie Lexie, it's so pretty! I wish I was there with you.' Her voice drops in pitch, rather glumly.

When I turn the screen back around, she's looking decidedly grumpy.

'I'll send you photos, I promise, so you won't miss a thing. Here, let me show you the living room behind me. I've turned the table into my desk though, so it's a bit messy – lots of paperwork. How was school today?'

'Good. We had strawberry shortcake for pudding,' she enthuses, her eyes shining again, and I start laughing.

'Well, lucky you!'

Shellie appears in the background, leaning in to see what's on the screen.

'Tea is ready, Maisie. I need to have a quick word with Auntie Lexie, so say goodbye.'

Maisie pulls a face but blows me a kiss before handing over the phone.

'Remember to send me some pictures,' she trills musically as she walks away.

'Hey, sis. Sorry I haven't had time to call to let you know I arrived safely. What with settling in and then trying to finalise this schedule—'

'Hmm... more like out of sight, out of mind. But I know you, your head will be full of the task ahead, so I didn't expect anything different. Neither did Mum.'

Oh, dear. Mega fail.

'I'll text her in a bit, I promise. She knows what I'm like. Nothing has happened... yet. When I have any news, I'll call her for a chat but we're still sorting the admin stuff. I'm due to meet our interpreter in about an hour's time and after a day hardly moving from my temporary desk, I need the distraction.'

She grimaces at me.

'Sounds lonely to me. I couldn't do that – head off to a place I've never visited before and set up a temporary home. Funny how, being the middle child, I'm sandwiched between two annoyingly successful over-achievers.'

I groan. 'Well, that remains to be seen for me. And anyway, you have one gorgeous little girl and another baby on the way. If I think my situation is scary, it pales in comparison to yours. All those sleepless nights all over again, and a husband who, let's face it, might be gorgeous and hardworking but needs a lot of organising. Behind every successful man and all that.'

'Remember when we were kids and I'd want to play tea parties all the time? You never wanted to sit down at our little pink plastic table and drink imaginary cups of tea. No, not you. You'd want to make something, and I'd have to sit there while you gave me a running commentary and then insisted I copy you. It always ended in a big squabble because you were so bossy, and I'd lose interest.'

She raises her eyebrows at me.

'I know. Is it any wonder my first job was presenting a kids' arts and crafts programme?'

'Nope. So, who is this guy you're meeting?'

'His name is Ronan O'Byrne.'

'Oh. I assumed he would be French. That's a shame.' She pulls a face. 'I'd conjured up a picture of some handsome, softly spoken man with deeply sensitive eyes whose smooth accent would sweep you off your feet.'

She giggles as I roll my eyes.

'He's an experienced interpreter and comes highly recommended. He's well known at the palace and has been involved in several documentaries over the years, apparently.'

'He lives in France permanently, then?'

'I assume so. To be honest I don't really know very much about him. Why do you care?'

I can see from the glint in her eye what she's getting at.

'Well, Elliot is taken, so I was just wondering—'

'Don't. Just don't. And with that I'd better go. Take care of everyone and don't go overdoing it. That morning sickness can't be fun.'

She screws up her face. 'I'm counting down the days, believe me. And, Lexie, don't forget to have some fun, will you?'

'Now who's being bossy?' I smile to myself as the call disconnects.

Fun? Who has time for fun?

* * *

'Alexandra Winters?'

The guy staring back at me as I hold open the door glances at me hesitantly. Clearly my slouchy leggings and sloppy jumper aren't what he was expecting, but he's not exactly dressed up. Wearing a fleece and an admittedly expensive pair of designer jeans, he's smartly casual.

I nod and he thrusts out his hand for me to shake.

'Ronan O'Byrne,' he adds, rather unnecessarily.

'Hello, Ronan, nice to meet you. Please come in. It's a little tight space-wise, so can you shut the door behind you?'

I move back, climbing onto the second step of the staircase to give him room to stand inside and then push the door closed.

'Follow me.' I throw the words over my shoulder as I turn and climb the narrow stairs.

'This is an interesting holiday home. I've driven by and walked down this road hundreds of times, but never realised these cottages were tucked away behind the row of shops.'

As he follows me into the open-plan area, I turn to get a better look at him. He's in his early thirties, I should imagine, with close-cropped, dark brown hair and hazel-green eyes, which are staring back at me with interest. It feels a little awkward.

'Can I get you a drink? Hot, cold, alcoholic?'

'I'll have whatever you're having,' he replies obligingly.

'Coffee it is, then. Please make yourself comfortable.'

I busy myself in the kitchen area, leaving him to settle down on one of the sofas.

'It's bigger inside than it looks from the courtyard. Quite a find.'

He watches my every move as I place two steaming mugs of coffee on the table and take a seat opposite him.

'So, it's all about to kick off, then.'

'Yes. I'm afraid Elliot couldn't make it this evening as he has a meeting about another project he's involved in while we're here filming, but we've thrashed out a draft schedule that fits in with the preliminary interview dates. I just need to run through it with you in detail, as the sessions that are asterisked are when we're likely to need your services. There are a couple of interviews where we've been informed the interviewees speak enough English for us to communicate without too much trouble. So, it's a case of dovetailing the other slots with your own availability.'

'When will this be agreed?' He lifts his mug off the table, cradling it in his hands although it must be extremely hot.

'At tomorrow's meeting, we hope. I should be able to firm up those bookings immediately afterwards.'

'Great. I like working with people who are on the ball and well organised. What's your background, Alexandra?'

Hmm. He hasn't looked me up online, then. 'Please, call me Lexie. I'm a TV presenter.'

He takes a slurp of coffee and rather quickly places the mug back down. It's as if he's nervous, maybe he's anxious to make a good first impression.

'Anything I'd know?'

'Not unless you watch either children's TV or mid-morning lifestyle programmes.'

'Ah, that would be a firm *no*, then. I've never had anything much to do with kids and I've never been a watcher of daytime TV. The history channel, some sport and mainly films, I'm afraid.'

'Well, you're not exactly our target market so I won't be offended! And what's your background?'

'I'm a freelance dabbler. I'm fluent in French, German, Italian and Japanese. I've translated a few textbooks over the last couple of years and worked as a translator for a number of different TV companies. But I'm also a writer, and I've published two books so far. And I have a reasonably successful YouTube channel where I upload videos of some of my favourite parts of France.'

Hmm. He's certainly not what I was expecting, at all.

'That doesn't sound like dabbling to me,' I reply. 'Eclectic, admittedly, but interesting.'

Ronan throws his head back and laughs.

'Well, if you listened to my mother, she would say I gave up a perfectly good career to *dabble* and she isn't impressed. The term is hers, because she's hoping to shame me into getting my act together again.'

I find myself laughing alongside him and he is charming in a sort of disarming way. A lot of what he says is accompanied by either a deadpan look, or a cheeky grin. And it's becoming clear with every word he says that he doesn't take himself very seriously at all, which makes him even more likable.

'Well, my late father was an internationally acclaimed wildlife photographer and film-maker, and my brother, Jake, is a successful producer living in Los Angeles. So, I know a little bit about the struggle to find your niche.'

'Struggle? Niche? Maybe that's where you're going wrong. Who wants to be pigeonholed? Life's too short for that, I've discovered. It's all about the adventure. I wasted a few good years trying to please other people and making myself miserable. If I ended up having to focus on just one thing now, it would probably drive me crazy.'

Oh, dear, I can't help worrying that perhaps this means he's a little flaky. I look up and realise he's staring at me.

'Don't worry, interpreting is something I really enjoy. No two days are ever the same. Plus, I know my way around the palace and I'm on nodding terms with a lot of the staff.'

We sit in silence for a few minutes sipping our coffees and then I stand up, beckoning him over to the table at the kitchen end of the room.

'Right. Let's look over this schedule, then.'

Disconcertingly, I notice he hasn't brought a diary with him, but as soon as we sit down, he pulls his phone out of his shirt pocket and begins looking at his electronic calendar. For all the joking around he knows exactly what dates he can fit in and it doesn't take long to run through the entire thing.

'Well, hopefully I will be able to confirm these dates very soon.'

'This interview here with Anton Mereux.' He points at the schedule on the screen in front of me. 'It won't require an interpreter. It would be a waste of time and your money, my being there. His English is very good and he's a very accommodating chap.'

'Oh, great, thanks for the heads up. We're simply going on the info we've been given. The asterisk alongside his name could be my error. This is probably the eighth version of this document,' I admit, glad he spotted it. Our budget is tight enough as it is, and we certainly can't afford to waste a penny on man hours that aren't necessary.

I give Ronan a grateful smile, and he stands, slipping his phone back into his pocket.

'Right. I'd better head off and leave you to it. I hope to

hear from you in the next day or two, then. Looking forward to working with you, Lexie, and to meeting Elliot.'

'You too, Ronan. I'll see you out.'

We shake hands and I feel sure we're all going to work well together as a team. I was expecting a serious, academic type but he's far from serious. In fact, he's left quite an impression on me, to the extent that my heart is thumping in my chest. *Calm down, Lexie,* that little voice of reason worms its way into my head. Yes, he's good-looking and intelligent and interesting... and maybe he is going to be rather fun to have around. But you're here to work and you need to focus, even if he does promise to be somewhat of a distraction.

4

FEELING THE BUZZ

'So, who is it we're meeting with this morning?'

Elliot and I walk side by side along the wide, tree-lined avenue leading up to one of the most famous landmarks in the history of France.

'Bertrand Tibault. He's the head of administration and security at the palace. I've spoken to him several times on the phone, but never met him in person. I did meet his predecessor and got on very well with him when I was here—'

Elliot is brought to an abrupt halt when he starts coughing again.

'Should we slow down a little so you can catch your breath?'

He shakes his head, walking on again. 'No. It's fine. It's worse early in the morning and late at night. Mia rang first thing and she's hacking away like a smoker, too. I hope you don't catch it. It could slow us down when filming begins.'

He makes a face. All it takes is one little thing like a cough to mess up our itinerary, but we're a few days away from our first session and hopefully Elliot will be over the worst of it by then.

'I'll be doing the honey and lemon thing as often as I can to appease Mia, so don't worry,' Elliot reassures me.

I know I must look worried so I take a deep breath. It's going to be fine.

'Will the meeting take place inside the palace?' I ask, hoping he'll say *yes*.

'Well, not inside the main building itself, I'm afraid. We're heading up to les Ailes des Ministres Sud, which is the first building on the left just inside the outer palace gates. We will also be introduced to Solange Forand. She'll be our on-site contact while we're filming.'

'Do you think we should have asked Ronan to come with us this morning?'

Elliot cocks an eyebrow.

'I'm sure we'll manage, as Solange Forand would probably have mentioned it in her email if we needed to bring an interpreter. All the required forms for our little team have been submitted and checked, so this meeting is hopefully just to get them rubber-stamped and to approve the proposed schedule.'

We exchange a look that lifts my spirits; Elliot is as excited as I am about this morning. We're really here, at last. Suddenly he slows, pointing to our right.

'This rather imposing building is la Grande Écurie, now the home of the Bartabas National Equestrian Academy of Versailles. Louis XIV commissioned one of his favourite architects, Mansart, to build this to house his horses.'

'It's rather grand for stables.' I laugh, taking in the majestic stonework of the building's façade; with elegant archways and immense proportions, it looks like a palace rather than an equestrian centre.

'On the left we're passing the Petite Écurie. It's a gallery exhibiting sculptures and mouldings and well worth a visit while you're here.'

While different in size, the buildings are mirror images. Ahead of us, the Avenue de Paris ends at the Place d'Armes, directly in front of the palace; two roads, one on either side, run like spokes in a wheel in a funnel-effect, culminating to form an arc. It closes off the large square in front of the outer palace gates. As we draw nearer, an imposing statue of Louis XIV on horseback is set high on a stone plinth, the huge bronze commanding everyone's attention. Every inch the omnipotent King, he sits astride the regal animal, whose head is proudly raised, as if he understands the importance of his role. King and horse overseeing not only their own army of men and beasts, but everything that inhabited French soil.

'It's everything I'd imagined and more,' I murmur in awe. Having studied so many of the books written about Versailles in preparation for this project, I wasn't expecting to feel so overcome with emotion.

'He was a man with an unshakeable resolve. This area was designed to accommodate six hundred horses, their riders, musicians, pages and onlookers. Louis held court wherever he went.' Elliot has visited so many times and even now the awe in his voice is discernible.

It's impossible not to stop in my tracks to gaze up at the statue and beyond, at the sheer spectacle in front of us.

Louis looms large, his commanding image set centrally to the sprawling palace behind him. There is no disputing the sense of ultimate power on display. Nothing was going to stop this man from turning a former hunting lodge, built on boggy unwelcoming ground, into the most unbelievably decadent palace imaginable. He succeeded in letting the world know there was nothing he couldn't achieve and even at a distance the scale and grandeur is hard to take on board. The astronomical amount of expenditure that must have been involved, at a time when many people went hungry in order to pay their taxes is unthinkable.

Even though it's only just after nine-thirty in the morning, the sun is already making the gold embellishments on the gates surrounding the palace glisten.

'It's breathtaking, isn't it?' Elliot's voice drags me back into the moment.

'You can understand why it became a symbol for the dramatic and bloody decline of the monarchy during the French Revolution, even though it was some seventy-odd years after Louis XIV's death. Did you know that the palace was besieged by an angry crowd in a march on Versailles, which was triggered by the scarcity and high price of bread? The then King – also a Louis – and his family were forced to return to Paris. The history books tell us how that ended – in front of the guillotine.' As I say the word it makes me shudder.

'All in the pursuit of elevating a man who believed he was untouchable; more than a King even, a resolute power chosen by God. He built something of incredible beauty, admittedly, but you can understand the anger it generated.' Elliot's words mirror my own thoughts. Beautiful, astounding, but at what cost simply to immortalise one man? Bold, audacious, visionary and bordering on the impossible. Few dare to dream this big for a reason.

We step through the outer gates, into an immense

cobbled area. A large queue has already formed in snaking lines, supervised by stewards. Either side is flanked by mirror-image buildings in the signature pale stonework, with the slate grey Mansard roofs repeated everywhere. The difference, though, is the lavish amount of gilding on the dormer windows set within the roofs, turning them into gleaming, golden eyes staring down at all who come to gaze up and marvel. Some are round, like myriad suns and not the more prolific rectangular style. Detail is everything, but the cost of the renovation work must be just as mind-blowing as the original budget.

To our left, the crowd of visitors mill around and as we head towards our destination it's clear it also houses the main ticket office.

Three soldiers wearing bulletproof vests walk past us, each purposefully nursing a machine gun, their eyes constantly roving around the mass of people. It's hard not to stare at them, and I realise I've slowed my pace while Elliot is talking to a member of staff.

'Bonjour. Nous avons un rendez-vous avec Monsieur Tibault.'

The man nods and we follow him inside.

Even though this building is outside the inner palace gates, it's impressive and very stately. As we walk across the entrance hall our footsteps have a hollow ring until we are led up a sweeping flight of stone steps, each one topped with marble. As we ascend, I look down at the constant coming and going below, marvelling at the intricate pattern of black and white inlaid marble covering the floor.

'Parlez-vous anglais?' Elliot asks, hopefully.

'Oui, a leetle. The director is this way,' our guide confirms. 'Your names, please?'

Elliot introduces us and receives a nod of acknowledgement.

Nervously, I smooth down the lapels of my suit jacket and give Elliot the once-over. We both look the part, anyway. Calm and professional – well, at least on the surface.

The man promptly stops to rap his knuckles on a door and, swinging it open, ushers us inside. He approaches a young woman, who rises from her seat in front of a computer desk, but he speaks too fast for me to catch much of what he says. He turns, giving us another quick nod of his head, before exiting and closing the door behind him.

The woman picks up the phone on her desk and speaks for several seconds before replacing the receiver. My French is rather basic, but she mentioned our names and asked if it was convenient to take us through.

'Please to follow me,' we are instructed.

On the wall to the rear of the room is a large painted mural of what I assume is a group of courtiers. Both men and women are finely dressed in the most opulent of outfits. Rich, colourful fabrics now slightly muted over time, but the attention to detail and embellishment are incredible. Either side of the door we're approaching is a stone column with intricate scroll work around the top. Our escort raps twice and as the door opens, we find ourselves entering a rather impressive-looking study.

The portly gentleman behind the enormous solid oak desk rises, extending a hand towards us.

'Ah, Monsieur Nielson et Madame Winters, welcome. Please sit.'

We shake hands cordially, delighted and a little relieved at such a warm welcome. Settling ourselves down, we wait as a few papers are shuffled on the desk in front of us.

Elliot clears his throat and I hope for his sake it doesn't turn into a coughing fit. 'Thank you for seeing us, Monsieur Tibault. It's an honour to be here.'

Much to my relief he recovers well.

'We have a few formalities, as you say, to attend to while we await Madame Forand's arrival. She will be a little late, I'm afraid, but I can sign off the paperwork for your team's passes ready for her to collect them later today. Unfortunately, I have one or two amendments to make to the schedule that was previously submitted to you, due to changes in our staff rotas.'

He produces a printed draft of the email attachment I sent across yesterday.

'Of course.' I pull the file from my backpack and he indicates for me to place it on his desk.

Scrutinising the planner, the amendments are fairly minor, mainly a few dates where the names of the people we will be filming have changed. He explains that the large team of gardeners is comprised of only a small core of permanent staff. A large contingent is hired on a set contract for specific months of the year. In addition, there is a small army of trainees and interns from various programmes and collaborations. It sounds like quite a task to organise the workload and Elliot interjects, adding that we can be very flexible throughout our entire schedule of visits. This seems to go down very well with Monsieur Tibault and it doesn't take long to run through the changes to everyone's satisfaction.

There's a tap on the door and a woman enters.

'Ah, this is Madame Forand from our marketing and partnerships department. She will be your guide and contact while you are here filming.'

The very petite dark-haired woman immediately steps forward, thrusting out her hand.

'Please call me Solange,' she confirms as we shake. Her smile is warm and friendly, and her English is good.

I shake her hand. 'I'm Lexie,' I reply, then take a step back.

'Elliot. Pleased to meet you, Solange.'

Monsieur Tibault stands, signalling the end of our meeting.

'I think we are done for now and I'm sure you would like to begin your tour. Welcome to the Palace of Versailles.'

* * *

'Have you visited before?' Solange asks as she escorts us from the building, and we head up towards the main palace gates.

'Yes,' Elliot answers. 'But it's Lexie's first time. I was involved in the filming of a series of documentaries here about two years ago. We were following the renovation work on the Queen's House in the Petit Trianon Park.'

'Ah, bon, I did not know that! I've only been here just over a year myself. It will finally be unveiled on the twelfth of May and we are all very excited about it.'

'It's an enormous task, but an important project and at some point, I'd like to get a peek, if that's at all possible.'

'Of course. Sadly, I only have an hour free today, but once your work has started, I will arrange for someone to give you the tour. I suspect it will be of much interest to you, Lexie. The first visit to Versailles is always special.'

Her accent is so charming, and I'm delighted at how welcome we're being made to feel. I nod, giving an appreciative smile. 'That would be wonderful, Solange, thank you so much.'

'And what is your first impression, Lexie?' she asks. I can feel her eyes scrutinising my face with interest as I gaze up at the magnificent structure in front of us.

'A lot to take in! Lavish, opulent – I wasn't expecting everything to be quite so... golden,' I admit. The gilding on and around the gates is even more magnificent up close and prolific – everything seems to glisten as the sunlight bounces around. Louis chose as his emblem a mask set within the rays of the sun. This heavenly body has always been associated with Apollo, the god of peace and arts. Louis saw the analogy as a fitting symbol for his own absolute role – a patron of the arts, a warrior king bringing about peace, and what he perceived as his God-given authority.

She laughs.

'The dreams of the Sun King were without boundary. The royal gates were torn down during the French Revolution. It took over two years and a hundred thousand gold leaves to make replicas of the eighty metre baroque-style gates. It was completed in 2008. But it is the crowning glory, yes?'

'Absolutely,' Elliot replies. I nod my head in complete agreement.

'We traverse now the Court of Honour and these outbuildings each side were the Ministers' Wings, originally housing the King's Secretaries of State. All of the government offices were here, not just the court itself.'

Ah, that accounts for the grandeur of the buildings. Solange inclines her head in the direction of the main gate in front of the palace.

'The area beyond that is known as the Royal Court, where Louis' equestrian statue was originally sited, and the other side of that is the inner Marble Court. Notice the distinctive black and white marble tiles adorning the terraced floor.'

'The attention to detail everywhere is incredible,' I affirm as I crane my neck to get a better view, given that the crowd in front of us is constantly shifting.

'We head to the Orangery now. Monsieur Tibault has arranged for some of your interviews to be conducted there. Others will be at Le Potager du Roi, which was the King's kitchen garden. It is run by the National School of Landscape Architecture and is close by.' She turns, extending her arm to point in the general direction to the left of us. 'It has two hundred landscape architecture students and in excess of three hundred continuing education students.'

'How many actual gardeners work here in the grounds?' I enquire.

'Today we have forty-eight permanent gardeners tending in excess of two-thousand acres, with as many as ten private companies supplying additional labour as the seasons dictate. During the reign of Louis XIV, it is said that seven thousand people were employed to work on the gardens alone.'

Solange is very knowledgeable and it's a lot to assimilate as she steers us between two buildings. We follow a path skirting the exterior of the palace. As we are drawn away from the crowd of people milling around, the snaking queue of ticket holders slowly shuffles forwards to gain entry to the palace itself. Leading us through a stone archway, Solange unlocks a tall wrought-iron gate. As it swings open, in front of us the vast panoramic spectacle extends out seemingly endlessly.

Words fail me as we walk forward, and I struggle to take in the sheer scale. My eyes automatically sweep across to our right, to gaze out over the beauty and grandeur of the famous canal and the various fountains.

'Les Jardins de Versailles.' Solange's voice is low as she watches my reaction with interest.

'It's... incredible, staggering.' I gasp.

Elliot has a little coughing fit and I glance at him anxiously. He recovers after a few moments and then chuckles at my initial reaction.

'Sorry. I must get some cough mixture. I've probably stood here surveying this view more than fifty times over the past few years and the sight of the Grand Canal still stops me in my tracks every single time,' he admits.

'I'm overwhelmed by it. I've studied the guidebooks and read so much about the palace and the gardens, but nothing prepared me for how commanding it is up close.'

Solange and Elliot exchange indulgent smiles.

'I know. I feel the same way, Lexie. And I get to see this every day of my working life now,' Solange adds. I can see that she is in love with Versailles.

I'm well aware from the research I've carried out that the Sun King's vision was audacious; many thought it was bordering on madness because of the problems that had to be overcome here. As Elliot said, turning useless, boggy land into acre upon acre of manicured gardens and parks seemed like an impossible task. But the creation of the Grand Canal and the ornate fountains was an even more staggering project by anyone's standards. Clearly, it was way beyond any possible definition of extravagance.

'The King's desire to move his court and government here to escape Paris saw him taking on the role of architect to give life to a vision few could grasp. The original cost was phenomenal – money was no object at all, it seemed, in the pursuit of the glorification of a king. Louis built a power base, distancing himself from his people and forcing the nobility to spend time at court, each year. His desire to establish absolute monarchy depended upon preventing anyone from establishing their own regional power. It was a clever move and it worked,' Solange explains.

'As fate determined, Versailles was only the centre of political power for just over a century. Some five thousand courtiers lived here at the very peak of its power, but Versailles was more than the overpowering beauty and grandeur of it all. There is still a tangible sense of the passions that have filled the air here throughout its turbulent lifetime. Political plotting, trysts and impossible love affairs; poisoning, jealousy and people's lives held in the balance on a whim. At court, being in, or out, of favour could result in either riches or ruin. Sometimes imprisonment, or even death for treason.'

We cross the lightly gravelled area, walking along, adjacent to the rear of the main palace building.

'The extensive renovation programme in recent years has brought the building back to its former glory.' She slows to a halt a short distance away to stand and admire the rear façade.

At ground and first-floor levels it comprises a long row of double French doors set within beautiful stone arches that seems to stretch out forever. Room, after room, after room.

'There are seven hundred rooms, in excess of two thousand windows and sixty-seven staircases,' she confirms.

At first-floor level it's slightly set back to accommodate a stonework balcony, only broken by blocks of staunch pilasters, which are rectangular projections. Above each of these is a wide plinth displaying a series of marble statues depicting Roman deities and emperors. Some are netted, undergoing renovation work still, and even from this level it's clear to see how damaging exposure to the elements has been over time. It serves only to make the condition of the building even more astonishing and a credit to the army of people who work tirelessly to preserve it.

Yet another floor houses a series of smaller rooms with matching windows in line with the full-length French doors below. These smaller rooms would be the quarters for the retinues and attendants accompanying the courtiers. I step back a few paces, tilting my head to get a glimpse of the roofline. In perfect symmetry to the low stonework of the first-floor balcony, slender stone urns are evenly spaced between clusters of statues that, once again, seem to mirror the outline of a King's bejewelled crown. In between, carved stone trophies are interspersed with slender flame pots to accentuate the elegant profile.

Feeling a little embarrassed when I realise that Solange and Elliot are now a few paces away and patiently waiting for me to catch up with them, I pull myself together.

'Sorry. It's beyond amazing. I've dreamt about coming here for so many years and now I'm here...' I tail off, rather pathetically.

'Lexie's grandma, Viv, was a horticultural student and spent some time here in the sixties,' Elliot explains.

'How wonderful! It is a real connection for you, then, Lexie. That was before l'École Nationale Supérieure de Paysage was set up in 1976, so one of the early programmes, no doubt. Sadly, that is not my area of expertise, though. I note that you will be using the services of Ronan O'Byrne when you are filming. He is very knowledgeable about the history of the gardeners who have worked here since the early 1900s.'

I nod. 'Yes. He said he knew a few people here.'

She raises an eyebrow. 'Indeed. He has worked on a number of projects, even in the time I've been around. Ronan will, I'm sure, know if any of the gardeners working here during that period are still alive. He has researched and written two books about different periods in the history of the gardens and the park, and is currently bringing it up to the present day in his latest book.'

'I wasn't aware of that. How fascinating. I suspect that once people come to Versailles, if they are captured by its spell, they find a reason to stay,' I muse, speaking more to myself than to Solange. But that wasn't true for my grandma and again I wonder why, because I know she would have been captivated by this.

To her dying day her windowsills were full of seedlings and cuttings; her garden was a joy to behold. As children we all spent time with her, weeding and planting, but I more so than my siblings. She said that communing with nature was good for one's soul.

I sigh. Being here must have been such a wonderful time for her and, now I'm here too, I feel a great sadness washing over me. I would have dearly loved to have heard her thoughts and learnt what she did on a daily basis. It would have been her dream; of that I have no doubt at all.

5

A LITTLE TÊTE-À-TÊTE

What people often fail to appreciate is the huge amount of planning and research required before an interviewer can get up close to an interviewee with a microphone. Preparing the right questions to draw out the information I want, when I have no idea how forthcoming the person will be – or how they will react to being filmed – requires a lot of forethought. Often, they are being interviewed for the first time and I've had a few people clam up on me, making the process painfully slow.

My biggest concern is duplication. With several changes in the list of people I'll be talking to, I'm worried I won't get the breadth of experience I was hoping for. From the newest trainees, to interns on a set contract, to the small core group of permanent staff who oversee the entire process, it has to be representative across the entire range of skills and horticultural disciplines.

I'm poring over my notes but I can't keep asking Solange questions as she's a very busy lady. My phone buzzes and I groan. After spending nearly an hour earlier in the day talking to Mum to reassure her that I'm fine, just busy, then sending a quick text to Elliot to check he's doing okay, I intended to knock this into shape without fear of interruption. It's Ronan calling.

'Hi, Ronan. How are you?'

'Great. I bumped into Solange Forand up at the palace this afternoon after escorting a party of Japanese horticulturists around the gardens. She mentioned your grandma worked at Versailles in the sixties?'

Well, it seems he must know Solange quite well to be so chatty with her.

'Yes. She was a horticultural student, but I don't really have any information other than she was on some sort of work experience programme. Elliot threw it into the conversation as he knows I'm hoping to find out something about her time working on the palace gardens. Solange did say I should mention it to you, now I come to think about it, as you might know if any of the gardeners who were here in 1961 are still alive. I didn't realise the two books you've written were actually to do with the history of the park and the gardens.'

'Well, what is it they say? Jack of all trades, master of none.'

He's doing it again; it's as if he doesn't want to be taken seriously.

'I, um, wondered if you fancied taking an hour or two off to come to supper at my place? I'm less than fifteen minutes away and hearing about your family link with Versailles has piqued my interest. I'm vaguely aware of a special programme pulled together in the early sixties that folded after only six months. The funds simply weren't there to justify the manpower. I'm wondering if this was what your grandmother took part in.'

I'm surprised he's that interested in a passing comment and aware my lack of knowledge is going to be somewhat of a disappointment. 'Unfortunately, I don't have any information at all that I can pass on. I'm literally starting with a blank page, myself.'

A soft 'hmm' filters down the line.

'That's a shame. Anyway, first things first. I'm known for making the best croque-monsieur you'll ever taste. I am part French, you know.'

Really? I start laughing, glancing at my watch and thinking, *what the heck?* I need a break, anyway.

'Okay. Text me your address and I'll punch it into the satnav.'

'Great. See you in, what, thirty minutes?'

'Sounds good.'

As soon as we disconnect, I begin to have second thoughts. I mean, he's a nice enough guy, although his attitude is a little disarming, but I have a rule never to mix business with pleasure. But then I doubt he would think that cheese on toast was a way to impress anyone, so I should stop jumping to conclusions.

I wonder if he thinks I actually do have information that could help his research.

Gathering together my papers, I close the laptop. I hope he isn't going to be very disappointed when he realises I don't know anything at all; I simply wish I did.

* * *

Oh. My. Goodness.

'This is *so* not cheese on toast!' I exclaim, cutting into the heavenly looking, golden-brown stack on the plate in front of me. I will admit that the accompaniment of a glass of red wine is rather welcome.

'What were you expecting? An English toasted cheese sandwich?' Ronan is laughing at me now and I look at him, raising my eyebrows.

'No.' I put a small forkful into my mouth, savouring the perfectly complemented flavours of home-cooked gammon, crisply baked bread and the oozy, cheesy, béchamel sauce, all coated in what appears to be a very thin mushroom omelette.

'Mushrooms?' I muse.

'Ah. Well. I'm not really a purist, although it was Solange who taught me how to cook this properly. I hope you're getting that hint of mustard on the Emmental cheese, but let's keep the mushroom omelette just between us. Although, some people serve it with a fried egg on top, but I feel that lacks a sense of refinement. Either could be construed as sacrilege, I suppose, but I prefer to view it as a modern twist on an old favourite.'

I burst out laughing.

'Okay. Your secret is safe with me. You and Solange get on well, then?' I'm just making conversation really – it's not that I'm interested.

Well, I don't think I am.

'Solange moved here from the South of France a little over a year ago and she didn't know anyone at all. I could sympathise with that. People assume it's hard for a foreigner in a new country, but for Solange, too, following her dream meant leaving everything behind. Her family didn't want her to come to Versailles and her father hasn't spoken to her since she left.'

I put down my knife and fork.

'I'm sorry to hear she's had to contend with that. She obviously loves what she does. I thought I'd researched enough to prepare me for the experience of being here in person but I was so very wrong.'

Ronan looks across at me and smiles knowingly.

'Eat. This is best consumed hot and not cold. Solange said you were hooked.'

'Hooked?' As my eyes flash over his face I can see he's enjoying himself, and I will admit that I'm feeling much more relaxed around him.

I wait while Ronan chews through an enormous forkful of croque-monsieur.

'Under the spell of Versailles. I came here seven years ago to record an audio version in several languages for an exhibition that was running at the time. I'm still here.'

He opens his eyes wide, indicating that it probably wasn't a part of his plan at the time.

'And two books later?'

'Yep. Still hunting for new information about the past. My research so far has left me with gaps. It's like a jigsaw puzzle where I don't have all the pieces but at least now I have a good idea of which ones I'm looking for. But I hate loose ends.'

Now I understand. Solange was doing Ronan a favour mentioning my connection. And maybe she thought it could be a two-way thing.

'That must be frustrating. I can sympathise with that, as my grandma was very secretive about her year in Versailles.'

He stops eating, a frown wrinkling his brow.

'Well, Versailles holds so many secrets. The more you uncover, the more you realise the surface has only just been scratched, even after all the years of intense scrutiny. I'm very lucky to have been given access to some of the mountain of records and journals relating to the gardens. If you're happy to give me a little more information about her I can see if I can trace her name.'

I'm a little surprised by his offer. I thought maybe he'd be firing questions at me, notebook in hand, but he seems very relaxed and genuinely interested in helping me out. What harm can it do?

'That would be great, thanks.'

He smiles and our eyes meet. I feel a little prickle of heat making the hairs on the back of my neck begin to rise. I think, with Ronan involved, digging a little deeper might just turn up a clue, or two.

There's more to Ronan than meets the eye, that's for sure. Any man who works so hard to give off that blasé, laid-back attitude, when it's clear that beneath that lies a very complex character, is protecting himself. I wonder what he's protecting himself from.

We carry on and finish our supper, chatting easily throughout. There is an unmistakably flirty feeling to the atmosphere now, as the wine we've drunk loosens us up.

'I'll clear the dishes and wash up,' I insist as soon as we've finished eating. 'It's the least I can do after that amazing supper. You grab a pen and some paper.'

He gives me a look of mild surprise. 'Okay.'

I load up the wooden tray perched on the end of the long, highly polished oak table and carry it through into the kitchen. The large and wonderful old house wasn't what I was expecting, especially its size when it's clear Ronan lives here alone. Just the kitchen itself is as big as the entire open-plan area at number six, and it has a magnificent run of modern bifold doors leading out onto a patio area.

Ronan reappears as I'm running a sink full of water.

'I do have a dishwasher.' He points towards the unit next to the sink, before settling himself down at the scrubbed pine table in the centre of the room.

I nod. 'I don't do dishwashers. I think it's better to do it by hand.' I smile at him and he rolls his eyes.

'The first thing I did when I inherited this house from my grandmother was to bring it up to date. I kept all her old furniture, because it's what I remember from my visits, but she preferred old school. No dishwasher and no shower, although she loved her washing machine. She was a very precise sort of lady; very proud of her Irish roots. Always cleaning.'

Swiping the plates with the soapy sponge until they sparkle, I work as I talk.

'So, your grandfather was French, then?' At last we're getting somewhere.

'Yes. My grandmother, Colleen, met him when she was in London, ironically. They were both on holiday at the time. Leaving Ireland to join him over here less than a year later was tough, as she was leaving behind her parents and four sisters. Irish families are close and I'm not sure whether my grandfather fully realised the sacrifice she'd made for him. But she was hopelessly in love and his ties were here. Versailles was his life, until it was sadly cut short.'

I vaguely remember thinking that Ronan is an Irish name the first time I saw it, but the French connection is a real surprise. I pull the plug out of the sink and wipe my hands on the kitchen towel, before taking a seat at the table.

'And your mother married an Irishman. So where were you born?'

He smiles. 'Ireland, but it's a long and complicated story, which I won't even attempt to bore you with. I spent quite a bit of the school holidays every year in France, as Mum took every opportunity she could to return to her childhood home.

'Even though I never knew my grandfather, who died in 1966 when my mother was only three years old, my love of languages grew from the time I spent here, I'm sure. When my grandmother's health eventually began to decline, we flew her back to Ireland. She died several months later, and we brought her ashes back, so they could be buried with my grandfather.'

'It's lovely to think that they were reunited in death,' I reflect.

'Her heart was always here because she had never truly got over her loss and she talked to me about him, often. She knew that my mother never mentioned him at all, but then she had no memories she could pass on to me. As the only grandchild, I inherited the house, although I rented it out for a few years. I only moved over here permanently seven years ago. To cut a very long story short, after years of seeming indifference, my father decided to reach out to me. I'd been working for his company, which was based in the UK, for a few years, but things became increasingly awkward. We had one argument too many and eventually I had to walk away in order to maintain my sanity.'

I can tell from his expression that whatever went on was a big deal.

'Right. So, you mentioned 1961?' he begins again, clearly wanting to change the subject. 'If you're happy to share whatever you do know, I love a challenge,' he says, picking up his pen.

'My grandma's maiden name was Hanley. Vivian Hanley, but everyone knew her as Viv. She was a student at Barker's

Horticultural College in Cirencester. My mum once mentioned that she thought Grandma's year here was a work experience type of thing, but even she didn't know any more than that.'

Ronan scribbles down a few notes and then sits back in his chair, tapping his pen against the side of his cheek.

'It's not a name I've come across in the records, but that's not to say I won't find it in one of the daily signing-in ledgers. Do you know what month she arrived here?'

'No, I'm afraid I don't. She married my granddad in the August of 1962, so I guess she will have returned in the late spring, early summer of that year. Sadly, she died in 2006, shortly after my sixteenth birthday. I've tried quizzing my mum, but I genuinely think Grandma Viv only ever talked about her childhood, or about her family. We have what she called her memory box, including a package of letters exchanged between my grandparents during Grandma's year in Versailles.'

Ronan's body language indicates an immediate interest, as he sits upright in his chair, his eyes on mine.

'Letters?'

I shake my head. 'Don't get excited. I skimmed through a few of them and quite honestly all she talked about were plants, the weather, the food and how captivated she was by her surroundings on her daily walks. Granddad's were in similar vein, mainly all about his work. But he did talk a lot about a new band, named the Beatles, he'd seen at a gig while visiting Liverpool.' I find myself chuckling. 'Granddad played guitar and was in a band at weekends. Considering they were married shortly after her return; I didn't even see any references to that. I saw no mention of people she worked alongside, or any friends she made over here. Maybe in a handwritten letter the whole point was to give a flavour of what was happening in one's life, not the nitty-gritty detail.'

He nods.

'I think we suffer from the opposite these days. I can't believe how many emails I send in a day. If I had to hand-write them, I'd write an awful lot less,' he admits. 'Anyway, a name is a start and as she was here between 1961 and 1962, that narrows it down considerably. I'm already aware from previous research that there was some sort of experimental work experience programme in relation to the trees, going on in the early sixties. It folded later that year, due to budgetary constraints. It was a time when opinions were divided, and emotions ran high.'

I look at Ronan in surprise as his tone becomes more serious and he shrugs his shoulders.

'Back in the sixties some experts believed that many of the trees at Versailles had been allowed to grow too tall, both for their root systems and the drained swampland area on which a lot of the park was established, to be able to support. Others saw it as doom-mongering, predicting a mass loss of trees being blown over in strong winds. A bid to grab more of the budget, let's say. The internal politics threw up general conflict as departments fought to grab as much funding as they could. The truth is that management didn't always get their priorities right and sometimes tough decisions had to be made.'

'But surely, the gardens have always been a major part of the attractions at Versailles?' I ask, rather surprised at his words.

'They are, but the building had fallen into disrepair and things like holes in the roof had top priority; much of the privately donated funding went to things like the statuary in the grounds and keeping the fountains working.

'One of the gardeners put forward a theory that the high water table associated with the boggy land resulted in the root systems growing very close to the surface. That, he proposed, was the inherent danger for the future as the trees aged, and that's what I think the tree survey project set about to prove for the first time. By looking in detail at the pattern of tree loss over the previous twenty years, it was hoping to trigger urgent action with regard to a major replanting programme.'

Ronan is very knowledgeable, and I'm impressed.

'I'm sure everyone was aware the solution wasn't going to be a simple one. If the money had been there, I assume it would have been a totally different story and the scheme would have had backing. I bet it was a bitter blow to those involved, though.'

His expression is one of exasperation.

'What was the point of wasting what little money was available, when from the outset no one was going to listen? That was the travesty.'

'Do you think my grandma could have been involved in this tree survey?' I'm a little taken aback at his in-depth knowledge. He knows his stuff, that's for sure.

'Possibly. It's all common knowledge, of course,' he adds quickly. 'No secrets being divulged here. Although it's a pity those early rumblings in the sixties were pushed to one side. Maybe some of the very old trees that should have gone on to stand for a long, long time could have withstood the storms. In tandem with a replanting programme, one proposal was to drill holes and inject nutrients into the ground to encourage the roots to go deeper. Whether that would have worked is anyone's guess.'

It's a sobering thought and I feel sad to think of what has been lost

'It will take several lifetimes for the park to be returned to anything like its former glory. In 1990, so many trees were lost in the first of two devastating storms which hit the park, that a restoration project was finally developed by a committee of experts. It was agreed that somehow the funds would be raised, because there was an outpouring from people around the world who wanted to help when they saw photographs on the news of the damage. At the time, no one could have predicted the further, colossal damage to come in December 1999. Over eighty per cent of the oldest, more rare species were destroyed in a two hour frenzy of tornado-strength winds.'

No wonder feelings ran high in the sixties, when there were those who foresaw how devastating the delay would be for the future of the landscape. If Versailles inspires anything in people, I'm starting to understand it's a passion for the beauty that was created at such enormous expense.

'I can't imagine what it's like to see a huge tree toppled overnight,' I admit. 'But I suppose it's a case of prioritising when there's also the fabric of the building to consider. That's such a difficult choice to make, though.'

Ronan gives a wry smile. 'The Sun King would simply have raised taxes when his coffers ran low.'

And look at how that ended, I can't help thinking, as he continues.

'The park is a lot less private these days, having lost so many of the tallest trees – some in excess of one hundred and twenty feet tall. We're mainly talking about some of the apartment buildings bordering the furthest extremes of the park's perimeter, though.'

He realises I'm looking at him with what is, no doubt, a look of fascination on my face.

'Sorry, it's one of my pet topics and that sounded a bit like a lecture.'

'No, it's interesting, really it is, and something that has never even crossed my mind. I can imagine how excited my grandma Viv would have found all of this. And as a passionate gardener herself, I know how strongly she would have felt about forward planning. A tree or a hedge takes a long time to grow and when something is lost overnight, suddenly the view changes quite dramatically. To my grandma the garden was an outdoor room and she always said that it required as much attention and dedication as anything inside the house.'

Ronan groans. 'Now I've made you maudlin and that wasn't my intention at all. Enough of this. Leave it with me and I'll let you know what I discover, if anything at all.'

It seems like a natural time to say goodnight and head home.

'Supper was delicious,' I compliment him as I stand, sliding the chair beneath the table. 'I'll invite you back very soon, but I don't think I can beat that, so I don't want you to set your expectations too high.'

We exchange a good-natured laugh. 'I confess the dishes in my repertoire are rather limited, but I cook what I know and leave the clever stuff to people with the right skills. It's been a nice evening, though, and thanks for the company.'

I feel myself blushing slightly as Ronan stands opposite me. I wasn't expecting him to be so open and honest with me, even if he didn't elaborate more on what happened with his father. As we get to know each other a little better I wonder if he will take me into his confidence. It's often easier to talk to someone you hardly know than those you are close to. Especially when that someone is only passing through. Ronan is turning out to be a man whose thoughts run deep and I like that.

6

A SURPRISING TURN OF EVENTS

After several very intense days of preparation and two meetings with Elliot, our sound man, Cameron, and Ronan, we're all counting down to the first interview. It turns out that Ronan's YouTube channel contains footage of a walking tour of various areas of the park and gardens around the palace. Together we watched a few of his downloads, as they were useful background information.

'Your camera work is good.' Elliot was full of praise. 'It's not easy to film and commentate at the same time.'

Both Elliot and I were intrigued to discover that Ronan's father owns a film production company. Ronan spent a number of years working for him behind the camera and then behind the scenes, as an editor. The company specialises in high-end animation and visual effects, as well as making video trailers. Being multilingual, as well as good with a camera, Ronan must have been a real asset. No wonder his father came back into his life, although I hope it wasn't just to use him. Ronan still hasn't mentioned the reason why he left the company, and I daren't ask, although my curiosity grows by the day over their falling-out. Business and family aren't always a good mix and the irony is that he'll probably understand the situation between me and Jake.

The palace doesn't open on Mondays, so today is a free day to catch up on my own admin as well as some office work. I've been to the supermarket to stock up on supplies, as I've invited Ronan over this evening to see if he's found out anything about Grandma's time here. After a leisurely stroll back to number six, even before I can turn the key in the door, I hear someone call out.

'Excusez-moi. J'ai une livraison pour vous.'

Turning around, an older woman is walking towards me with a parcel in her hands. Her silver-grey hair is tied neatly in a bun and she's dressed entirely in black; her skirt is ankle-length and even though it's an unusually warm spring day she's wearing a long black cardigan over her blouse.

'Ah. Merci, madame,' I offer, as I take the parcel from her, wondering what on earth it could be. She indicates that she had to sign for it, and I can see a Royal Mail special delivery label with a bar code. I give her a warm smile of thanks.

'Je m'appelle Lexie Winters,' I add, feeling it would be rude not to introduce myself.

'Ah. English!' she exclaims. 'I am Renée Duval. You stay here long?'

'Twelve weeks,' I reply, and she frowns. 'Douze semaines,' I clarify.

'Ah. Bon.'

She nods her head in acknowledgement, then heads back to the cottage, opposite.

I open the door then slide the sizeable box under my arm as best I can, in order to grab the carrier bags. It isn't easy negotiating the stairs as I puzzle over the unexpected delivery. Not many people know I'm here and I haven't ordered anything. I'm so curious that I dump the bags down and carry the box across to the table before unpacking the shopping.

It's obviously from the UK and when I turn the box over, I see it has one of Mum's little flowery address labels on it. Grabbing a knife to slit it open, I end up sitting down on a chair with a bump as I stare at the contents. It's full of palm-sized, spiral-bound notebooks. I pick one up and see that the paper inside is plain, like an art pad, and, flicking through, I see it's full of Grandma's stylish handwriting, interspersed with drawings of flowers, plants and trees. These little vignettes jump out, tantalisingly. Tucked alongside them is a folded sheet of white paper, which I slide out.

Hi Honey

Your dad once said I was being silly hesitating over when exactly was the right time to hand this box over to you. Now you're in Versailles, walking over the very ground your grandma walked so many years ago, the time has come. I will admit I am nervous about what you might discover. But history can't be rewritten – it is what it is.

When I had the awful task of going through her things, I found this hidden away at the back of a drawer. There was no letter but if you look closely your name is written in pencil inside the lid. I opened one of the small notebooks and realised that France was a dream my mother had to let go, but it still meant a lot to her. Oh, her passion for plants and nature in general always shone through and she shared that with us all, but I still can't bring myself to go through the contents of this box.

In the end, what's contained here turned out to be the sum total of her career. After she returned to the UK, she made the decision to devote her time to supporting the man she loved and to have and nurture a family. Unlike the memory box, which contained a wealth of old photos, letters and general items she happily shared, this is different.

I believe that she kept her notebooks because at some point she wanted to share her adventure with you, honey. That's why I could never bring myself to pore over them; maybe she didn't want to upset me. Or maybe it was because you had a very special bond with her.

You know that I don't really believe in all that psychic stuff... too airy-fairy for me, but – and it's a but that sent me scurrying to parcel this up and send it off to you – last night I had a dream. I rarely remember what happens once my head touches the pillow, but I woke up to find tears on my cheeks, convinced your grandma had come to visit me. As I opened my eyes, I swear I could still feel her presence and smell her perfume.

Shellie said you were intent on trying to discover whatever you can about your grandma's time there. So, I'm sending this to you by recorded delivery because I think it was a sign. Even if it was only my conscience telling me it was wrong to hold out any longer.

At some point, depending upon what you discover, maybe we can talk about the part of her life she kept very quiet. Without a doubt, you are the one who is most like her in so many ways. If there are lessons to be learnt, then maybe that's why she kept them. Perhaps Versailles was meant to be a part of your journey, too, although how could she have known that? It all sounds a little silly, but I'm feeling very emotional about the past, today.

Anyway, honey, please don't go putting too much pressure on yourself. I'm so proud of what you've achieved already. I worry that you will follow in your brother's footsteps. Always remember that success shouldn't come at the cost of one's happiness in life.

Enjoy experiencing spring in a wonderful and very special setting. But I'm marking each day off on my calendar until your safe return, because life isn't quite the same without you here.

Love Mum. x

I swallow a lump that has risen in my throat. My heart is thumping in my chest and my stomach begins to churn. I stand, busying myself by putting away the contents of the carrier bags while I try to get my head around Mum's letter, and the level of trust she's putting in me. She's torn about whether or not she wants to know what really happened. Reaching for the lid and turning it over, sure enough I see my name staring back at me.

What if this reveals not just the contents of a box, but a secret that changes my perception of Grandma Viv forever? Is it possible that the wonderful memories I have of her could be tarnished by what I might find? Do I have the right to do what even her own daughter can't bring herself to do? But then again, Grandma could so easily have destroyed the notebooks, and no one would have been any the wiser.

With so much apprehension and doubt swirling around in my head, I go over and place the lid firmly back on the box. There's a supper to prepare and I want to impress Ronan after he was kind enough to put so much effort into our cosy little meal. Reading the notebooks is something I'm going to have to think long and hard about before I go any further.

* * *

When Ronan arrives, he steps inside with a big smile on his face and thrusts a small bunch of pretty pink tulips and a bottle of wine into my arms. We're beyond shaking hands now, I realise as he's leaning in to kiss my cheek. The space is so confined it's impossible to avoid each other anyway. I return his smile, tilting my head to alternate cheeks. I can feel myself blush as I turn to head up the stairs.

'Well,' he comments as he follows behind me, 'something smells good.'

'I hope you're hungry, I'm cooking my mum's favourite recipe from the seventies, based on a French classic.'

He laughs out loud, slipping off his jacket. 'That would be coq au vin, then. Actually, the modern version has barely changed and it's still very popular.'

I will admit the smell is amazing and it's my go-to dinner party dish. I'm pleased at Ronan's response and I head over to the kitchen area to put the flowers in a vase of water.

'Thank you, these are lovely, but you shouldn't have, really.'

'Oh, it's my pleasure. It's been a while since—' He pauses, awkwardly.

'Since you had a date?' Heck, there's no point in avoiding the obvious.

Ronan casts me a rather nervous glance. 'Well, yes, a date – I was rather hoping that's what this is.'

'Take a seat. Maybe you can uncork the wine while I dish up? I think the bottle you brought will be a safer bet than the one I randomly picked off the supermarket shelf.'

That raises a smile too. Ronan is wearing navy trousers and a slim-fit white shirt, which really suits him, and I can see he's made an effort tonight. I think he's even styled his hair, as it's usually a little wayward on the top. I pull out the plates that are warming in the grill, trying not to look his way as he rolls back his sleeves and turns his attention to uncorking the wine.

We work in a companionable silence as I ferry the casserole across to the table, then the dish of crispy roast potatoes. After pouring a little wine, Ronan picks up the small box of matches next to the candle in the centre of the table to light it.

'I like that you're a candle person,' he says, his words softly spoken. 'This is vanilla?'

I nod. 'Yes. I think it's my TV brain and the years I've spent being reminded about lighting, and the mood of a room.'

We're side by side staring down at the table and I turn my head to look up into his eyes. My mouth has gone dry.

'Um... well, take a seat and let's eat!'

I was a bit nervous that acknowledging this was a date might make things a little awkward between us, but I needn't have worried. In between two helpings we chat almost non-stop, mainly about childhood memories. Ronan admits he yearned to travel.

'You've obviously always been curious and an explorer,' I add, as I watch him finish clearing his plate.

'Now that was good.' He sighs, relinquishing his knife and fork. He wipes his mouth on a napkin, sitting back in his chair to relax. 'My mother, Eve, was over-protective, and the truth is that there were occasions when I felt hemmed in. I spent a lot of time in my room either reading or watching films and it opened up a whole new world.'

'It sounds like a rather solitary existence for a child.'

He shrugs his shoulders.

'It was all I knew. I was the centre of her life. I guess in my head I wanted to become this intrepid explorer, wielding a machete as I stumbled through the jungle discovering ancient ruins. Or white-water rafting, to reach some far-flung village, away from the beaten track.'

'Ah, now I understand. And that wasn't such a bad thing in your case.'

He cradles the wine glass in his hands, staring down into it.

'I felt it was my job, well, my role, to keep her happy; to make up for the fact that she loved my father, but he didn't love us. They were never married and had never lived together, so she only ever used her maiden name, Arnoult. When, eventually, he did marry he had two daughters, but there was no contact and hadn't been for years. I doubt they even knew of our existence at that point. To my cost, much later I came to learn just how badly he wanted a son, but one who was under his roof and his control.'

The undertone of bitterness he can't hide is poignant. To be rejected once is hurtful, to be rejected twice is unforgivable.

'She must miss you, even after seven years, but I'm sure she understands why France was such a draw,' I offer.

He raises his head. 'There were two reasons I turned my back on the UK and my mother's well-being was one of them, ironically. It forced her to take a step back and start living her own life before it was too late, but it was tough on us both for a while. We're gradually repairing our relationship, but she hasn't totally forgiven me yet. But it did force her to look for ways to get out and meet people, including a widower named Frank, when she joined an art class. They've been seeing each other for two years now and he's good for her. In all honesty, there were times I felt I couldn't breathe, if that makes sense.'

It's a sad story, but something he said has made me think about my own family rift.

'It must be a relief for you. Family stuff can be hard to deal with sometimes. I haven't seen my older brother for a few years now and it does hurt; the family no longer feels complete. It's heartbreaking for my mum. Being on her own, she tends to spend a lot of time worrying about us all, even though we try to encourage her to lead a full life. My dad spent most of his working life travelling, so she was very much the rock in our family. It worked for us, but maybe for my brother, Jake, being brought up in a household full of women, he was the one who missed Dad's influence the most. It never occurred to me that as the oldest he might feel he had to step up. I thought he was just full of himself. He's a bit like that.'

The candle between us flutters as the melted wax swamps the wick. The light dies and the last few puffs of smoke are blackened, filling the air with an acrid smell.

'Hmmmm. Time to clear the table, I think. Are we going to sit and finish this wine, or did you drive? I could put the kettle on.'

'I came by taxi as parking isn't the easiest here,' he admits.

We clear the plates between us, and I quickly run a sink full of water, washing as we talk. On several occasions our arms brush as we work around each other in the confined space. I'm certainly not complaining and neither is he.

'If you carry the glasses over to the sofas, I'll dry my hands and find another candle. Can you turn the side light on, too? Thanks.'

The evening is going so well and I can't remember the last time I felt this level of connection on a date. I find Ronan fascinating to talk to and there is definitely that little physical thrill thing going on between us. Maybe it's because I'm not on my home turf and France adds that frisson of being able to let my hair down, away from anyone who knows me. Whichever, it's clear we are both enjoying it.

When I walk over to Ronan, I hesitate momentarily about whether it will look presumptuous to sit next to him on the sofa rather than opposite him, but there's something about the twinkle in his eye and I decide to take a seat next to him. He hands me a full glass of wine and raises his in a toast.

'To a fabulous evening with great food and wonderful company. Thank you, Lexie!'

We touch glasses; our eyes are on each other as we each take a sip, before settling back in our seats.

'So, are you ready for tomorrow?'

'Yes. There comes a point when you can't really do any more and you just need to get on with it. The nerves are beginning to kick in, but it's been a weird afternoon, if I'm honest with you, and I've been a little distracted.'

He frowns, putting his glass back down on the coffee table in front of us.

'Distracted? There isn't a problem, is there?'

'No. Everything is fine. This is family stuff. A part of the reason why I'm here, as you know, is to do with my grandma.'

He raises both eyebrows. 'I'm glad you mentioned that. I trawled through some of the info on my database, but I haven't found anything as yet. Have you discovered some new information?'

'Maybe.'

I didn't mean to raise this and I'm annoyed with myself for breaking the mood. I'm also not sure how much to tell him. What's in the box has never been seen by anyone other than Grandma herself and I don't want to betray her memory by sharing her thoughts and reflections too soon.

Ronan is watching me intently and it's time to make a quick decision. He has told me a lot about himself and he needn't have shared that, and my gut is saying that he's someone I can trust.

'My mum has sent me another box she found hidden amongst my grandma's things. No one has ever opened anything inside it as far as we know, but she wrote my name on the underside of the lid.'

'And it contains?'

I slide out the drawer of the coffee table and grab hold of the box, putting it on my lap.

'It's full of notebooks and there was a heartfelt letter from my mum.'

I'm hugging it to me, as if it's valuable. Which it is, to me.

'Do you want to share that, or is it too personal?'

My hand hesitates for a moment before I prise off the lid, lifting out the folded sheet of paper and passing it to Ronan. I think I trust this man, and what I need is an impartial opinion. If I'm any judge of character at all, I do believe he's capable of that.

He takes a few moments to digest the contents before looking up at me, wide-eyed.

'Okay. This isn't an easy situation you find yourself in, then.'

I close my eyes, momentarily, so relieved that he seems to understand my dilemma.

'I know.'

'So, what are you going to do?'

I sigh. 'I'm scared I'll discover something that could end up breaking my heart. My grandparents love for each other was a romance that never ended – even after his death he was still the one for her until the day she died. If I kept whatever I discover from Mum, I think she'd sense something was up. My sister warned me about my obsession with Grandma and Versailles, but I thought that if I found out where she stayed when she was here, I'd feel closer to her. However, this box changes everything, and, well, who knows what secrets there are in the notebooks? Do I take the risk and read them because that's what she wanted, or do I let the past lie?'

'You can't right now and that's obvious, just looking at you and the way you're hugging that box as if someone is about to snatch it away from you.'

I'm feeling tearful, not least because Ronan seems to understand. It's not my imagination; there is a real connection between us that seems to grow with each encounter.

'But a part of me has to know. Why didn't she just burn the contents of this box when she knew she was dying? If I'd been older at that point, maybe she would have sat me down and told me the story in full. Grandma Viv believed in passing on some of the lessons she'd learnt. Many of them repeated so many times, they're imprinted on my mind, and it has helped to guide so many of my decisions as an adult. It's like she's still with me, if you can understand that.'

He cups his chin in his hand, running his fingers down each side against the light stubble, in thinking mode.

'You have reason to believe there's a message in there she wanted you to discover?'

Shrugging my shoulders, I stare down into the open box. There's no order to anything, no conveniently numbered covers. Just two rows of spiral-bound notebooks about six inches by five and a few keepsakes, by the look of it, wedged in between them.

'Look, I can see this is upsetting you. Why not pop the lid back on and stash it away in the drawer until you're ready to make a start? Wait and see if I can uncover anything at all about what she was involved in at the palace. Maybe even find out where she stayed and take you there. How about that?'

I nod gratefully, then almost without thinking I close my fingers around one of the small notebooks and I lift it out of the box.

'Can you just do me one favour?'

He looks at me, unblinking.

'Open the first page and tell me what it says, but don't go any further.'

There's a hint of reluctance as he takes the book from me, then slowly opens it, his eyes scanning the words written on the page.

'Goodness.' His glance confirms he's intrigued. 'It's a title page. "Nature is a formidable teacher. Embrace the lessons if you want the seeds of your life to grow and be fruitful. My personal journey." She's signed it Vivian Hanley and that's it.'

I hesitate for a moment, then pop it back into the box before closing the lid. I can tell he's curious and would like to investigate further, but I'm not ready to trawl through Grandma Viv's personal collection quite yet.

'I'm sorry, I bet it's a bit frustrating for you, Ronan, as a researcher. I know that her time here is a part of the history of the garden in a very small way. If I bring myself to read through the contents, then anything I think might be useful to the work you're doing, of course I'll share with you. Maybe that's what it was all about, anyway. But without a clue over where this might lead, I need to be cautious and not merely curious. I hope you can understand that.'

He turns slightly in his seat, reaching out to place his hand over mine as it languishes between us on the sofa. As our skin touches, the warmth of him is exciting and I can feel my pulse begin to race.

'You could be right. There was a lot of tension at Versailles at the time and tussles over what should be given priority. Egos came into play and the internal politics really affected the people to whom the gardens were their life's work. But it's all history now, and the majority of the people involved are long gone.'

He's right, of course.

'But not all of them,' he adds suddenly. 'There is someone I could arrange for you to meet, who was a trainee here in the early sixties. He retired at the age of fifty-three, after being involved in a terrible car crash. He's in his late seventies now, but I've visited him on numerous occasions over the years. It's true that our relationship is a bit strained at the moment, but I think he'd enjoy talking to you, given the connection.'

'That would be incredible, Ronan. I'd love to know if someone remembers my grandma when she was here. She might have given up on her dream career for the love of my granddad, but that doesn't mean it's not worth celebrating her other big achievement. And that was for a whole year to be a part of the team of gardeners helping to tend one of the most famous gardens in the world.'

7

DAY ONE IN THE CAN

I'm buzzing this morning, fuelled by nervous energy and excitement. Elliot arrives looking tired, but his cough seems a little better than it has been and he's more like his old self. It takes just over an hour to set everything up.

We're filming in the North Parterre this morning and we want to get the majority of the interview out of the way before the gardens are at their busiest. We need to wrap by noon at the latest, but it's going to be a complicated first session. Monsieur Theron Picard is a senior gardener and very knowledgeable, but he doesn't speak any English at all.

It's finally time to film the intro for this episode, after which I'll be briefing Ronan, ready for the interview.

'Okay.' I run my hands through my hair, flicking it out at the back where it tends to fall a little flat and straightening my collar. A quick check by Cameron that the wireless microphone is firmly attached to my lapel and I'm about as ready as I will ever be.

'I'll count you down from ten,' he informs Elliot and myself. I draw in a couple of really deep breaths to help me focus. Forcing a smile and then relaxing my facial muscles several times in quick succession, I'm all set. This has been a long time in coming and the moment has finally arrived.

'... four... three... two... one!'

'I think few would argue that André Le Nôtre was one of the most famous and influential landscape architects in French history. As we take you... argh!'

I catch a sudden movement out of the side of my right eye and take a quick step backwards, almost losing my balance, as two squabbling birds swoop out of the towering hedgerow, dipping and missing my cheek by the merest of whispers. Cameron, being the nearest to me, instinctively grabs my flailing right arm to steady me and in the process dislodges his headset. Having steadied my legs, he slowly releases his grip and I give him a grateful nod.

'Thanks. That was unexpected. Guess it isn't people we're going to be dodging today but the birds, who clearly love this hornbeam hedging.'

He nods, stepping back and taking a minute or two to readjust his headphones before checking he didn't yank on any of the leads when he sprinted forward.

Elliot has lowered the camera from his shoulder. 'Are you okay?' he asks, and I can see he's anxious to get on. A sudden fit of coughing catches him unawares and we wait patiently, trying not to put him under pressure by watching him. It's a painful sound, but he recovers well.

'Sorry. You're all set now?' Elliot checks, his voice sounding rather gravelly.

'Yes, I'm fine. The birds just caught me off guard. Count me down from three this time, Cameron. I'm good to go, really.'

Cameron strides forward to double-check my mic first and then steps back, giving Elliot a thumbs up.

'Three... two... one.'

'I think few would argue that André Le Nôtre was one of the most famous and influential landscape architects in French history. As we take you on a journey around the magnificent park and gardens at Versailles, designed to complement the Sun King's sumptuous palace, the question is – was this Le Nôtre's finest achievement?'

I half turn, indicating the vista behind me, and Elliot pans around to capture the magnificent backdrop.

'I'm standing in front of the North Parterre, one of four areas situated to the rear of the palace. These level spaces house the formal gardens, separated by connecting pathways and occupied by ornamental flower beds. The symmetrical displays are flanked by vast rows of iconic hedging and we will be looking in depth at the work involved to maintain these wonderful, living structures.'

The words just seem to flow, but I've practised them so many times over the last few months that I could probably repeat a lot of it in my sleep. We move on to do several short promotional pieces that we are hoping to use to demo the series. Then a run of fifteen-second break bumpers, that can be shown before a commercial break. These are one-liners that will have the same soundtrack and will advertise other episodes in the series.

Finally, I'm done and I can relax my face once more. Elliot pans back around to capture the rear elevation of the palace building before lowering the camera from his shoulder, a little awkwardly.

'How did it look?' I ask and his smile is reassuring.

'Good,' he confirms. His voice has recovered, and that rasp has gone.

'It looked perfect to me too.' Ronan's voice suddenly fills the air and I turn round to give him a welcoming smile.

'Great timing,' I reply, glancing at my watch. 'We have about an hour until Solange appears with our expert. Elliot, are you happy to get some footage of the walk down to Neptune's Fountain while it's still quiet?'

He nods. 'Yep, no problem. See you in a bit.'

As I stand here and gaze around, it's the sheer scale of the layout that screams bold, audacious even, planning. It's quite a walk to follow the straight path between the mirror-image sections to the left and right-hand sides of the North Parterre. Beyond this is the fountain named the Pyramide, a very elaborate affair comprising statuary and stonework. It's a central focal point but also an art form. It leads on to the water walk, which stretches off into the distance and the main event – the infamous Dragon Fountain. Beyond that, the enormous Neptune Fountain completes the picture.

'Now you're done with me for the moment, Elliot, I'll head to the Grand Café d'Orléans to grab a coffee and run through the interview questions with Ronan. Anything we can bring back for either of you guys?'

Elliot and Cameron both shake their heads. Cameron has already removed my mic and I know he won't wander far from his kit. He's already fiddling with knobs and settings on the sound box, one hand pressed against his right ear as he listens intently.

'Give me forty-five minutes and I'll be ready for you,' Elliot confirms.

'See you in a bit, then.' I nod to Ronan and we head off in the direction of the café.

'It's such a relief to be making a start,' I admit to Ronan as we walk. 'I feel as if my head might explode with the information buzzing around inside it. How are you doing this morning?'

He casts me a glance and I wonder if he's a little nervous.

'Great,' he says, sounding confident. 'I'm sure we'll get all the information you need, but I'm a little concerned about making sure the answers don't go off track. How do we handle that, given that you won't really get the gist of Theron's replies?'

The gravel beneath our feet is a little annoying when you're wearing heels, especially as Ronan is striding out.

'Don't worry too much about that. I'd rather have too much material to trawl through than not enough. Obviously, if you feel he's missed something crucial then by all means jump in and give him a steer, but we'll just keep rolling. It's going to be a massive editing and voice-over job anyway, once we're in the studio.'

Any doubts I had about Ronan are long gone; his background, working for his father, means he knows the score. As long as the questions I pose today are well constructed, hopefully we'll have a happy interviewee who can give us everything we need, and more.

* * *

After a long session filming, we all chink bottles, raising our cold beers in a toast to what has been an amazing first day.

'Well, guys, I don't think that could have gone any better,' Elliot says, beaming from ear to ear.

'You did a brilliant job, Ronan and Cameron, especially putting Theron at ease. My heart did start pounding for a moment at the start, especially when I asked that first question. Theron looked at me, then at the camera and back again as if nothing was going to come out of his mouth! As soon as Ronan jumped in to interpret, Theron didn't take long to find his stride though.'

There's a real buzz in the air as I glance around the table.

'Yes, I thought the exact same thing. The seconds began ticking by and I thought he'd frozen, but he recovered well,' Cameron adds.

'Once he relaxed a little it really flowed and I'm pretty sure we covered everything you needed, Lexie,' Ronan says. 'Maybe not quite in the right order, but it's all there.'

'You did well redirecting him on several occasions, Ronan. I picked up bits of it, but I can't wait to get into the studio because it all sounded fascinating. I'm sure it will piece together well and make a cohesive interview. I'm looking forward to filming the second half, when we get to follow the team as they trim the hedges and shape some of the wonderful topiary.'

We're all on a high but I know that when the adrenaline begins to slow down, I'm going to feel shattered and just want to sleep. But for now, it's all about enjoying the high.

'That's some camera you have there, Elliot,' Ronan enthuses. 'Nice bit of kit – bet that put a dent in the bank balance, for sure.'

Elliot smiles knowingly. 'You get what you pay for and Lexie and I saw it as a necessary investment. Think big, I say, and it doesn't get any bigger than Versailles as a starting place,' he muses.

They have a little back and forth chat about frame counts and Ronan seems very impressed when Elliot informs him it can handle up to two hundred and forty frames per second.

At that point my eyes glaze over, and I zone out for a few minutes, taking in the ambience of our surroundings.

We're sitting outside one of those cosy little bars that isn't quite a café but isn't a traditional *tabac* either. It's lovely to be able to enjoy the warmth of such a beautifully sunny March day, even with the sound of traffic and honking horns in the background.

'So, the next interview for you lot is in two days' time, then,' Ronan reflects, looking around the table at Elliot and Cameron, his eyes coming to rest on me.

'Yes. Anton Mereux. We'll be filming in front of the Orangery. You said he won't need an interpreter?' I query, double-checking.

'Anton speaks several languages rather well. It's important in his role, as his team comprises a lot of foreign students who come to hone their skills in topiary. And you're off to Paris tomorrow, then, Elliot?'

Elliot nods his head. 'Another pre-production session. The bigger the budget, the more meetings it generates. I'm not sure all of them are necessary or productive, but it pays the bills so I'm not complaining. How about you?'

Ronan shifts a little in his seat, easing back his shoulders in a circular movement, and I realise he was probably a little tense today. I hope he's getting the message loud and clear that both Elliot and I are extremely happy with his part in today's filming.

'I'm working on book three in my *Versailles – The Living Garden* series. But I'm struggling to find the catalyst to help me focus on this one. Both of my other books are based on anecdotal information gleaned from interviews, which I then researched. The history is well documented, of course, but I'm concentrating on modern-day characters and the personalities who have been instrumental in shaping and running the horticultural programme here since the early 1900s.'

Elliot and I exchange a quick glance. Ronan is turning out to be more of an expert than either of us expected.

'If I'd realised beforehand, then I would have read your books as a part of my research,' I reply, feeling remiss.

Ronan shrugs his shoulders. 'I doubt it would have been relevant. Much of it focuses on internal politics and why certain decisions were made at various points over time. The books are a celebration of the dedication of key characters in the modern history of the gardens, who I think were unsung heroes. Passions have always run high at Versailles. When someone dedicates their entire working life to something it's more than a job; it's a legacy for everyone who has a hand in the process.'

'I can well believe that after today's interview. Even though I couldn't understand very much of what Theron said, it was his intensity and the way he kept reaching out to touch the hedging around him as he spoke. Like a proud father talking about his children,' I muse.

They all nod in agreement. Elliot suddenly begins coughing again and has to lean forward until he can catch his breath.

'I'll be glad when this clears up,' he eventually voices, sounding jaded. 'It's a damn nuisance. Right, I should head back to prep for tomorrow, as I'm up at the crack of dawn to do battle with the traffic.' He jumps to his feet in a sudden burst of energy. Elliot knows I'm worried about him and he's trying to allay my concerns.

Stooping to give me a hug, he then turns to shake Ronan's hand, thanking him for his efforts today, and leans across to fist-pump Cameron.

As I watch Elliot walk out, I can't help thinking that what he needs is a few days of rest.

'What's up?' Ronan asks, picking up on my concern.

'He's been overdoing it. And now his girlfriend, Mia, has caught this flu thing too. Was it my imagination, or was Elliot struggling a little today with his left shoulder?'

Our eyes meet. 'I thought the same thing, but he didn't mention it, did he?'

I sit quietly, mulling over my thoughts.

Cameron clears his throat before speaking. 'A couple of times I saw him wince,' he throws in, stopping for a moment to drain his bottle of beer and glance at his watch. 'When you went off to the café, he admitted that he thinks he's pulled a muscle. Sadly, I should head off too, as I need to pack a few things and get on the road. It's a five a.m. start for me tomorrow. Onwards and upwards from here, guys.'

He stands, leaning across the table to shake hands, and says he'll be back on Thursday.

As Cameron walks away, Ronan turns towards me, making eye contact.

'It was obvious that Elliot was struggling a little at times,' he agrees. 'Look, if he needs a bit of a break from filming at any point I can easily jump in and cover for him when you don't need me to interpret. Book three isn't going anywhere fast, at the moment, to be honest. Obviously, I won't step on any toes, as it looks like Elliot is determined to power through, but if it comes to that then the offer is there.'

'Thanks, that's really appreciated. If the opportunity presents itself, I'll suggest he sees a doctor. You can't be too careful, can you? And I'm sorry your research isn't going well. It must be frustrating, ploughing through endless records to glean a little information you can really latch on to. Do you ever miss working for your father?'

That thought randomly jumped into my head, but as I look across at Ronan, I can see he wasn't prepared for it.

'I, well, no. We rowed, constantly. You see, I won't take his name and he sees that as the ultimate betrayal.'

I'm stunned. 'Oh.'

I don't quite know what to say to that. Ronan presses himself back into his seat, toying with the glass of water on the table in front of him.

'I said it was complicated and it is.'

'Well, I'm here and if you feel like sharing then I'm happy to listen.'

He inclines his head, indicating that I might be sorry I asked.

'When my mother, Eve, was sixteen years old my grand-mother wanted her to get in touch with her Irish roots. So, my mother left France and went to live with my aunt in the town of Killarney, County Kerry. She enrolled at St Brendan's College and, while she missed her mum, suddenly her life got a whole lot more exciting. A year later she met my father, Oliver Traynor. He was four years older than her, although at the time I suspect he had no idea that was the case. They had a very brief affair, from the little I can gather.

'I have no doubt at all that my mother had fallen madly in love at first sight, but for him it was a transient thing. His future career path came before everything else at that time. When my mother discovered she was pregnant, he didn't want to know. She ended up quitting college and my aunt had a tough time with her, as she was an emotional wreck. My father made no attempt to contact her at all after hearing the news and when she registered my birth she used her name, Arnoult, and his name didn't appear on the certificate.

'Eventually, out of guilt no doubt, he did get in touch and began supporting us both financially. I think he was worried my mother, or my aunt, might make trouble for him and the last thing he needed was the threat of gossip.'

'How awful for your mother,' I say, sadly. 'She was facing an exciting new future, only to end up broken-hearted at such a young age. That's tragic, as having a baby is a joyous event and a blessing.'

Ronan nods.

'That's life. These things happen. She was so young and rather naive. It was an unfortunate twist of fate, because suddenly Mum's options were limited. My father was promoted around the same time and it was making people sit up and notice him, raising his profile. Whether he realised that money was such an issue for us, I don't know.

'My aunt looked after me, as my mother had to work two jobs just to keep a roof over our heads until he finally stepped in to help out. She never got over my father's rejection and she's a proud woman, so when he did offer to help it would have hurt her to accept it. In the small community in which we lived no one was aware of our link to him and she wanted to keep it that way.'

'But you don't use your mother's maiden name any longer?' Now I'm really confused.

He gives a little smirk. 'Hell hath no fury... as the saying goes. When I was old enough for my mother to sit me down and tell me the whole story, she talked a lot about Ireland. Grandma Colleen was very proud of her Irish roots. Sadly, after numerous miscarriages my mother was her only surviving child. Grandma herself was one of five girls and although there were five cousins, only one was a boy. Tragically, he died at the age of six after falling out of a tree. There was no one to carry on the O'Byrne name. Now, my grandfather had two brothers, one of whom had two sons, so the Arnoult line continues to thrive. I'm sure my mother was only trying to honour my grandmother, but the sting in the tail in asking me to change my surname by deed poll was that she knew it would be another slap in the face for my father. He hated the fact that I had never carried his name and this sent a clear message that I never would. I was old enough by then to appreciate that fact, and I suppose I, too, was exacting a little revenge for the way he rejected her... well, us.'

My jaw drops slightly. That's quite an admission and yet it demonstrates very clearly how close Ronan, his mother and his grandmother were. I supposed that was only natural, given what they had been through.

'I was a young teen at the time, and I told you it was a long story. Inevitably, the day came when he made contact with me. My father said he regretted some of the decisions he'd made in his younger years and offered me a job. He's a very persuasive man in many ways and I thought he was genuinely reaching out to me. This was my chance to get to know him, as well as an opportunity to hone my skills. I wouldn't simply be learning something from him, but my ego kicked in and I wanted to impress him, I suppose. So, I went for it. And that's when the real horror story began. He has a ruthless streak when it comes to business and he's a bully if people don't simply jump to attention and do his bidding.'

I take in a deep breath. 'How did your mother take the news?'

'She was torn, I think. I was fresh from university and the job market was saturated at the time, so we both knew it was an offer anyone would have jumped at. She might not have wished him well, exactly, but she has always put my interests first. Like it or not, he's my biological father and Mum hoped his intentions were good. This was his chance to make amends, if you like.'

'After having had virtually no involvement in your life, I presume his family understood his sudden desire to get to know you?'

'I really don't know. I didn't have much to do with them, and his wife made it clear she had no intention of recognising me formally as a part of the family. I had my own place and I was happy enough once I'd settled in and made friends.

'His girls, my half-sisters, are a few years younger than me; one was hoping to become a fashion designer with the help of our father's cheque book and the other one was off backpacking around the world with her adventurer boyfriend. At the time my father was very annoyed to have funded her trip to Australia, in what was supposed to have been her gap year before going to university. He hasn't seen much of her since, I gather.'

Ronan is very matter-of-fact about it all, but it sounds like a war zone to me. No wonder he turned his back on them, just to get a little peace.

'Well, that's karma for you,' I remark.

'My thoughts, exactly. It's just easier for me being here now, as I don't get pulled into any of it any more. My mother is finally making a life for herself and learning to let go of the past. Living with resentment constantly welling up inside you isn't good for anyone and it nearly destroyed her for a while. My father has no need to contact her and now she knows I'm happily settled, she can at last relax. That's not to say she doesn't phone me all the time to chide me about being more focused, but she knows I'm content.'

It must be difficult to share such a harrowing life story, and I'm glad Ronan seems happy to put his trust in me.

'Right. That's enough about that. Did you drive or walk? I have the car and can give you a lift back, if you like.'

'Thank you. I wasn't relishing the idea of the walk.'

Pulling into the entrance in front of the gates, Ronan insists on driving in, parking up while I search around in my backpack for the key. When he follows me out of the car and walks round to the front door of number six, I wonder if he wants to come in for coffee. He hesitates for a moment before stooping to kiss my cheek, and then turns to kiss the other. His body language indicates that he was considering kissing me on the lips and as he turns to walk away from me, I catch his hand.

Ronan turns round and I lean into him, resting my head against his shoulder.

'What's wrong?' he murmurs into my ear.

My arms instinctively wrap around his shoulders and I give him a gentle squeeze.

'You're a good man, Ronan, and I'm sorry for what you've been through. I just felt you needed... a hug.'

He laughs softly, leaning back a little to place his hand under my chin. Tilting my head, he gazes into my eyes. His smile is warm and tender.

'Hey, you don't miss what you never had. Besides, we were better off without him. I only needed to look at his present-day family dynamic to see that.'

'Well, I'm glad you weren't fooled, as it's human nature to give people the benefit of the doubt. Sometimes that's a good thing; sometimes it isn't.'

Ronan continues to stare down at me, his eyes scanning my face as if it's a page in a book.

'There's a soft heart beating beneath that highly professional exterior of yours, Lexie Winters. My instincts are telling me that it's something you try to hide. And that's a shame.'

I don't know quite how to respond, until he pulls me even closer. Which turns out to be a good thing. As our lips touch, I begin to feel a little light-headed. The gentleness is sweet, but I think it's obvious we're both holding back. A noise on the other side of the courtyard sees us drawing apart and we exchange slightly embarrassed smiles. Words lie, but kisses don't.

'Well, I, um... had better let you get some rest.'

8

BEING NEIGHBOURLY

After every adrenaline high comes the fall, and when I wake up this morning, I'm glad it is a day to chill out and go through my notes in preparation for tomorrow's filming. By lunch time I'm pretty much up to speed and, grabbing my iPad, I decide to download Ronan's two books from Amazon.

Clearing a space amongst the piles of paperwork on the dining table, I figure I might as well have a little read while I eat. I should have popped to the boulangerie, but I have half a large baguette left over from yesterday. It's lost its crunch but it's the perfect accompaniment for creamily soft Pont-l'Évêque cheese, a handful of walnuts and some apple slices. Heaven on a plate.

Turning on my iPad, I flick past the cover and go straight to the dedication page of the first in Ronan's series and, despite the huge piece of bread I've just popped into my mouth, I stop chewing for a second.

In memory of my grandfather, Fabien Arnoult,

whose spirit lives on in the gardens
he loved more than life itself.

The words jump off the page and my head involuntarily jerks backwards a little, as if I'm having to dodge them. *More than life itself?* I wouldn't even say that of my dad, who I'm sure loved his work just as much as he loved his family. It's one thing to give whatever you are doing your complete attention, but another to place it above all else. I swipe and begin reading.

When lunch is done, I saunter over to the sofa with my iPad still firmly grasped in my hand. Stretching out on the sofa rather lazily, I only intend to continue reading for a little while before doing some laundry, but an hour passes and another. It's fascinating reading, but what I'm really looking for is any reference to his grandfather. Before I know it, I'm already a third of the way through and there's no mention of him at all. I was expecting a formal textbook charting the history of the key people involved, but instead Ronan has woven a rich narrative, based on in-depth interviews conducted over quite a period, and his detailed research. It is as gripping as any good novel; he has been able to give a real insight into the lives of a succession of gardeners.

What stands out already is that the behind-the-scenes politics didn't end when Versailles was no longer a seat of power; the disagreements, differing viewpoints and the constant struggle with money were a real battleground and even today there are still tough decisions to be made.

The first half of the book talks in length about Versailles in the early 1900s. The palace was going through a period of restoration and conservation, led by Pierre de Nolhac, interrupted, of course, by two world wars; in the 1920s, philanthropist John D. Rockefeller donated in excess of two million dollars to the project.

The latter half of the first book takes the reader through to the late 1950s. The second book, by the looks of it, is based almost exclusively on the working life of Maurice Perrin. After a long career spanning forty-one years, he ended up being one of the most influential of the chief gardeners during his time at the palace.

He joined the team in 1945 at the age of twenty-four. Sadly, he died, at the grand old age of ninety-four, a year after Ronan's series of interviews with him was completed.

My eyes are beginning to grow weary and reluctantly I press the off button.

Walking over to the window and peering out, I'm surprised to see Madame Duval, throwing what looks like a bundle of dripping items out through her front door. She immediately disappears for a second or two, rushing back with her hands full of even more saturated items. I turn and head straight for the stairs.

Hurrying across the courtyard towards her, I call out.

'Is everything all right, Madame Duval?'

She throws up her arms to the heavens, a babble of words coming back at me in a very agitated tone of voice. I don't understand exactly what she's saying, but I can see that there is a pile of sopping-wet towels in front of her.

'Leak? You have a leak?'

She looks at me, frowning. 'Water,' she declares, drawing it out so it sounds like *waterrrr*. 'Dans ma cuisine,' she adds with desperate urgency, before hurrying back inside. The hemline of her skirt is heavy and dripping.

I stride out to catch up with her, negotiating the narrow

hallway and following her into the ground-floor kitchen. I'm surprised by the very different layout, but I guess not having a garage opens up the options. But even before I step through the inner doorway, I can hear the sound of water flooding out of a tap. To my horror, there's an arc of water shooting up into the air. Only some of it is falling back down into the sink itself, the rest is hitting the floor in a constant stream. Madame is on her hands and knees with even more towels to absorb the waterfall.

'Where do you turn off your water supply?' She looks back at me, uncomprehendingly. 'Où fermez-vous l'eau?'

Madame blinks and points to a small cupboard in the corner and I head straight for it, pushing aside a bucket and some mops and turning the stopcock with all my might. It's impossibly stiff and I can see why she hasn't managed it herself, as I'm struggling to move it even a millimetre. After some encouraging and much pressure, it finally releases and the sound of the rushing waterfall in the background quietens.

When I turn around Madame Duval is leaning against the sink unit and she visibly sags. Rushing over, I put an arm around her and walk her across the kitchen to sit her down, pulling a chair out from beneath the old pine table.

'It's fine. Just sit quietly and let me clear up,' I tell her, not sure she is even listening to me.

I notice there's a hammer lying on the worktop and next to that is the top part of the tap.

She nods. 'Merci, oh, merci,' she groans. I'd love to stop and make her a cup of tea, but I need to mop up the puddle of water before it does irreparable damage to the bottom of the kitchen units.

It takes about twenty minutes of toing and froing to take

the sopping towels out into the courtyard, wring them out and return to soak up some more of the water. Eventually, after throwing open both windows above the sink unit and keeping the front door wedged open, there's no surface water left. Thankfully it's not chilly today and there's a warm breeze being drawn through the cottage, which should soon begin to speed up the drying process.

'Slippery, madame. Dangereux,' I advise her as she sits watching me. But at least she has a little more colour in her face now. For one awful moment I thought she was going to faint. I lift the kettle, glad to feel it has water in it. 'Thé?' I enquire, thinking that there's no point in doing anything about the tap until the floor has dried out a little more.

She nods. 'I make. Je suis très reconnaissante... thankful. Please to call me Renée.' She stands, giving me a warm smile, and begins bustling around the kitchen. Opening cupboards, Renée pulls out cups, a delicious-looking homemade tart and some beautiful little china plates decorated with roses.

I continue running a dry mop over the dampest part of the floor, as I'm worried it's still a bit of a hazard, but at least she seems calmer now.

'I wish my French was better,' I admit out loud. 'I can understand a little more if you talk slowly. But when it comes to replying I've forgotten a lot of what I learnt at school.'

She gives a little laugh and I turn my head to look at her, realising she got the general drift of what I was saying.

'Please. Thank you. Hello. C'est tout ce que je peux dire en anglais!' she explains.

Now we both laugh. I gesture towards the tap, using my hand in a turning movement and frowning. She walks across to show me the problem. Picking up the hammer, she indicates a swift blow and shrugs. It looks as if she wasn't able to turn it off for some reason, so she used a little force. The tap is very old and if it was as stiff as the stopcock in the cupboard, then I doubt her wrists would have been strong enough; goodness, even I struggled and thought for a moment I wasn't going to be able to shift it.

'Plumber?' I make a gesture of holding an imaginary phone to my ear and suddenly her eyes light up. She turns and walks over to one of the units, pulling open the drawer. When she walks back to me, she has a pair of glasses and a phone in her hand. Well, that's a good place to keep your phone if you don't like being interrupted. Within a few minutes Renée has made a call and gives me a huge smile, nodding her head very happily.

'Oui. Il arrivera dans une heure,' she informs me. It's followed by several sentences obviously telling me something about the plumber she called, some of which I do manage to piece together. Mainly that he lives close by, but he's at work at the moment.

Over tea and a slice of meltingly gorgeous pear tart, we have a conversation of sorts, using odd words and hand signals. It causes much laughter between the two of us. But as I tune into her voice, I find I can understand a lot more of what she's saying; the frustration is that I can't talk back to her as fluently, only in part sentences.

Afterwards she takes me out into her little garden. Both cottages on this side have similar sized plots to the rear and Renée's garden has a spectacular display of spring bulbs. Daffodils, lily of the valley and even wood violets create a wonderful splash of colour.

As far as I can tell, Renée lives here alone, but she does go on to tell me about the other neighbours. The property adjoining hers – number two – and numbers three and five are simply pieds-à-terre. Renée, it appears, is employed as a housekeeper, keeping the properties clean and checking them on a regular basis in between infrequent visits throughout the year.

Number four is empty right now. The man who lived there, whom she refers to as simply Pierre, died a few months ago. I can sense the sadness in her and maybe I misconstrue her babble of words, but I feel she was close to him. His family haven't decided yet what they are going to do with the property and her frown tells me it is a change she isn't looking forward to.

'Et numéro six?'

It's a holiday let, and it's run by a management company. She rarely sees the owner, a young man who lives and works in Paris.

When we part, she gives me a very warm hug and I point towards her phone. She passes it to me, and I pop in my number.

'Call me, any time. Appelez-moi si vous avez un problème,' I say, handing it back and holding my left hand up to my ear so she understands. 'If you need water – de l'eau.' I mime turning on a tap and filling a jug.

As she sees me out, she doesn't say anything further, simply placing her hand over her heart for a moment and giving me a look of sincere thanks. I make a mental note to visit her tomorrow and I'll make sure I bring my phone, so I can look things up if I struggle to find the right word.

Heading back, I prepare a quick chicken salad and work while I eat, re-reading my notes for tomorrow. When, eventually, I slip into bed, I'm feeling very sleepy and it doesn't take long before dreams claim me. I'm back at Versailles. Laughing, I launch myself into the Grand Canal, splashing around as if I am a child with no cares in the world. In my head, the only sound is that of running water.

9

I'M LIVING THE DREAM

It's shortly after seven a.m. when I lock the front door and set off. The birds are particularly noisy this morning, a little group of them chasing in and out of the small trees in the courtyard. Every day it's more evident that winter is over, and nature is already awake and showing the world its glory.

I glance across at number one, but there's no sign of any movement and it's too early to knock on the door. I did hear a car pull into the courtyard around six o'clock last night, so I think it's safe to assume that Renée's plumber managed to fix her tap.

Taking a left turn, I walk past the little boulangerie, called La Cuisine des Boulangers, waving when one of the ladies appears in the window as she leans across with tongs to grab a couple of croissants. I get a hearty wave back, and the tempting smell of freshly baked bread and pastries filling the air makes my feet long to take a quick detour. Instead I take a deep breath, which makes my mouth water, and keep walking.

All the staff are very friendly and the café on the other

side of the gateway is owned by the same family; it's only second generation, but it's a thriving little business and is always heaving with locals.

I'm beginning to feel very comfortable now I'm actually doing some real work. As I walk, I'm excited about today's interview, but I'm also anxious as it is still early days. And despite feeling as if I've settled in, I'm still missing home a little; just the chance to pop in and see Maisie and check on my sister or drop in for a coffee with Mum. Just then my phone pings, and I grab it from my pocket to see it's a text from the lady herself. She must have been thinking of me at the exact same moment!

✉ Morning, honey. Just to say good luck today and I hope the first interview without your lovely interpreter guy goes well. Ring me tonight if you get a chance and tell me all about it. Break a leg! x

Sidestepping a metal sign outside the last little gift shop on the Avenue de Paris before the three roads converge at the Place d'Armes, I hear my name being called out. Glancing around, Solange is waving at me and I stop so she can catch up.

'Bonjour!' I greet her with a smile. I didn't realise she lived within walking distance of the palace.

'Bonjour, Lexie. What a beautiful day again.'

She falls in alongside me as we continue on.

'How are you?'

'I'm good, and you?'

Her smile is warm and engaging, and I see that she's

rather gingerly carrying a little box from the boulangerie in her hand.

'Wonderful pastries.' I smile at her, nodding at her parcel.

'Oh, the best!'

'I didn't know you lived so close to the palace,' I add.

She gives me a rueful look. 'I don't. But I know a young man who does.'

I kick myself mentally for the offhand remark, but she simply grins back at me.

'Another day of filming. How is it going?'

'Very well, thank you. There are moments when it all makes me catch my breath. I've dreamt of being here for such a long time.'

She turns to look directly at me as we stop for a moment to look both ways before crossing the busy road in front of us.

'I can tell. When there is a personal connection it has even more meaning,' she enthuses.

'You knew someone who worked here in the past, too?' I hazard a guess but can see that I'm right.

She nods. 'My first boyfriend, several years ago. We met at a seminar and he invited me for a visit. Versailles grabbed my heart on that trip, and I knew that someday I would end up making my way back. However, it wasn't to be with him, and he no longer works here.' She laughs out loud and I give her a smile. 'Life moves on and now I'm seeing someone who lives close by.'

Interesting. I did wonder about a possible relationship between Solange and Ronan, but it seems I was wrong about that.

'Do you have a partner back in the UK?' she enquires matter-of-factly.

'Um... no. I'm married to my work.' Why did I say that? It

sounds lame. 'Guys come and go, but I haven't found anyone I consider a keeper yet.'

'Ah, that's sad, but we have to live in hope. I'm hopeful at the moment and I think he is, too. You're staying in the little courtyard behind the boulangerie. I was in the shop when I spotted you walking past.'

'Yes. It's a perfect little place to stay and an easy stroll away.'

'And you have met Renée,' she replies.

I look at her in surprise. 'Yes.'

'She is my boyfriend's grandmother.'

Well, that's unexpected. 'A lovely lady, I just wish my French was better. But we manage to chat a little,' I reflect.

'And I want to thank you; Philippe is a plumber and replaced her tap last night when we went to see her after work. As soon as she mentioned your name, I made the connection. She's very independent, but she isn't getting any younger, I'm afraid. I call in on her from time to time when Philippe is away working. To be honest, if number four comes on the market, he has it in his head to buy it and I think it's a wonderful idea.'

'It must be hard being away from your family.'

'It is,' she admits as we walk through the outer gates of the palace and she slows, indicating that she's heading into the ticket office. 'My father and I haven't spoken since I left. But my life is based here now and he must learn to make his peace with that if he truly wants me to be happy and not just be a dutiful daughter, pining away for dreams that remain unfulfilled.'

'Well, if you're ever in need of a chat, you know where I live.'

She looks at me intently. 'Thank you, Lexie, that is most kind. I will remember that.'

As we part, I walk away thinking that following one's dream isn't always easy. How can anyone be sure that the choices they make will turn out to be the right ones? Or how different life would have been if they'd gone in another direction? I suppose it's about listening to what your gut instincts tell you and making the best of it, whatever happens.

I've lost my pride a few times over the years and it does shake your confidence, but the lessons I learnt were invaluable. Hardest of all though is when a family member turns on you – it's a hurt that never goes away.

* * *

'Three... two... one!'

My eyes shift from Cameron to face the camera, my expression easing into what I trust is an engaging and welcoming smile.

'Louis XIV ruled France for seventy-two years and the palace and gardens are a testament to his belief in the absolute power of monarchy. His aim in creating a fitting environment for his divine presence was to showcase the power and wealth of his nation.' I half turn as Elliot pans around, then zooms in to take a close-up of the magnificent spectacle below us.

'We're standing on a balustraded terrace in the South Parterre, overlooking the magnificent Orangery. Below us, reached by a flight of stone steps flanked by statues of sphinxes with bronze Cupids astride them, the South Parterre is sheltered from the prevailing cold winds.'

I step aside now, to allow Elliot unrestricted access as he

continues to zoom in on the extraordinary detail as I resume my narrative.

'The gardens take the word "manicured" to a whole new level. Separated by the gravel pathways are intricate swirls of lush-looking grass set in a pattern, so meticulously trimmed that the attention to detail is astounding. It really is akin to looking at the finest example that ever came from an embroidery needle; almost too perfect to be real. Each of the six swirling patterns are edged with low-level hedging, the lines of which are crisp and even.

'In the centre of the first block of four of these areas is a circular pond. On one side it's bordered by the immense edifice of the Orangery itself. To my left, in the distance is the Lake of the Swiss Guards.'

It's captivating. My imagination conjures up hazy images of ladies in elaborate wigs and beautiful gowns, escorted by dashing young men. A time when a stroll wasn't simply about getting a little exercise; there was intrigue, romantic liaisons, plotting, social climbing and the necessity to make oneself visible. It was a very different world here for the courtiers and, while privileged, it came with what was often quite an onerous and restrictive set of rules.

Elliot brings the camera back around to face me.

'In creating a microcosm, the Orangery parterre covers three hectares in total. Many of the twelve hundred planters are kept inside the building during the winter months.

'Today some of the palms, citrus and pomegranate trees are still inside the Orangery, protected from the early-morning and late-night chill. Traditionally, the placement of the containers on the wide, gravelled pathways is regimented. Long straight lines of trees and shrubs, interspersed with a host of specimen topiary for which Versailles is renowned.

Spaced and arranged so meticulously that it takes hours to reconstruct when all of the containers are brought back out after their spell indoors.'

I half turn, indicating for Elliot to zoom in.

'The circular pond behind me breaks up the straight lines beautifully, cleverly focusing the eye and lending yet another dimension. Here the containers add a second concentric circle, the height of which reflects the outline of the trees upon the watery surface. It is, most certainly, a garden fit for a king.'

I draw to a close. Elliot gives me a thumbs up, lowering the camera and kneeling down to make a few adjustments.

'Great job, Lexie, and we're really lucky today as there's hardly any breeze. It's so exposed up here. No sound problems, Cameron?'

'No, mate. It's all good. It looks more like a computer graphic from up here, doesn't it? I moan about cutting the lawn at home in the summer and my wife says I never do the edges properly. She'd love this.' He laughs.

'It doesn't make you yearn to change profession, then?' Elliot jests and it's good to see him looking a lot more like his old self today. He hasn't coughed once, and he doesn't look quite as tired as he has done recently.

'Don't get me wrong, I can stand here and appreciate the work that goes into it, but it would do my head in fussing over all those straight lines and edges.'

Solange approaches and we turn to greet her as she introduces today's interviewee. Monsieur Mereux is a genial-looking man, in his late fifties and dressed rather smartly, I presume because he will be in front of the camera. His hands, though, reflect those of a true gardener as he leans in to shake mine.

After a little small talk, Solange heads back in the direction of the palace and, while Elliot swaps batteries and Cameron sorts a mic for Monsieur Mereux, I run through the list of questions with him.

'Please, call me Anton,' he insists.

'And I'm Lexie. No one calls me Alexandra, except my late father whenever I exasperated him – which was often,' I admit, with a smile. I can see that Anton is going to be a good interviewee; he's relaxed, and his voice is clear, his speech well-paced. Sometimes it's hard to slow people down and, thankfully, his English is very good.

We begin with a general overview, building on my short introduction, and I can see that Elliot is content for me to let Anton do his thing before I wade in with specific questions.

A quick glance in Cameron's direction confirms he's more than happy and there isn't too much background noise as we finish up this segment. We all head down the steps to the lower level next, and I'm really looking forward to the live demonstration as we talk in detail about the art of topiary.

The four gardeners we're going to be filming are waiting for us, their equipment already laid out on the gravelled path around them. Elliot suggests that they simply go about their business as usual, working in teams of two, while he films. Part way through the process we'll stop and continue the interview while they work away in the background.

As we watch the guys lay boards on the gravel at the base of the planters to catch the cuttings, Anton turns to me.

'It is said that a friend of the Roman emperor Augustus invented topiary and that *topiarus* is actually the Latin word for landscape gardener.'

'It's certainly an art form,' I agree.

The two shrubs being trimmed each have three separate

sections. One large ball shape at the bottom, above which is a slightly smaller ball, and at the pinnacle it ends with a pointed cone shape. It's a very elegant design and I'm surprised to see one of the pieces of board on the floor is a template.

'I wondered how on earth it was possible to maintain that perfect spherical shape,' I exclaim.

'As the shrub is delicately clipped with the shears, the template is moved a few inches at a time until it's back in the original starting position. You will note that the new spring growth is uneven and straggly. So, it requires careful attention. Too severe a cut would leave exposed woody patches, but failure to trim regularly would destroy the perfect shape. It is a slow and methodical process, repeated many times over throughout the year.'

I nod, impressed by the diligence and attention to detail as the men focus on the task in hand.

'How many different shapes are there, Anton?'

'Over sixty and we have almost seven hundred topiary hedges and trees in total.'

Anton speaks so passionately about his work that he's instantly engaging. For those who can only dream of a visit to Versailles, his enthusiasm is bound to transport them here through the screen.

What viewers can only imagine, however, is the warm sun beating down on us. We are also contending with the birds squabbling and chasing each other in and out of the vast array of trees and shrubs in their spring frenzy. On the terrace above us, the crowd of people is beginning to grow, and we now have an audience. Any background noise from above carries overhead so hopefully the only sounds we are capturing are those of the repetitive clippers and the crunch of gravel underfoot as the teams continue to work their magic.

By the time we're ready to wrap I'm starving and looking forward to a leisurely lunch with the guys. The sun is high overhead and the warmth is very welcome; but what I need now is a nice comfortable chair in which to while away an hour or two.

While Elliot and Cameron pack up the kit I saunter off, mingling with the tourists who are now filtering into the Orangery parterre in increasing numbers. Heading towards the lake to get a closer view, I can't help thinking about Grandma Viv. I know she would have been enthralled by all of this. Why did she never talk about it? Even to share with her family the wonders of her foreign adventure and tales of the fascinating people she met while she was here.

I realise that it's time to make a start on Grandma Viv's box.

10

REACHING OUT

Midway through our late lunch a series of pings emanates from Elliot's phone. He excuses himself from the table and I decide this is a great opportunity for me to get to know Cameron a little better. He has quite a sense of humour, I discover, and has me in fits of laughter when he shares some of his worst moments.

On one occasion he had to crawl on his stomach across a studio floor during a live interview after someone's mic had become dislodged. Apparently, every syllable they uttered sounded like Darth Vader on a bad day.

I'm not really aware of how long Elliot has been gone, as when you're languishing over a cheese board at the end of a perfect lunch, time seems to stand still. However, I find myself glancing out of the window and now I even have Cameron turning his head on the lookout, too.

'Do you think I should go and find him?' he offers.

Before I have a chance to reply, I see Ronan stride in through the door and he rushes up to the table.

'Hey, guys. Lexie, I've just had a quick chat with Elliot.

He's outside on the phone but he needs to talk to you for a few moments.'

I can see by his face something is wrong. Very wrong. Throwing my napkin down, I sprint between the tables and out through the door. The warmth of the beautiful spring sunshine is dazzling after the cool, intimate ambience of the bistro restaurant.

One look at the strained pallor on Elliot's face and my heart plummets. 'What's happened?'

'It's Mia. She's just been rushed to hospital in an ambulance. They don't know what's wrong yet, but she's having difficulty breathing. I'm just online trying to arrange a flight as the drive will take too long. Look, I have to go, Lexie, and I'm sorry. Ronan says he'll step in for me but at the moment I can't think past getting home as quickly as I can.' His voice is distraught.

I throw my arms around his shoulders and he allows me to hug him as if that's exactly what he needs. I hold him for a few moments until I feel him relax a little and then draw back.

'Just go. Head off and pack your things. I'll get you a flight and text you the details. Go. GO! If you need a lift to the airport, let me know and we'll sort it.'

He shakes his head as if in disbelief at what is happening. The look that he gives me in that instant is one of real fear, before he turns and strides away.

Back inside the restaurant all three of us get on our phones and twenty minutes later the flight is booked. Ronan arranges for a friend of his to pick Elliot up and take him to the airport. We're all in shock and my hands are trembling; I know there is nothing else I can do.

The restaurant staff are amazing when it's clear that we

are dealing with some sort of emergency. They haven't disturbed us, even though we're the last people still at lunch, until a waiter appears bearing a tray of coffees.

It's hard to relax, even though the immediate panic is over, and we're all wondering what Elliot is going to find on his arrival at the hospital. It's going to be an agonising trip back for him, for sure.

'You never know what's just around the corner, do you?' Cameron remarks, pensively. 'I mean, one minute everything is fine and the next—'

The cold feeling in the pit of my stomach doesn't warm, despite the coffee. I suppress a shudder.

'I've been worried about Elliot, but I didn't realise Mia was suffering quite as badly as she must have been. He seems to have turned the corner, but I know it's very easy for these viruses to turn into pneumonia.'

I can feel two sets of eyes on me and when I look from one to the other, they share the same miserable look.

'She's his world,' Cameron declares.

The silence around the table is heavy and we continue to sip our coffees, feeling a sense of disbelief and confusion.

'So, what happens next?' Cameron asks. 'I mean, every-thing is all set up. This is costing you guys a lot of money and the last thing Elliot needs to add to his worries is the thought that this project will grind to a halt.'

I was thinking the same thing and I straighten in my seat, then lean in purposefully.

'If we push back the schedule we'll run out of time. I need to be back in the UK by the fourth of June, because I have a contractual commitment I have to honour. Ronan, the fact that Elliot rang you tells me he wants us to carry on and get it done. How on earth we are going to do that,

I don't know. You can't be both interpreter and cameraman.'

Ronan drains his coffee cup then sits forward in his seat, looking at me resolutely.

'I'll find someone to step in for me, don't worry. I've never filmed with a Sony PMW-F55 CineAlta before, but I'm sure I'll pick it up quickly. The fact he'd trust me with his prize possession is a big deal. I might be a bit rusty to begin with, but my father taught me well. Do you think we can do this?'

I glance at Cameron, who thrusts his hand into the centre of the table, and I follow suit. Ronan's face relaxes into a smile as we do a triangular fist pump.

'One for all, and all for one!' I declare. 'Failure isn't an option. We know what our job is, and Elliot's job is to be there by Mia's side and see her through this.'

God willing.

* * *

'Well, that's a stroke of luck,' Ronan says as he pulls up parallel to the boulangerie, giving way to the car with the blinking indicator.

My phone pings, and I jump, dropping it on the floor and having to scrabble around for it rather inelegantly. With nerves still on edge, I'm feeling a little frayed. As Ronan switches off the engine, he turns to look at me anxiously.

'It's Elliot. He's at the airport,' I confirm. 'Mia has been admitted and will be undergoing some tests. In the meantime, she's on a drip to rehydrate her and is on oxygen to help her breathe more easily. He says he'll be in touch as soon as he can to let us know what's happening in the longer term.'

'Poor guy. It's everyone's worst nightmare, isn't it?'

Ronan can see I'm reeling and he leans in to give me a brief hug, before fetching my backpack from the boot. He insists on carrying it for me.

'I feel bad. We've pulled you away from whatever you were doing. It's so good of you to say you'll drop everything to step in for Elliot.'

Now this is all beginning to sink in, I'm conscious that I'm going to have to really squeeze the budget to accommodate a cost we never envisioned having to cover. Short-term I can use the contingency fund, but it won't last very long at the going rate for a cameraman.

'It's fine. Actually, when he rang, I was driving back home after visiting George.'

We walk and talk, weaving in and out of the shoppers as we make for the gates. Stopping to punch in the code, I frown.

'George?'

'George Sanders. I told you I was going to speak to him about your grandma.'

'The gardener from the sixties? You didn't mention his name. I'm just surprised he's English.'

'Oh, sorry, I didn't realise. His wife was French, but she died many years ago. He's been on his own a long time. Ironically, language isn't an issue in this case, but George puts up his own barriers.'

I look at him questioningly and he raises his eyebrows. 'That's another long story,' he adds.

'Now I'm curious. Do you need to get off, or do you have time to come in for a while? I was going to ask for your assistance, actually.'

As our eyes meet, I can't help noticing that his lips are twitching as he tries to hold back a little smile. There's more than a hint of amusement in those hazel-green eyes of his and my stomach does an involuntary flip as I struggle to remain cool and collected.

'I'm all yours,' he declares boldly. Is that an innuendo? I stifle a groan. It's never as simple as just giving into your most basic of desires, is it? If there's one thing experience has taught me it's to be careful who you encourage, especially when it's a colleague.

'My work is in the doldrums at the moment and I hate it when the research comes to a grinding halt. The upside is that I'm available.'

Maybe he's just fooling around to make me laugh, but his banter is hard to resist.

As we swing the gates closed and turn to walk across the courtyard, my mood has lightened considerably. I feel easy in Ronan's company; everything is rather effortless, as if he's an old friend. An interesting, charming and rather good-looking friend, at that. My stomach does another little involuntary flip and I'm suddenly very conscious of how near we are to each other.

Am I going to keep on kidding myself that I can control this undeniable attraction I feel? Calm down, Lexie, my inner voice is yelling at me. It's time to use your head and not give in to... well, it would be foolhardy to throw all caution to the wind with someone you're employing.

Putting the key in the door, I move inside so that there's room for Ronan to join me.

'If I lived here, I'd convert the garage and the storage space that runs through to the rear of the ground floor,' I say, thinking out loud. 'I've been inside number one and that's what they've done with it.'

Ronan looks up at me. 'Goodness, you've only been here for a bit and already you can imagine living here.'

'Yeah... but, sadly, that's just in my dreams. My latest contract is what is going to pay the bills for the next year.' I laugh, gazing down at him from my vantage point three steps higher.

Judging by the heat I can feel slowly rising up into my cheeks, I'm beginning to look a little flushed. 'And both Elliot and I are well aware that it could take at least six months to complete this project before we see any return. So, we decided to be realistic about it and have more work lined up. If this pays off, then it could change our careers; if it doesn't, then at least we gave it a go, but we won't be completely broke.'

'Oh,' he replies, sounding just the teensiest bit disappointed as he follows me upstairs. But it's best to make my position clear.

I dump my bag on the floor and walk over to throw open the windows to let in some air. It's stuffy as the heat has built up during the day, but a little breeze is enough to bring some instant relief. With the sun sideways on to the building it's the best of both worlds. Light, bright but not in our eyes.

'It is a lovely cottage,' he comments, turning to glance at me. 'And a pity.'

Pity? That I can't stay?

I can't resist gauging his reaction, but when he doesn't elaborate, I jump straight in to change the subject.

'I'm curious about George. Tell me more.' I indicate for Ronan to take a seat.

He flops down on the sofa opposite me, extending his legs to the side of the coffee table and crossing his feet at the ankles. I like the fact that he seems to feel so comfortable here.

'Oh, where to begin? Well, he's not an easy guy to talk to at the best of times. He gets a little cranky sometimes and he's quite opinionated. That's fine, because he's seen and done a lot in his time but, being in his seventies, what really rankles with him is the quality of life that was snatched away at the peak of his career.'

'Car crash, wasn't it?'

'Yes. The brakes on a lorry failed and ploughed into several cars. George's right leg was shattered. They reconstructed it using plates, screws and even a bone graft, using a piece of his rib. At least they saved his leg, but he can't bend his knee more than an inch or two and he's had to learn to live with the constant pain.'

'That's horrible, Ronan. The poor man.'

'After months of recovery and rigorous physiotherapy he was able to get around with just the one stick. He received a good payout, but money doesn't mean a lot when in a split second your whole life is turned upside down. George was a very active man who spent most of his life out in the open. He became reclusive for a while and wouldn't let any of his colleagues visit him. His version of events is slightly different. Whether the pain, or the drugs he was on at the time, affected his memory, I don't know, but his story is that people simply forgot about him.'

'How sad if he believes that and it wasn't actually the case. So how did you get to meet him? Didn't this happen quite a long time ago?'

I sprawl out on the sofa opposite Ronan, happy to put up my feet at long last.

'Nineteen years ago. Most of this I gleaned from my

interviews with Maurice Perrin. George was one of the trainees Maurice employed back in the early sixties. He was the person who put me in touch with him in the first place, as he felt George could fill in some of the gaps in my research.'

There's something in Ronan's tone that tells me George hasn't been too forthcoming.

'George doesn't like talking?'

'It's not that – it's personal. At first, I think he was grateful for the company and it was clear he enjoyed talking to me about old times. Then, when I told him I was Fabien Arnoult's grandson, he ordered me out of his house. You see, in all the time they worked together in the same team, they were never the best of friends.

'It was another eighteen months before we spoke again, very briefly at Maurice's funeral. I think it began to dawn on George that with every passing year more of the details about life as a gardener in times gone by is lost forever. Like it or not, he had a role in that past and I could write him out of my account, or he could give his version of events and have it on record once and for all.'

'So, he did start talking to you again, then?'

'Unfortunately, no. He said he would when he was ready, and I've been patiently waiting ever since. But I decided to visit him to ask if he remembered your grandma and he said he'd like to meet you. Thanks to you, it looks like he might be ready to share a little of what he knows.'

Perhaps it's time to ask the question that's been floating around in my head since the day I stood at the sink in Ronan's kitchen; the moment when he admitted that Versailles had been the centre of his grandfather's world. So important, that his wife was torn away from the network of her large Irish family without him seemingly realising what she was giving up for him.

It reminds me in a way of my grandma. Selfless women without whose support I wonder how well the men would have fared if they hadn't been in their lives. They gave up so much, but then it was that way for many women of that era.

The way we live our lives now is more conducive to allowing each other the freedom to enjoy both family and career. Or maybe the burden, in some cases, when husbands and wives end up stressed, trying to juggle too many things at the same time in order to achieve their goals. My fear is that something is lost in a world where people are so judgemental of each other.

'You're deep in thought.' Ronan peers across at me.

'Our grandmothers gave up a lot to support their men, didn't they?'

'I guess by today's standards they did, but life was much simpler then, or maybe the truth is that it was more basic. Less expensive technology and a make-do ethos. Household chores took a lot longer and everything had to be cooked from scratch. Besides, women were traditionally the back-bone of family life and if they worked, they often ended up doing jobs simply to bring in some extra money, rather than following a career path. The sixties were an exciting time for young people. Change invariably brings new opportunities and for some a new sense of freedom that was exhilarating and empowering.'

I don't think I ever looked at it in quite that way, but that was exactly what Grandma Viv was trying to get across to us when we were young.

'My grandma always said that we should follow our dreams because we wanted to, not because we felt we had to.

I never really understood what she meant by that. Maybe she was alluding to her own situation. Yes, she could have had a fulfilling career while raising her family and supporting her husband. But what strain would that have put on everyone and everything? She managed to keep the grand passion alive, fawned over her family and was everyone's rock, while ensuring nothing held Granddad back. His success was also hers.'

Ronan's expression is one of acknowledgement of a sacrifice borne out of love and I find that endearing.

'In those days when a woman with children was interviewed for a job, she would have been asked what childcare arrangements she had in place if they were sick. And no allowance was made to accommodate taking leave, only in the school holidays. It was tough for women with children then. I know, because I saw first-hand what my mother had to endure just to keep her two jobs going. Fortunately, my aunt usually stepped in to look after me, but there were times when she wasn't available, and my mother had no option but to ring in pretending she was sick. Every time she did that, she risked losing her job if it had been discovered.'

I shake my head in dismay. Swinging my legs off the sofa, I pull open the drawer of the coffee table and reach inside to pull out the box. Ronan looks at me, frowning.

'I think before we go to see George, we need to make a start on this. Would you help me? There's no one else I'd feel comfortable sharing this with, to be honest, as I have no idea what I'm going to find. If it's a chronological record of the work she did, then maybe that could prove helpful to you in your research. But if it's too personal, then it might have to stay buried forever. I know that's a lot to ask, but that's how it has to be.'

He sits forward eagerly.

'Agreed.'

As I lift off the lid, we both incline our heads to peer inside.

'How many notebooks are there?' he asks.

I quickly count them. 'Fifteen. And this little bundle of documents.' I hold up a small wad of neatly folded papers; some of them appear to be cuttings from gardening journals, but some of the papers are handwritten.

Pulling out the first two notebooks, I hand one to Ronan and he carefully opens the cover.

'It says, "My year of discovery begins. Treasures don't always sparkle; some are covered in mud." Wow – that's a statement to make.'

Our eyes meet and I nod, swallowing hard. Placing my hand on the cover, I pause for a moment, but Ronan is already eagerly leafing through the pages.

'I'd say it's a diary of the work she was involved in while she was here. Maybe she intended to share these with someone if she'd lived longer. Perhaps it had to be the right someone,' he continues.

Goosebumps run up and down my arms, as we both settle back to begin reading.

11
_____

SILENCE IS GOLDEN

As the evening progresses, it soon becomes clear that it's going to be necessary to make notes in order to keep track of, and share, relevant information we glean. Grandma Viv's handwriting is small and the notebook I'm reading contains many drawings of flowers with detailed descriptions, but interspersed, and often without a date, are little snippets of her daily interactions.

I stop only to throw together some small baguettes with ham and cheese, while Ronan makes drinks. There is a further text from Elliot just before eleven p.m. saying that Mia is sleeping, and they will know more in the morning.

When Ronan leaves, we hardly speak, just exchanging a very genuine hug as we are both so exhausted. We agree to pick it back up tomorrow night and he stoops to kiss my cheek softly before he leaves. It's different. Personal. Meaningful. We are delving into someone's life and I guess he's used to that, given the nature of the work he's doing, but I can also see that he's fascinated by some of what he's read. It seems that our shared interest is cementing the connection between us and there's no denying that.

Shutting the door behind him, I lean back against it deep in thought, until I suddenly remember that I'd promised to ring Mum. I immediately climb the stairs two at a time to go and text her, feeling like the worst daughter in the world.

✉ Sorry, Mum, ended up being a late one. I'll ring you in the morning — promise. Sleep well! x

* * *

I ring Mum during breakfast because there's so much to do today and I must head up to the palace first thing to see Solange. In between mouthfuls of fresh croissant, I pass on Elliot's update and she says to let him know she is thinking of them both. Then I explain why I didn't call her last night. As soon as I mention that I've made a start on Grandma Viv's notebooks she doesn't make any attempt to acknowledge that and the line goes ominously silent.

'I'd better go. Today promises to be a hectic one. Take care, Mum. I miss you and I'll be in touch very soon.'

'I hope it goes well for you, Lexie. I'm proud of you, honey.'

There's a hint of loneliness in her voice and I know just how much she's missing me.

I find it hard to shake off thoughts of her and, even though it's a beautiful morning and the walk is very pleasant, my heart is heavy. After such a good start, everything was looking so promising, but now all we can do is plough forward as best we can.

Solange isn't in her office and I wait rather anxiously while someone pages her.

'Problems?' she enquires as soon as she appears, inviting me to take a seat.

'Yes. I'm afraid Elliot has had to return to the UK. His girlfriend was rushed into hospital yesterday and he's with her now.'

Her face drops. 'Oh, Lexie. I am so very sorry to hear that. What a terrible worry for him. Will she be okay?'

I'm trying to remain positive, but I can't hide my concern. 'His latest text says she's very poorly. Something to do with the lining of her lungs. They are still waiting for some test results to come back but she's in good hands.'

She sighs. 'Such awful news. Hopefully she will respond quickly to treatment. The National Health Service is good, I believe?'

'Yes. We're very lucky in that respect but Elliot will want to be by her side until she's well enough to go home. The reason I wanted to speak to you was to let you know that Ronan will be stepping in for Elliot. I'm awaiting confirmation of who will interpret for us in his place. If he can't find someone who can step in for tomorrow's interview, then we might have to postpone it, or see if we can swap interviewees. I don't know if that's possible, as I realise this one was scheduled for a Saturday because of problems with availability.'

Solange frowns, then nods her head. 'Leave it with me. No one could have predicted this would happen. I will ring you later to let you know what is happening. Maybe by then you will have found someone to step in for Ronan and I can get a security pass sorted. When you speak to Elliot next, please do express my sincere hope that his girlfriend recovers very quickly.'

As I rise up out of my seat Solange gives me an encouraging smile.

'I will walk out with you. There's a press meeting taking place shortly and I'm making a presentation about a new exhibition we are putting on in the autumn.'

'It's a busy time for you and I'm sorry to add to your workload, but your help is really appreciated.'

'It's fine. This is why I'm here, to help smooth things along. But, yes, it is a busy time and there is always something new happening to keep those visitors coming back. Did Ronan have any luck with George?' Solange asks as we make our way down the marble staircase and out into the open.

'He did. We are going to see him, but I'm not sure when.'

She seems pleased.

'That is great news. I hope that you can help each other.' I raise an eyebrow questioningly.

'Ronan is a good man. I think you two have many things in common,' she adds. 'He is stuck at the moment, and it frustrates him. I'm glad he was able to step in and help you both personally and professionally. Aside from getting some answers, I think you two will make very good friends.'

'You know, Solange, I think so too.'

We exchange a brief knowing glance before heading out in opposite directions. I wonder what exactly Ronan has said to her about me. Whatever it is, she's decided we need to be encouraged. I guess the days of plotting at Versailles aren't over...

* * *

'Hang on a moment, Shellie, there's someone at the front door.'

I run down the stairs to let Ronan in.

'Hi, sorry, I'm on the phone with my sister – come up and get yourself settled. I'll make it quick.'

I race back up and take my phone off hold.

'Right, I'm back. You were saying?'

Shellie sounds a little anxious

'There's something going on with Mum, Lexie. She was fine last night and said she'd come round to take Maisie to school this morning, as I had a doctor's appointment first thing and it would be tight. Just routine, nothing special, but the sickness slows me down a bit. She rang just before eight a.m. to say she had woken up with a bad head and was going to have to take some tablets and go back to bed.'

'Oh. That's odd. I spoke to her myself shortly before seven this morning and she was fine then. But headaches are like that – they just come on, don't they?'

'The thing is, she didn't sound unwell, she sounded unsettled – enough to tell a fib. Something has happened and she didn't feel she could share it.'

'Really? Mum? I mean, she loves taking Maisie to school and she would know that Maisie would be disappointed, aside from the fact it put you in a bit of a spot.'

'Precisely. That's why I found it rather odd. I don't know whether I should pop in to check on her.'

I feel a little uneasy.

'I did mention that I'd made a start on Grandma Viv's notebooks. She didn't say anything, but she did go quiet. Maybe after she put the phone down it set her thinking. You know, going over old times. I didn't mean to upset her, obviously, and I feel bad if that's it. I'll be more careful in future. Sorry, Shellie.'

There's a brief pause. 'I suppose that could account for it.

Yep. That could have been it. I'll give her a call a little later, then. So, did the notebooks throw up anything you can share?' Now she sounds curious.

I don't want to admit that Ronan is helping me. I'm not sure what Shellie would think about that as to her he's basically still a stranger. 'I've only just started reading them and all I can say so far is that Grandma was quite the artist. Her drawings of various plants and flowers are incredibly detailed and lifelike. I think it's going to be a baptism into the world of the green-fingered,' I muse, and she laughs.

'Well, when you get back you can come and apply your newly acquired knowledge to my garden. This morning sickness is now extending throughout the entire day. It's a sign of a good pregnancy, I'm told, but it's such a drag.'

'Look, I have to go, but ring if you find out what's going on with Mum at any time, okay?'

'Will do. Miss you, sis, and take care!'

Ronan has taken a seat on the sofa and is making notes in an A4 book. He looks up the moment I switch off my phone.

'Not problems at home, I hope?' His enquiry is tinged with concern.

'I don't think so. I told my mum I'd made a start on the box and think it probably brought back some memories. We all get days where the loss of someone weighs particularly heavily on our hearts, no matter how many years have elapsed.'

I finish speaking and realise that I'm welling up. Ronan jumps to his feet and approaches, placing his arms very gently around me.

'Hey. Everything I read last night was written by a lady who had a real zest for life. Many people don't realise how important it is to savour each and every day; to appreciate all of life's experiences, the good and the bad. From what I can tell, your grandma lived her life to the full and that's something to be celebrated. She passed that vibrancy, that... determination, on to her daughter and her grandchildren. Of course, she's missed, and that's fine. Sadness isn't always a bad thing, though, you know.'

I swipe away at a solitary tear that is beginning to slither down my cheek. Ronan hugs me to him for a moment and then relaxes his grip.

'Come on. Let's swap notes,' he says, his smile full of encouragement. 'And I have some news. George left a voice message on my phone. It seems he's very impatient to meet you. So, we need to set a date.'

'Oh, I nearly forgot,' I reply, making a concerted effort to contain my emotions. 'Come and see what I found amongst that little wedge of loose papers tucked into the box.'

I reach in to grab the bundle, slipping the item from behind the pale cream lace tied around it. 'This is her. On the back she's written *"summer 1961"*. Look at the background.'

Ronan takes the faded colour photograph from my hand and stares at it, almost in disbelief. 'It's the Orangery. Or, at least, a close-up of one of the glass panels.'

'She looks so young wearing capri pants and a striped cotton shirt, wrapped around at the waist and fastened with a bow.' I can't help sounding a little bemused. 'She does look amazing, but it's sort of shocking – she so reminds me of Olivia Newton-John in *Grease*. I only ever remember Grandma as being rather reserved when it came to clothes. She always looked smart, but in that picture, well, she looks a bit like a model.'

I can see Ronan agrees. 'You have her smile. She smiles from her eyes like you.'

'Do I?'

He hands it back. 'Did you only find the one?'

I nod. 'Sadly, yes. Oh, we have loads of photos at home, but none taken at Versailles or even around that time, as far as I'm aware.'

'Then it wasn't taken by a camera she owned, because films usually came in twelve, twenty-four, or thirty-six exposures I think, although don't quote me on that. Unless she threw the rest away, of course. That's great though, because it's something with which to jog George's memory. Given his reaction, I'd say he recalls the name but being able to put a face to it is something else entirely. It's a great start. So, what else did you discover?'

We settle ourselves down on opposite sides of the coffee table so we can have our notes in front of us. I'm impressed that Ronan has now transferred his into a hard-backed notebook and I shuffle the couple of sheets of paper with my own notes scrawled over them.

'Well, she wasn't big on using people's names, which is a shame. Or specific dates. I'd say it was spring 1962, because most of what I've read so far is about cuttings and propagation. There are lots of detailed little drawings and technical information. The Latin names for the plants, habitat, soil type – that sort of thing.'

Ronan shrugs. 'Hmm. That's a shame. As the title page indicated, the one I'm reading records her first days here. It's the sort of record you would expect from a student with nothing really personal in it. Mostly observations and the same as you're finding, really. Lots of notes about trees, so that's possibly something we can ask George about, if it turns out that he remembers meeting her. It's a pity her handwriting is so small, but then these little books would fit neatly into a pocket, so it's understandable.'

I don't know whether to be glad these aren't diaries, or sad about that.

'Well, hopefully we can piece together what she did while she was here, and George might be able to add to that. What I'd love is to be able to write a little piece and get it printed up, so I can give a copy to some family members. A little record of Grandma Viv's life here at Versailles on a timeline. I know in the grand scheme of things she's not really a part of the story when it comes to your research, but for our family it's something I don't think we should lose sight of. Can you understand that?'

'Of course. How many families can say they have a connection to the Palace of Versailles? It's a part of the history of your family. Who knows? A future generation may well discover they have inherited her green fingers and be curious where that trait came from. I think I can get through the remainder of this one in about an hour, allowing me to add to my notes. I only recognise two of the names she's mentioned in passing so far, but I'm keeping a list. Some of them will have been students, of course. As she settled in, I'm hoping we'll learn something more about the permanent staff she worked alongside. How about you?'

I give him a wry smile. 'If I have a glass of wine to aid my relaxation, I'd say that's doable. Then I'll pop something in the oven, and we can relax over dinner.'

Pushing the box to one side, I lean back and put up my feet; it's fascinating and the attention to detail in her little drawings makes me think I should take copies and frame some of them. Suddenly the chime of the doorbell breaks the silence. Ronan doesn't look up as I head downstairs.

When I ease back the door the first thing I see is a large plant and, standing behind it, holding it out to me, is my lovely neighbour.

'Renée! Bonsoir.'

'Bonsoir, Lexie. Merci de votre aide.'

I take the plant from her, with a look of delight, and she does a hand gesture like turning a tap, which makes me laugh.

'Ah. Merci bien. It's fine! Is it good now?'

It takes a few minutes, a babble of French, some shared laughter and a few more hand signals, but I think I understand. It sounds like she has a replacement tap and a new stopcock, as well.

'Good,' she confirms, finally, nodding and smiling.

'Merci bien,' I reply, gazing at the beautiful plant filling my arms.

'Je vous en prie,' she says as she turns and walks back across the courtyard. It's not much of a conversation but she's happy enough and it makes me smile.

When I return upstairs Ronan does a double take.

'Nice plant. What is it?'

'I think it's some sort of fern. Lovely minty-green colour, isn't it?'

But he doesn't respond; his head is once more bent over as he squints a little to focus on the written page before him. I take the plant over to stand it in the sink, adding a little water and leaving it to drain. Suddenly, Ronan calls out rather excitedly.

'There's an address written in the back of this one. It might be the place where she was staying. Result!'

I close my eyes for a moment, hoping that is in fact the case. Imagine being able to bring Mum to France for a holiday to retrace the steps of her mother. To be able to let her know that Grandma was happy here and it was a year of fulfilment, full only of happy memories, would mean so much to me.

'Well, if you've finished, and as I still have a good few pages to go, would you like to rustle something up for dinner?'

Ronan stands, walking towards me with the biggest grin on his face. 'I knew you secretly admired my culinary skills. Let's see what I can do to impress you tonight. You have half an hour tops, so get out of the kitchen and get reading.'

I'm beginning to see a very different side of Ronan emerge. Stretching out on the sofa, notebook in front of me, I face the other end of the room so I can surreptitiously observe him. He scratches his head for a moment as he swings open the fridge door to inspect the contents. He grabs eggs, some vegetables and a block of cheese; it looks as if he's going to rustle up an omelette. He's so attentive and caring; it isn't all about him all the time, and that's refreshing because I've spent a lot of time around men with whom that wasn't the case.

He's humming something under his breath as he grabs a bowl from the cupboard and searches around for some utensils. Nothing is too much trouble and he's eager to please. I'm trying hard to focus on Grandma's handwriting, but my eyes keep straying. He's so damned good to look at as he moves around the small space. Every little movement seems to affect me and I realise that I'm holding my breath. When I expel it, his head turns in my direction.

'Are you okay?'

'Nearly finished,' I lie. The last thing on my mind right now is Versailles.

Ronan whisks the contents of the bowl, unaware that I'm watching him. The way he tilts his head and the little mannerisms he doesn't even realise he has.

Whenever he finishes a task, he leans his palms on the countertop, fingers splayed and drumming lightly as he considers his next step. Then those powerful arms push back, as he turns away to grab something else. Some herbs, the cheese grater, a pan... mundane little actions that make me want to go up and throw my arms around him. Just because he's here, in my little world, and I'm feeling things I never, ever expected to feel.

12

WITH A LITTLE HELP FROM OUR FRIENDS

Ronan's potential stand-in, Yvette Gilliard, calls to confirm she is available on Monday.

Ronan immediately dials Solange, and it isn't long before we both receive a text from her to say that she has arranged to reschedule the interview. We've been given special permission to film even though the palace itself is closed to the general public on Mondays, but she will be there to ensure we have access to whatever facilities we require. I immediately text Cameron to let him know and he replies with a thumbs up.

It's a huge relief this morning to talk to Elliot and be able to reassure him everything is under control.

'And how is Mia doing?' I ask tentatively. He sounds so tired and anxious that I'm almost scared to hear his answer.

'She's heavily sedated at the moment. She has pleurisy, but overnight they discovered she also has a blood clot in her right lung. That's what has been causing the low oxygen levels and the shortness of breath. She's on a drip with antibiotics and blood thinners to break it down. We'll know more in a day or two. They've warned us that the clot can leave scars and other damage, but, assuming they've caught it early enough, her body will take about six weeks at least to recover from this episode.

'She's been lucky, Lexie. Mia had no idea how ill she was and if she hadn't collapsed in the presence of a friend who had popped in to see her on a whim, it could have been a very different outcome.'

'Well, just focus on being there for her and staying positive. Once she's home she'll pick up a lot quicker. Everything is fine here, really.'

'Thanks, Lexie. Not just for seeing this through, but for being you and not making me feel awkward about dropping everything. Ronan, Cameron and Solange, they're all stepping in to help out and it's because they admire your determination. Without that, there's a real chance we'd end up losing every penny we've invested. I can't even begin to consider the impact of that on top of everything else. When you care about others, people care about you. I couldn't ask for a better partner and I will make this up to you. I promise.'

'Well, we've made a great start and I'm sure we'll end up captivating our audience, especially those who will never get a chance to visit in person. Try to get as much rest as you can, Elliot, because Mia is going to be relying on your strength to see her through this. Everyone has asked me to pass on their best wishes for a speedy recovery for lovely Mia. Take care, my friend.'

* * *

'I don't know what I'm more excited about – meeting George,

or the thought of seeing the little place where my grandma stayed, today,' I remark, as I stare out of the car window.

We pass large swathes of daffodils and tulips, and already there's a tiny hint of green on the skeletal trees as the buds begin to swell. Everything is beginning to come alive and it really helps to lift my spirits.

Ronan kindly offered to drive today, and he even waited around patiently while I took the call from Elliot. It means we're running late, so we're heading straight to George's first.

'Is it very far?' I ask, as we head out of the city.

'Not really. About half an hour's drive. He had a second-floor apartment a walking distance away from the palace, but bought a single-storey cottage in Buc, a commune in the Département de l'Yveline, after his accident.

'You might have read about the Aqueduc de Buc? The huge structure was built to supply water, drained from the ponds of Saclay, to the fountains and basins at Versailles. It's disused now, of course.

'Originally, the gardens and park around Versailles were almost twice as big as they are today. The grounds extended this far out, which is incredible to believe, isn't it? George has family close by and there's a stream that runs along the bottom of his garden. He enjoys a little fishing to while away the time.'

'You seem to know quite a bit about him, considering he's not that chatty,' I reflect.

'He was well respected in his time at Versailles. I learnt a lot about him from other people while doing my research. It was clear that he didn't suffer fools gladly. But he was passionate about his work. George isn't afraid to voice his opinions, even when it goes against the flow, and people remember that. Unfortunately, there were some pretty heated arguments over the years, and he doesn't forgive easily. A few of them seemed to have been with my grandfather, hence his caution around me now.'

'Do I have to be careful what I say?' Now I'm beginning to wonder what sort of reception I'm going to get.

'The fact he's allowing us to visit him is a real surprise. For me that's great, I will be honest, as I'd virtually given up on him. But his interest shows he might be coming round. Slowly. Maybe this is step one towards accepting that you can't change what happened in the past. All I want is to get the facts straight for the record. So, let's see what happens.'

I'm happy that Ronan is pleased about this visit. If it helps him to begin building bridges with George again, then that's a real bonus. It gives me a warm feeling hearing the positivity in his voice and knowing that I'm instrumental in that.

As the scenery whizzes past the window and with the air con blasting out, it's a wonderful relief from the afternoon sun filtering in through the windows. Eventually we turn off the main road and, after a mile or so, Ronan indicates before turning into a concrete area in front of double gates.

'I usually park around the corner, but George gave instructions to pull onto the drive, so you're an honoured guest. Talk of the devil.' As we get out of the car the front door opens wide.

The house stands alone on a larger than average sized plot. Bounded either side by tall hedges that have been immaculately trimmed, the garden to the front is a delight. Wonderful little pathways meander between waist-high, raised flower beds brimming with spring colour. There's no gravel here, but solid concrete paths to give a firm footing.

Ronan strides forward and I trail a pace or two behind

him, unable to stop myself from gazing admiringly at the beautiful displays.

'I might not be able to get up the ladder to trim the hedges,' George's voice booms out, 'but there's nothing stopping me putting on a good show. When the bulbs start dying back, I'll be busy with the bedding plants.'

'It's breathtaking. Hi, George, I'm Alexandra Winters, but everyone calls me Lexie.'

I hold out my hand and take a giant step forward as he slows, leaning heavily on his stick.

'Pleased to meet you, Lexie.'

'This is quite something,' I add, gazing around and smiling, noticing too that he has totally ignored Ronan.

'Well, there's little else for me to do and it keeps me going. I won't last long once I get to the stage where I can't come out and potter. But I figure I have a few years left in me yet. Come and have a look at the gardens round the back.'

He turns and I fall in behind him, looking over my shoulder briefly to glance at Ronan. He gives me a thumbs up. I can't help but notice that still George hasn't really acknowledged him, at all.

'I pay someone to keep the grass and the hedges in order, but the planters allow me to keep my hand in,' George continues, sounding really rather friendly.

It's a very formal layout and I instantly think of the grounds in front of the Orangery. Albeit, this mirrors it in a more simplistic way.

Running down the centre of the garden is a wide, gently sloping path. On the left-hand side a long row of large metal planters stand, rather proudly, each one housing a specimen shrub. All are beautifully clipped, although not in the more formal topiary shapes, but the natural shape dictated by the plant itself.

To the right-hand side the smooth, slightly downhill sloping lawn is weed-free. But one long line of fruit trees mirrors the planters on the opposite side of the garden. The hedging bordering the property continues on down to the bottom, affording a lot of protection to George's display of miniature trees. Stopping for a moment, I can hear the sounds of the water, loud enough to know it's not merely a small, meandering stream.

'Oh, my. I keep thinking about the Orangery. This is truly delightful, and the sound of flowing water is a perfect back-drop,' I remark, taking in the wonderful ambience.

George looks pleased. 'It's all about scale and symmetry. And simplicity. Some of the most restful areas of the gardens at Versailles are those where the hornbeam hedging encloses a quiet area. A simple stone bench, some flowing water and the sound of birdsong is all anyone requires to switch off from their troubles. Or sit and plot the downfall of a courtier.'

Gazing up at him, I'm amused by his comment. He begins to laugh.

'It's funny you should say that, George. Whenever I get to wander around the garden between takes, I'm always drawn to those hidden areas. Discovering something new every time is such a delight. It's so easy to sit for a while and imagine the trysts and plotting.'

He raises an eyebrow, his eyes narrowing as he stares at me intently.

'A kindred soul. Have you toured the palace yet?'

I shake my head, sadly. 'I'm hoping to, very soon. The preparation has been time-consuming and my partner, Elliot, has had to fly back to the UK on a family emergency. Ronan has very kindly stepped in for him and I'm so very grateful as this project means a lot to me.'

Hearing his name uttered, Ronan draws closer. I realise he was giving us a little space, but if there's a bridge to be mended here, then Ronan deserves a little help.

George glances at Ronan and finally gives a little nod of acknowledgement.

'Let's head down to the water. My housekeeper will bring us some tea, shortly. Did you two know each other before this visit?' All of a sudden, his tone isn't quite as friendly as it has been so far and I'm a little taken aback by his question.

'No. A contact of Elliot's provided a list of interpreters and Ronan was one of them.'

Falling in alongside George, we continue walking at his gentle pace. It's easy to see that his discomfort grows the further he walks, as even with the help of his stick his lopsided gait must really pull on his back. He's a proud man, that's obvious, and I try my best not to show the pity I feel for him.

'Seems we all have a connection to Versailles.' George turns his head to look directly at me and I can see he's a little suspicious, which puzzles me.

'We do. It was a long time ago, though, and there's no way of knowing whose paths might have crossed at the time. I have a photo of my grandma to show you, actually.'

George indicates for us to take a seat as we draw near to a large circular wooden table looking out over the river. Clumps of tall trees, shimmering in the light breeze, fracture the rays of beautiful spring sunshine, covering the grassy area with glints of flickering light. It's heavenly. The only sound is the bubbling water as it swooshes by and the birds, noisily foraging in the trees overhead.

'This is a beautiful spot, George. Gosh, that's quite a flow, but what a joy hearing the water cascading over the rocks. I see you enjoy a little fishing.' I nod in the direction of the smart-looking jetty to our right. There's a reclining chair with a folding canopy over the top, a large plastic box and a rack housing two fishing rods.

'Yes. There's plenty of river carp and bream here. Usually the river can be fished all year round, but the winter storms and constant downpours made it flood. It washed away my old jetty but this new one is a sturdier construction and should see me through a few good years.'

Ronan and I take a seat, both making a concerted effort not to watch George as he eases himself into the only chair with a foot rest. It takes him a minute or so to make himself comfortable.

'Ah, here she is,' he says, and I turn to see a young woman walking towards us carrying a tray.

Ronan leaps up to go and help her as the tray is rather loaded. They exchange a little light-hearted banter and there's some laughter. I notice George gives her a beaming smile before she heads back up to the house.

As I pour the tea and pass around the plates, George motions to her retreating back.

'My wife's eldest brother's granddaughter,' he informs us. 'I don't know what I'd do without her. She works a morning shift at the local vet's and is here every afternoon. Her and her boyfriend are saving up to buy a house.'

Ronan had said George's wife died years ago and it would be rather sad if he didn't have anyone close by to help out when needed. I notice Ronan is very quiet and there's little eye contact between the two men as I pass around a platter of tiny French pastries and cakes.

As soon as our rather subdued little afternoon tea session is finished, I decide to pull out the photograph, sliding it across the table towards George. He picks it up, holding it in his hands for a few moments and stares down at it.

'Her name was Viv. Vivian Hanley at that time, as she didn't marry my granddad until after she went home to the UK. As far as I can tell she arrived at Versailles in the May, or possibly the June, of 1961. She was married in August 1962, shortly after her return.'

He continues to stare down at the photograph in silence.

'It was linked to her coursework at a horticultural college in the UK. I think maybe to do with a study of the trees here? I'm afraid I don't really know any more than that. Do you... do you recognise her at all?'

George slides the photo back across the table.

'Sorry, I don't recall having met her. It was a long time ago and my memory isn't what it was, I'm afraid.'

He's emphatic and tight-lipped now, but I don't believe him. I glance briefly at Ronan, who is trying to observe subtly in order not to deter George, I suspect. But now George, too, is looking directly at Ronan and this is all beginning to feel very uncomfortable indeed.

'Oh. That's a real pity. I would dearly love to know a little more about her time here and the people she worked alongside.'

I pause and George says nothing. It's as if he's switched off and we are no longer here.

'Well, thank you for inviting me here, George, and thanks to Ronan for introducing us. I know this period in my grandma's life meant a lot to her and, while she did keep some notebooks, I've only recently begun the task of going through them. It seems a shame that this period of her life should be lost to my family. It was quite a thing to do to uproot herself for a whole year, as family was everything to her. She gave up her career shortly after she married and that must have been a tough choice to make, but her husband and her daughter always came first.'

George's face gives nothing away, but I can see by his eyes that he's growing agitated. I can feel Ronan looking at me and he furrows his brow, indicating we've overstayed our welcome. And he's right: George is communicating that loud and clear without needing to put it into words. He's grown aloof and distinctly chilly towards us.

Ronan and I stand, and I walk around the table to offer George my hand.

'Please, don't get up, we can see ourselves out. But I must thank you for the most delightful afternoon tea in such a beautiful setting, George. I feel privileged to have been able to experience it.'

He reaches out to shake my hand and I edge forward to save him overstretching. Rather unexpectedly, he places his other hand over the top of mine. Holding it for a few, lingering moments he adds, 'The pleasure was all mine, Lexie.'

A lump rises in my throat as we walk back to Ronan's car. I hadn't realised how much I was hoping that George would look up and say he'd crossed paths with my grandma, even briefly. To speak to someone who knew her while she was here would have meant so much to me. He obviously isn't easy around Ronan, I already knew that, but I honestly don't think he was telling the truth. But why would he lie about it?

13

We are both feeling so dispirited on the return trip that I ask Ronan to drop me off at home and suggest that maybe we could check out the address where Grandma stayed another time. He does look a tad disappointed and I wonder if he'd hoped we would do some more research this evening.

'Do you want me to pop inside and fetch the notebook you're working on? I need to crash and get an early night, but I don't want to stop you if you wanted to plough on.'

Ronan gives me an understanding look and nods his head enthusiastically. 'That would be great, if you don't mind. I promise to take great care of it.'

'I trust you.' I laugh, slipping out of the seat and slamming the door behind me.

When I return, he's managed to slip into a parking bay, but he says he has to head straight off as he has work planned for the remainder of the weekend. A quiet Sunday will allow me to clean the cottage, do the laundry and do some prep for next week; but I am a little disappointed.

'Well, see you on Monday, then.'

'Yep. Bright and early. Let's get another interview in the can. Give Elliot my best when you talk to him next and text me if there's any good news.'

'Will do. And thanks, Ronan. For everything. I know that wasn't very comfortable for you this afternoon.'

He screws up his face, his forehead puckering as he shakes his head sadly. 'I'm not sure I did you any favours there, Lexie. George has a selective memory; I've grown to discover. I don't understand why he doesn't want to go on record, or voice what I've been told were some very strong opinions at the time. He was a part of it and that sort of thing you don't forget. Whether he ever met your grandma, well, he studied that photo for an awfully long time. I can't help wondering if his recall would have been different if I hadn't been there.'

I wasn't going to say anything to Ronan, but he's snatched the thought right out of my head.

* * *

I'm lazing on the sofa, nearing the end of the first book in Ronan's series, when Shellie calls to ask me to ring Mum. She's clearly exasperated and worried that something is wrong but seems unable to get her to talk.

Of course, if my sister is worried then I'm worried too, although I half wonder if raging hormones are making Shellie a little paranoid. When I spoke to Mum on Friday morning, she seemed fine to me, just a little subdued. Everyone is entitled to have their off days; I'm having one myself today.

'Hi, Mum. Just checking in. I'm not interrupting anything, am I?'

'No. I'm just channel-hopping. There's never anything good to watch these days. I loathe these reality programmes and quiz shows. I might end up popping in a DVD. How are things there?'

'Good, all things considered. Everyone is pulling together. Mia has pleurisy and a blood clot, it turns out, but thankfully they caught it in time. Elliot sounds exhausted and it's a difficult time, naturally, but fingers crossed the treatment will see her improve a little every day. They said if there are no complications it could take up to six weeks for her to recover from the effects of the clot alone.'

'Oh, my!' Mum takes a sharp breath in. 'Well, she's in the best place and there's not a lot to do other than support her while she gets stronger and her body heals. But I know he'll be anxious, as you both have so much on the line. How are you managing?'

Mum's right, of course, and as we chat, I can't hear any sign of her being particularly down, just sympathetic about poor Elliot and Mia.

'Our interpreter, Ronan, can operate the camera and we've found an interpreter who can at least step in on Monday for the next interview.'

Mum sighs softly. 'I meant for money, Lexie.'

'Well, we have a small contingency fund, but not enough to cover the costs of an experienced cameraman if Elliot is away for several weeks. As soon as I have a good idea of what time period we're looking at, then I will consider what options are open to us.'

Mum clears her throat before speaking. 'Look, Lexie, I know you aren't going to want to hear this, but I have money that isn't doing anything. I don't want you going into debt.'

Bless Mum's heart.

'It will be fine, I'm sure, and I don't want you worrying about it. I'll go through the budgets line by line and see if I can do a little trimming; it's business, that's all. Budgets are meant to be flexible.' I try my best to sound light-hearted, but it's not easy as, to be honest, I'm worried.

'Well, the offer's there if you need it. There's something I should tell you, though, and I fear that whatever I say it's bound to upset both you and Shellie, so I don't know quite how to handle it.'

I swing around into a sitting position. Now Mum is sounding agitated and that's not like her at all.

'Mum, what's going on?'

If I was relaxed, I'm not now. A chill is working its way up from my stomach into my chest.

'Oh, dear, oh, dear,' she sighs, sounding in two minds about taking this conversation any further.

'Mum, stop saying that. Just talk to me.'

'You won't like this, and neither will Shellie. She's very up and down at the moment with her pregnancy and I had hoped to wait a while, but things are moving quickly.'

I let out a frustrated 'aargh' and she begins speaking again, almost immediately.

'Jake flew home to the UK a couple of months ago. He sold his house in LA and has bought something over here. I've agreed to move in with him and be on hand if he needs any help. Yesterday he rang to say he's found a purchaser for my house. Eventually, everything I have will be split between the three of you anyway, and even without the sale there's enough in the savings account to give you all a reasonable lump sum now. And now is when you need it, Lexie.'

I don't know what to react to first. The fact that my

brother is home, Mum is selling up, or that she's offering to bail me out. They are all equally shocking and unexpected.

'Mum, I am not taking your savings. Besides, you love that house. You've been there forever. Why would you let Jake talk you into selling it?' I exclaim, my mind quickly visualising a picture of it and refusing to believe she'd let those memories go and sell it to a stranger.

'I rattle around here all alone, when some other family could be making new memories and using it to the full. I'm quite content with the plan Jake has laid out. I will have my own separate accommodation within the grounds of the delightful old property he's purchased.'

I can see it in my mind's eye – Jake has no doubt bought a huge country house with a little cottage in the garden for Mum. But as for being at his beck and call, that makes me angry.

'You might as well agree to take the money, Lexie, because I'm going to give the same to your brother and sister. When the house sells, I'll invest the capital somewhere safe to earn a little interest, but if you need it at any time, then it's there for you all. I'm looking forward to having a smaller place to call home and something meaningful to do, which will be helping out whenever I can. I will admit there have been times recently when I've felt a little redundant. I know that's my own fault, but by nature I'm a stay-at-home person. If my children could just make up and move on, I'll be the happiest mother in the world.'

'So why haven't you shared this news with us before now? I mean, this hasn't happened overnight. And why has all of this been done in secret? Shellie will be as shocked as I am about it.'

Another sigh. A big one. 'I didn't say anything because I

knew how you would both react and Shellie's got enough on her plate at the moment. Plus, you were heading off to France and I told Jake straight that he had to wait until the right time for us all to get together. Oh, it just seemed too overwhelming to tackle and I didn't know where to begin, or how to break the news without upsetting you both.'

Well, she has a point because neither Shellie nor I are likely to give him the same open-armed reception that Mum has.

'When Jake left the UK there was bad feeling amongst you all, I know that,' Mum admits. 'But you, in particular, should be able to talk to Jake about what happened and clear the air. Shellie is only upset with him because of the argument you two had.

'He's coming *home* because he's setting up a new company on his own. Doesn't the fact that he still regards this as his home tell you something? He could so easily be doing this in the States but, at long last, he's admitting that he misses his family. That old saying *blood is thicker than water* isn't just a few silly words strung together, it means something. For all he's seen and done, for all the people he's worked with, your brother has missed being a part of our family.'

I could scream. There has been no contact with either Shellie or myself in the intervening years and that's typical of Jake. He's a manipulator and Mum is a pushover. I take a huge breath to calm myself down and am relieved at how evenly my voice sounds.

'If you don't ring Shellie and tell her, then I will, Mum. As for talking to Jake, well, tell him when he's ready he knows where to find me. I love you so much for wanting to dip into your savings, but I know what I'm doing. This is business and there are ways and means of raising funds. I'm happy to risk what's mine, but I'm not happy to risk your legacy and please don't take that the wrong way.

'Now put down the phone and call Shellie, because she's imagining all sorts of things, but it doesn't include the possibility of Jake coming back to the UK. But please, before it's too late, just stop and think about what it means to let go of the house. So many memories; so much of the past wrapped up within those walls. If it truly is the right decision for you, then I'm happy, but I don't want you to have any regrets, Mum, that's all.'

There's a moment of silence and I wonder whether my honesty has made her stop and think.

'My mind is made up, honey. Sometimes there are too many memories here for me to handle. Besides, I'm looking forward to a new challenge.'

My heart sinks in my chest.

Afterwards I'm wracked with guilt, as what I noted in her voice was a level of enthusiasm I haven't heard in a long while. I appreciate that Mum would do anything not to upset any one of us, but she should have opened up about this and not kept it to herself until the last minute. Was I guilty of being so consumed by my own problems that she didn't feel she could talk to me? And Shellie obviously has so much going on at the moment. Did we leave Mum feeling out on a limb, with no one to talk to, and unwittingly pave the way for Jake to swoop in and take advantage of her?

Hand on heart, I can't say an influx of cash wouldn't be highly convenient at this moment in time, but no business venture is a sure bet. Elliot and I are putting in what we can afford to lose; if we don't sell the series then we've blown our savings, but we won't lose everything. I wouldn't risk a penny of Mum's money, even if she is buying into this totally absurd idea of Jake's. If it doesn't work out, then I want her to be in a position to have options.

My fingers dial quickly.

'Shellie, Mum's going to ring you any minute with news. Jake returned to the UK a while ago, it seems.' There's a weird sort of screech. 'Pretend you don't know. She's going to sell the house and move in with him to become some sort of housekeeper, by the sound of it. Just listen and don't go off on one, because that won't help. We'll talk more about this tomorrow. I'm putting down the phone as you can expect that call at any moment. Hopefully it's not too late for us to talk some sense into her, but we need to tread carefully.'

I can imagine Shellie sitting there, phone pressed against her ear and her face draining of all colour. You messed everything up once, Jake. I'm not going to sit back and let you do it again.

* * *

It's just after eleven p.m. when Shellie calls me back. I've been sitting here in the semi-darkness, trying to focus on the last couple of chapters of Ronan's book to distract me.

'I'm speechless,' she groans.

'You haven't been on the phone the entire time?' I quiz.

'Yes, I have.' She sniffs.

'Are you crying?'

More muffled sniffs and some nose-blowing.

'How can Mum have sold the house without telling us? I can still visualise Dad in every single room and now strangers are going to be moving in. Jake clearly is a cold-hearted bastard to have talked her into this without consulting us.'

I've been mulling it over, off and on for the last two-plus

hours. Mum won't have taken this decision lightly. There are things going on with her and it's clear that both Shellie and I haven't been paying attention. We each have excuses we can make, but when it comes to it that's all they are – excuses. Mum's well-being comes first and she never makes a big deal of anything, so we have to be on our toes and it's more about what she doesn't say than the words she uses.

'Look, Shellie. Mum told me there are times when she feels redundant. Mum, *redundant*! She's not one to throw herself into hobbies, is she? As much as I dislike the idea of her appearing to be almost like an employee of Jake's, maybe something is missing from her life.'

'So, what do you suggest we do?'

Oh, this is so hard, given the distance between us all at the moment. 'Look, I can't get back, even for a quick visit. Why don't you pop round to Mum's for a chat over a cup of tea? My biggest fear is what happens if Jake meets someone and they don't want his mother running his household? Then she really would be redundant, in the worst possible way. Without actually *saying* that, could you get her to talk through the bigger plan? If she doesn't mention future changes in Jake's life – personal, or business-related – then maybe ask if this is a long-term thing. In the excitement of imagining us all as one big happy family again, she might not have thought this through properly.'

The sniffing has stopped.

'Brilliant idea! I'll drop round with Maisie tomorrow after school. Maisie will want to invite Lizzie from next door in to play and that will give me the perfect opportunity to have a leisurely chat with Mum.'

'Try to keep calm about this, Shellie. We might have to accept that there's nothing we can do because the decision is

Mum's, after all. But we need to be sure that she's aware that there are no guarantees we'll ever bond again as siblings and that there's an element of risk in her walking away from the life she has now. I mean, what if she comes to regret selling the house? She won't be able to buy it back again and that's the harsh reality.'

We sigh in tandem. 'I promise to be gentle with her and not to let my anger at Jake spill over. I'll let you know how it goes, but it might not be until the day after tomorrow. Drew and I are going out to dinner tomorrow night with some friends, so it will be rather hectic. Sleep well, sis. I've got this, don't you worry.'

How can I possibly sleep after that? Well, the truth is that I can't, so I try to empty my mind and continue reading Ronan's book.

Maurice Perrin was, it seems, amongst the most influential of chief gardeners at Versailles by the time he retired in 1986. Having a quick leaf through the second book in the series, I see Ronan makes a brief reference to the dreadful storms of 1990 and 1999, and the ensuing devastation that will be covered in the final book, apparently.

Maurice had dismissed the idea that delaying a massive replanting programme could potentially result in a complete change in the landscape of the park, as far back as the early sixties. But he did support a project looking in detail at the pattern of tree loss going back to the forties. Immediately I saw that, it grabbed my attention. A project about the trees – could Grandma have been a part of that?

Obviously, one could say that storms of the magnitude of the two in the twentieth century are an act of nature. If the park had been on the edge of either of those storms it could so easily have been a very different story. But the fact that so many trees were at risk and succumbed had been predicted.

Ronan explains that one of the gardeners in the sixties was adamant that many of the trees had been allowed to grow too tall for the high water table. The roots had travelled along the ground, rather than downwards, which in his opinion was a serious concern as it compromised their stability. The inherent danger for the future was that trees wouldn't die because of their age, but because they would become unstable.

But Maurice, for some unknown reason, had a sudden change of heart and the project was abandoned before a conclusion could be drawn. It's becoming apparent to me, that is the puzzle Ronan is trying to solve. What really happened, because it feels as if there might have been a conspiracy going on. One that targeted Maurice, perhaps as he was a lone voice at the time, daring to challenge the people above him. Having committed to the idea of the survey, was pressure then applied to make him stop?

Diving into Grandma Viv's box once more, I decide to try to put the notebooks in some sort of order. To my amazement, as I look at the inside covers and then skim the first page or two, not only does it become apparent that there is a natural order, but also that some are much less about her work. I find one detailing a day trip to Paris and another a picnic by a river.

Halfway through the exercise, one inscription on the inside cover jumps out at me. It's an old saying. *There are none so blind as those who will not see.*

I always thought it was those who *cannot* see, which, now I think about it, is actually something very different indeed. In actual fact it's referring to people who choose to ignore what they already know. Is that because they are arrogant, deluded or have no choice in the matter? It's possible that Maurice was a realist and had no choice other than to be pragmatic because of funding issues. But I can't help wondering whether the real reason was that he was ordered to stop and he hadn't wanted to lose face by sharing that information.

The first page of Grandma's notebook reflects the frustration of that time.

The arguments get worse by the day. We've spent too many hours cataloguing, measuring and testing soil to throw away all that hard work and yet today we were told the project has been shelved.

My heart leaps in my chest. She doesn't specifically mention trees, but this seems to fit in with the period Ronan was talking about in his book.

Tempers flared yet again and this time it came to blows. I fear that someone will be sacked after the incident today. Who knows what tomorrow will bring? I have been sent to work in one of the greenhouses and our little group of three has been disbanded for the time being. It always comes down to the same thing. Money. I fear they are in danger of making a grave mistake. But my voice is nothing, because this isn't my battle. My heart is heavy for those to whom this represents a major defeat. People care so passionately, and I feel privileged to be here, but useless.

My eyes begin to smart. Grandma felt a real part of what was going on; Ronan and I must piece this together somehow, even if we aren't going to get any cooperation at all from George. Maybe he didn't have anything to do with Grandma when she was here, but I'm convinced he recognised her from the photograph. Perhaps they didn't get on; I veered between glimpsing a wry sense of humour in him and feeling as though we were trespassing, and he wanted to throw us out. Grandma wouldn't have warmed to that sort of reception, either.

I make a start on the second notebook in the newly ordered row and read late into the night, making copious notes as I go. If these weren't so very precious, I'd highlight sections, but one day, when Maisie is grown up, I want her to read them, too. To see this other side to a lady we loved because of her kindness and selfless nature is humbling.

If Grandma hadn't returned from Versailles, I have no doubt at all that her life would have been consumed by her work here. She might never have had children and it makes me wonder how much choice we each have in our own destinies. Is it, indeed, mapped out for us? And if that's the case, did she ever have even the teeniest tinge of regret in her heart for what might have been? Sadly, that's something we may never know for sure, unless I can successfully piece together the clues.

14

Driiing. Driiing. Driiing.

I open one eye and shift the pillow off my head. The light slanting in through the partially open blind tells me it's not that early and I vault out of bed. Did I arrange to see Ronan this morning? It's... Sunday, isn't it?

Throwing on a baggy T-shirt over my cotton camisole and shorts, I hurry down the two flights of stairs to swing open the door. Rather surprisingly, it's Solange's smiling face I see in front of me. As soon as she glimpses my bed hair, her smile begins to fade.

'Oh. So very sorry, Lexie. You were enjoying a lie-in and I should have considered that fact. Another time, maybe?'

'No, not at all. It's lovely to see you and I said feel free to pop in for a chat. Coffee?' I turn and begin walking up the stairs so that Solange can step inside and follow me up.

As I head straight for the kettle, I indicate for her to take a seat at the table.

'This is a lovely layout up here – very open, I like it. Really, though, I shouldn't interrupt you. It's just that I stayed at Philippe's last night and as I had to walk past... well, I promised you a tour of the palace and I have an hour and a half free this morning.'

I do a double take.

'Now?'

'I know. I did not think this out.' She laughs softly. 'Philippe asked me to move in with him last night, so my head is full of *fluff?* this morning.' She looks at me question-ingly, checking she has the right word.

'Good one! *Cotton wool* is the most commonly used saying. But that's wonderful, Solange.'

'Our secret. Renée does not know yet.' She puts her finger up to her lips, keeping them tightly shut.

'Of course! Look, if you're happy to make the coffee, because I can't function without the first one in the morning, I can be ready in fifteen minutes.' It's times like this I bemoan not having a shower, so it will be the quickest dip in history.

'Great. That will give us enough time for a quick tour of a couple of the rooms before I have to escort a party of VIP guests around.'

* * *

We slip in through one of the staff entrances and Solange gives me a running commentary as we walk. Although I pride myself on the depth of my research for any project in which I'm involved, I quickly come to understand that even the most professional of photographs simply cannot do more than give an impression of the grandeur and opulence here. It's experiencing the scale up close, and knowing one is walking on ground traversed by some of the most important royals, nobles and dignitaries in France's colourful history, that gives me the chills.

'We're lucky, we timed it well. I feel that the experience of the Hall of Statues is often diminished, as eager tourists file through here quickly in vast numbers after queuing patiently for, often, a couple of hours. Everyone is eager to get to the more celebrated rooms like the Hall of Mirrors, the various salons and the bedchambers of the King and the Queen.'

In front of us is a row of magnificent archways supported by buff-coloured marble pillars. Between each archway is a statue on a plinth. The matching marble floor is like a carpet runner, with an inset chequerboard pattern in alternate black and white marble squares set diagonally. It runs the entire length of the row of archways. At the end of the long run is a full-size statue set back within an alcove and it stands out because, unlike the others, a dark grey cloak adds a splash of colour.

I step forward eagerly to look in detail at the imposing representation of a man named Jean Racine, according to the plaque; the folds of his cloak and the finely chiselled features show his nobility. His fashionably curled wig adds a touch of grandeur and his eyes, although devoid of any colour, are so well carved you have to marvel at the artistry. I can imagine this man standing in front of me and I almost want to curtsy.

Solange gently touches my arm, leading me to the left, down a few steps where the same black and white tiles traverse a large open-plan area. There's no furniture at all in here and presumably this is simply one of the large hallways, a place where courtiers congregated to pass the time of day. Or maybe awaiting their attendance at one of the Sun King's many daily ritualistic ceremonies.

As we walk along parallel to the arched gallery, I

continue to glimpse to my right to view the statuary. We're alone, except for a member of staff wearing a dark blue uniform and sitting on a tall stool at the far end of the room. Our footsteps have a hollow ring to them and it's impossible not to think about the feet that have trodden this floor before us.

'Come,' Solange says, steering me across to the far left and the massive wall of French doors that look out over the Water Parterre at the rear of the palace; away in the distance is the Grand Canal. There are a few visitors already traversing the large gravelled expanse outside, but in my mind's eye I imagine what it must have been like when this was the home of the French court.

'To see and be seen was the order of the King and those who did not make their presence felt would quickly fall from his grace,' Solange half whispers in the hollowness, our minds thinking the exact same thing. 'This is one of my favourite places. It's not as ornate, or ostentatious, but I love the simplicity of the stone ceiling and the arches. But when it's packed with visitors it spoils the effect for me and I know I should not say that. Revenue is essential to maintain and preserve this, so that future generations can come to marvel at the achievement of so many.'

We head off quickly as Solange glances at her watch. 'You need to allocate a few hours at least, to come as a visitor and saunter through at your leisure, Lexie. The crowd around you tends to dictate the pace at which you walk and in some places that unfortunately obscures what you can see at busy times. I suggest mid to late afternoon, when it's a little quieter.

'Maybe spread your visit over two days. This morning I want to take you to experience a few of the most popular rooms before they begin to fill up. We won't use any of the main staircases, as we are taking a shortcut,' she informs me.

Solange strides out and it quickly becomes apparent that comfortable shoes are essential in her job. She leads me up a wide marble staircase and I find myself holding onto the metal handrail, held up by twisted ironwork spindles with the obligatory gilding. The steps beneath my feet are worn down in places. If this isn't one of the main staircases, I can't even begin to imagine how grand the others are going to be.

There is a clear path that has been trodden next to the handrail. The deep depressions show just how many feet have passed this way in order to wear away the hardest of material and leave such an impression. People who climbed this staircase, maybe fearful of the fate that awaited them, or to meet up with a collaborator to plot someone else's downfall. Or to hurry to one of the salons, only to return a few hours later having lost a substantial amount of money that could result in their ultimate ruin.

We veer to the left and Solange unhooks a plush velvet rope barring our way. There's a sign on a stand forbidding access by the public.

'This is the quickest route,' she explains.

On the walls either side of this long and rather dimly lit corridor is painting after painting. Various scenes from battles mainly, some of which are protected by glass because the colours are no longer rich and vibrant. We keep going and turn into yet another corridor and around a corner. In front of us are two huge, wooden doors.

Swinging one of the doors open, we step inside. Ornately carved wooden shutters have been pulled back, allowing the light from the French windows to brighten the room. But even with the sun low in the sky, the shaft that filters in between the gap in the curtains only lights a small area. With this level of detail and decoration it lends a heaviness to the ambience of the room. Or is it the history contained within the walls that weighs heavily?

So many joyous and also life-changing moments have happened in this room; is it possible for something to be left behind forever, I wonder, like a shadow so faint the eye can't see it any longer? As with the paintings, over time they lose the bright contrast of the colours until all one sees is a dark representation that belies the original. Even kings must feel fear, as much as they feel the euphoria of the power they wield. That's the trouble with life: everything waxes and wanes.

'The King's bedchamber,' Solange declares solemnly.

The chevroned parquet flooring beneath our feet is a golden-brown colour, set in diagonal squares. It contrasts well against the heavy brocade curtains, which remain part drawn to help restrict the amount of sunlight filtering in to preserve the contents of the room. They were essential, no doubt, to keep in the heat during the cold winter months, too. It's a temptation to reach out and touch the fabric, but I know I mustn't. I turn around and walk towards the bed.

'The French Minister of Culture revived the eighteenth-century weaving techniques to reproduce the drapery and wall hangings in accordance with the original designs, at great cost,' she whispers.

'Is the furniture original?' I ask, enthralled.

'Yes, but much is missing. Considerable amounts were spent in tracking down and re-purchasing as many of the bespoke pieces as possible. But, as you can imagine, anything connected to the palace and designed especially for it is a prized acquisition for a wealthy collector. The market is international and not everyone is sympathetic to the benefit of returning an item to its original habitat, even for a good price. Money is sometimes of no object, sadly.'

Half of the room is merely a walkway for visitors, as the rooms interlink – one flowing into another. There is a cordon to stop visitors going too close to the side of the room that is furnished to give an indication of how it would have looked back in the day.

To our right a marble bust and two tall candelabra are displayed on the mantelpiece of the magnificent marble fireplace.

The bed is enclosed by heavily embroidered brocade curtains in the same pattern as the wall hangings. It is possible, just, to glimpse the bed itself nestled inside but it affords some privacy at least. It is a bed fit for a king indeed.

Aside from the modern-day roped cordon, the other side of that is a gilded balustrade that runs the entire length of the room. It looks original because it's so beautifully carved. Did courtiers stand as close to the King's bed as we're standing right now?

'The gilded railing denotes the King's own space; a sort of line that could not be crossed unless the King expressly wished it,' Solange explains as she follows my gaze.

'I've read the accounts of the grand getting-up ceremony *le grand lever*, one of his many ceremonial rituals. It seems bizarre that he turned the mundane into a spectacle just to demonstrate his power and celebrate what he perceived as his divine majesty. I doubt there was anyone who was not either in awe, or fear, of him.'

'The number of spectators was anything up to a hundred, comprising the most important members of court as well as the King's closest royal servants. Females were not allowed, as would have been expected. The final ceremony of the day, which took place at 11.30 p.m. was yet another public ritual as the King retired to bed.'

'There's no air in here.' I remark. Solange is now a few paces away, studying the bust sitting on the mantelpiece and I walk towards her.

'It's warm today and the sun is already on the back of the palace. The heat builds up even at this time of the year,' she replies, turning back to face me and then gaze the full length of the room.

Did the King ever feel he couldn't breathe in here? I wonder. It feels heavy, close, almost oppressive and a little claustrophobic to me, but I can see that Solange doesn't feel that way.

'Can we see the Hall of Mirrors?' I'm eager to move on. If the room were full, would I be feeling a sense of panic now instead of mere discomfort? It's all in your mind, Lexie, I tell myself, and then I think of Grandma. What did she think when she stood in this room?

The door opens and a member of staff walks through followed by a group of visitors. The morning rush is about to begin.

'This way,' Solange says, and we head in the opposite direction.

'Some people feel it: the history. As if it's almost tangible,' she remarks, turning to look at me as we walk fairly quickly through a series of opulent rooms. 'I do not and I'm grateful for that. Some have seen things amongst the shadows, but all I've ever seen is the tiny dust particles when a shaft of sunlight escapes between the semi-drawn curtains on a brilliantly sunny day.'

I nod in agreement, but the truth is that I'm open-minded.

The rooms and corridors are beginning to fill with both staff and visitors. When we reach our destination any sense of heaviness has left me, and I'm enthralled. It's a giant ballroom with huge, sparkling chandeliers. The imposingly tall mirrors reflect the daylight flooding in from the wall of French doors opposite them. Made up of a series of large sections, these mirrors stand between pink marble pillars and have beautifully gilded, floor-standing candelabra in front of them.

The French doors lead out onto a balcony overlooking the magnificent gardens and park. It's impossible to stop myself from slowly circling around to take in the dazzling beauty of mirror, gold and crystal.

It's truly magical and if anyone doubted the boldness of the vision, as soon as their eyes stray to the windows and see that magnificent view, they are left in no doubt at all. Who could dare to dream about this level of lavish indulgence, let alone bring it into being? Only a Sun King, I think.

The vaulted ceiling heralds the most wonderful paintings, all set within gilded plaster decoration that frame them like the individual pieces of art that they are.

'This is unbelievable,' I whisper to Solange, looking around at what is now quite a crowd filtering into the room.

'It's almost two hundred and forty feet long and thirty-four feet wide. The paintings are scenes from Louis XIV's life. Breathtaking, isn't it?' She pauses as we both stare upwards. 'The Treaty of Versailles was signed in this room on 28 June 1919, ending the First World War. Most of the paintings celebrate either France's political, economic, or artistic successes under Louis' command.'

Solange checks her watch once more and shrugs.

'We should start making our way back now, I'm sorry to say. There is so much to see but this is by far the most ostentatious room within the palace. The number of mirrors, some 357 of them in total, was a purposeful demonstration of wealth at a time when items like these were a great luxury, indeed.'

As we pass through the door, I am now having to dodge people to keep up with Solange, who is still talking to me, but doesn't realise several people have stepped in between us. It takes a few seconds for me to weave in and out and I'm only grateful not to have been separated from her.

She turns and her eyes rest on my face for a second. 'I'm so glad we could do this today. Your first visit is always special, but you must come several times while you are here. I hope, though, that I have not thrown too much information at you.' She grins.

'No. It's fascinating. Thank you so much, Solange.'

We part in front of the ticket office and the queue is snaking down and around in long lines that are three or four people abreast already. It continues to edge slowly forward.

'It's going to be a busy day, but I fear rain is on the way,' she reflects, looking up at the grey clouds forming in the distance. 'I'm only here for a few hours and then I'm off for a leisurely afternoon with Philippe. I will see you in the morning, Lexie.'

I lean in to give her a hug before she heads off, then I stand and people-watch for a few minutes. The sun disappears briefly, but when it reappears the rays bouncing off the gilding on the inner gates and the façade of the palace turn it into a glorious, glinting crown once more. I stare in fascination, knowing that this moment will be forever locked inside my head. It's the moment that I realise I was meant to come here. Is it just to make the series we're working on, or is there another purpose, too?

Walking back to the cottage, I wonder if I will ever succeed in getting any answers at all about Grandma or have to accept that the past is now a closed book and look to the future. But being here has made me feel close to her again and perhaps that's what I needed in my life right now. She would have been championing my decision to push forward boldly and not be afraid of taking a few calculated risks. Maybe a little reminder of that is all the comfort I need to re-energise my sense of self-belief.

Reaching the courtyard, I feel something flick against my cheek and as I look upwards the first raindrops begin to fall. Within seconds I'm scrabbling for my keys as the clouds empty. Please, please, please, don't let it rain tomorrow. Losing time and money we simply don't have isn't an option right now.

15

PULLING TOGETHER

As we all anticipated, it takes longer than normal to set up this morning, but at least the sky is clear and there's no threat of rain today. Elliot had given Ronan the key to his apartment so he could pick up the kit, but it's clear from the moment he arrives that Ronan is feeling the pressure.

He's working with a camera he hasn't operated before, but I'm impressed at how quickly he's sussing it out. It's obvious he's annoyed with himself when, after he has unpacked everything, it turns out that there's only one battery in the aluminium transport case. Even so, after a quick practice session he gives me a thumbs up. His forehead is beaded with sweat, even though there's a slight chill carried on the breeze.

Cameron is being very supportive and chatty, at one point both of them leaning over the camera, frowning. I leave them to it as I can't be of any help on the technical side of things, so instead I engage Yvette Gilliard, our stand-in interpreter, in a little chat before going over a brief overview of today's proceedings. We agree that she will do a running commentary, as today we're focusing on the greenhouses and will be watching a series of demonstrations before touring the nursery.

It's fascinating learning how various plants are propagated and gaining an idea of the scale involved. Already this year's seedlings are being repotted, like a production line; three students chat as they work, their fingers deftly nipping off tips and the odd leaf or bud. It's as automatic as if their hands have been pre-programmed.

A little later one of the English-speaking, full-time gardeners joins us.

'Anything up to fifty thousand flowers are planted out every year, including tuberoses, jasmine, pinks and carnations. The very positive effects of the move away from the use of pesticides, more than ten years ago now, has had a huge impact on the various plants and shrubs. Indeed, on the survival of everything that lives within the gardens, too. It has encouraged the birds to return in greater numbers, attracted by the insect life.

'The variety of plant species is the key now,' he tells us, 'to avoid major losses from disease or pests in the more natural environment that now exists. It was a bold decision for Versailles to turn its back on the use of chemicals. At the time some considered it to be a risky move. But as with all change, that's often the case, and as the years have passed and the organic movement has grown, it is now regarded as a visionary decision.'

By the time we're ready to begin packing up I can see that Ronan is feeling much more comfortable. Yvette did a good job and her narrative flowed really well. I hope the play back confirms that it worked.

We don't hang around long as Solange has this afternoon off and Ronan offers to give me a lift back. I wish I had anticipated that and popped to the supermarket to get something interesting for lunch.

'How about we grab some things to eat and find somewhere quiet to have a picnic?' I suggest instead, as we drive away from the palace.

'That sounds like a great idea. Do we need to call into your place to pick anything up?'

I shake my head. 'No. We'll manage. A rustic lunch will be fun.' I muse as he raises his eyebrows.

'Bread, cheese, water and a little fruit. Simple.'

In fact, we end up with a carrier bag full of treats and Ronan finds the perfect place, less than twenty minutes' drive away.

'This is very pretty,' I remark, swinging open the passenger door. Leaning back in, I grab my jumper and tie it around my waist. Ronan is rummaging around in the boot and hands me an old waterproof tartan blanket. I half hope the next thing in his hand will be a comfy sun chair, but no such luck.

Walking over to the grassy bank, I pile everything on the floor in a heap and then begin spreading it out, slipping off my shoes to sit cross-legged. Ronan places the bag next to me and I begin to lay out our feast. My mouth waters as the aroma of the meltingly soft, ripened Brie I'm unwrapping mingles with the saltiness of sliced, dry-cured ham.

'Can you pass my backpack?' I call out to him and he returns, shutting the boot and joining me on the rug, easing off his shoes with a satisfying little groan.

When I notice his odd socks, I can't help laughing.

'What?' Ronan asks.

'That's some combo you have going on there,' I declare. One has a black and white stripe, the other is a cobalt blue.

He grins back at me as I finish off emptying the contents of the lunch bag. I watch as he cracks open a bottle of water to wash off a couple of apples.

'This could be a little messy to eat, but doesn't it smell divine?'

Ronan looks at me and his eyes travel over my face, making me break into a nervous smile. 'You look lovely and relaxed. It's good to see,' he says softly.

I look away, feeling a little self-conscious suddenly, and begin ripping half of the enormous baguette into chunks, stacking them up into a pile.

'A feast fit for a king,' he adds.

We sit facing each other as we tuck in, hungrily. It's messy, tearing the chunks of bread apart with our fingers and scooping up the soft cheese, but fun. Chewing in silence, I scan around to take in the gentle babbling of the small brook at the bottom of the grassy bank we have found.

In the background an intermittent stream of cars flashes by but, in between, all we can hear are the birds busily chasing each other as they fly in and out of the branches overhead. The spring madness has begun in earnest and after the long winter there is much to do as they prepare their nests.

'This is a gorgeous little spot. Only in France could you pull up alongside quite a busy road and experience a little piece of heaven.'

Ronan looks across at me, pausing for a second before he bites into an apple.

'Simple pleasures,' he agrees.

I watch as he savours the piece of fruit, then leans forward to grab some ham. He can feel my eyes on him, and he shrugs his shoulders.

'Sorry, I know I probably look like I haven't eaten for a week, but I'm starving. That was quite a morning and I will admit I was feeling the pressure, but I think I've sussed out the camera now. I'll pop back to Elliot's and pick up the spare battery a bit later. Any more updates about Mia?'

Holding my hand in front of my mouth as I finish savouring the delights of the creamy cheese, I shake my head. 'Not really. It's a case of rest and letting the drugs do their work until she's well enough to recuperate at home. It sounds like the worst is behind her, but Elliot says she's very weak. He doesn't know when he can fly back, and I reassured him that we're managing.'

Ronan nods, wiping his fingers as he glances across at me.

'It looks like you have a halo,' he muses. 'There's a shaft of sunlight behind me reflecting off the tips of your hair.' He pulls his phone out of his pocket and before I know it, I'm laughing and he's snapping away.

He places the phone down on the blanket next to him and turns his attention back to the picnic platters, lowering his eyes.

'You never said if there was any significant other, missing you while you're here working.'

When he raises his eyes to meet mine, I can see he's serious.

'No. Not even a cat,' I add, emphatically.

'But you do go on dates?'

I nod. 'Of course. I just haven't met anyone who succeeded in holding my interest for very long,' I reply truthfully.

'Oh, so it's not a conscious decision to remain single forever, then?' Well, when he has a question he certainly doesn't hold back.

'When the right someone comes along, then my sister reliably informs me that it turns your life upside down. One's priorities change, I guess.' I watch Ronan's reaction with interest, as he draws his hand along the light stubble on his chin while he considers that.

'Yes.' He pauses for a moment. 'Life-changing, for sure, once the commitment is made.'

I can see he's preoccupied by whatever is going on inside his head. There's undeniable chemistry between us that we're both trying to keep in check. For me it's a self-preservation thing. Who wants to be the first to make that move and face possible rejection? I can't help wondering whether Ronan is treading carefully because he fears it could upset our working relationship, or because he isn't sure what's going on between us.

'Until that happens, I'm a firm believer in setting oneself goals. I have my sights set on diversifying. Presenting is fine, it pays the bills, but it doesn't satisfy that creative streak within me.'

'You find this project exciting, not just because you have a connection to this place, then,' he reflects.

'Exactly. My mum and sister don't understand the pull. I can't help myself, really.'

He toys absent-mindedly with a piece of baguette, then discards it, his eyes scanning my face with genuine interest.

'I can understand where you are coming from. In my case I think I'm searching for something and I haven't found whatever it is yet that will make my life fall into place. All I do know is that being here feels right for me, as I've distanced myself from the things that were causing me stress. But admitting that makes me feel like a bad son. This lifestyle suits me, but whether I can continue to earn enough to support it is another thing.'

I can empathise with that.

'We can't live our lives just to please other people, even if they do have our interests at heart. My sister is expecting her second child and my mum is now despairing of me ever finding someone who will succeed in tying me down.' I confess.

'Mothers always worry about their children, no matter how capable they are. They don't realise that it's an added pressure, in a way. Not everyone has a clear picture of their future stretching out in front of them and if you're one of those people then it makes you feel a little lacking sometimes,' Ronan admits, frowning.

'I guess it would. I've always had a dream and I don't want to settle for anything in life, unless it really fires me up. So, did you have someone meaningful in your life before you came here? Was the move to get away and start over again?'

It's a question I've been longing to ask but, rather than appear to be a little too eager to find out, I begin clearing up. Ronan helps tip everything back into the carrier bag as he continues.

'Just my father and his dysfunctional family life. I was seeing someone off and on. But they weren't too impressed when I chose to walk away from a well-paid job to come here and it wasn't a tough goodbye for either of us. We wanted different things out of life and it was time to part company. There's no point being in a relationship if you end up simply going through the motions. I guess the truth is that loneliness is scary at times and it's easy to hang in there for the wrong reasons. Besides, who would put up with me long-term?' He turns to look in my direction, holding my gaze as if inviting me to comment. It's a playful look, but he's waiting for a reply.

'Well, I enjoy your company.' My pulse suddenly quickens.

A smile creeps over his face as our eyes remain locked.

'I was rather hoping you'd say that, because I was thinking the same thing about you.'

It's a relief to hear him say that, but I wish he hadn't stopped there.

'You turned out to be quite a surprise, Ronan. I like a man who isn't afraid to share his innermost thoughts. And I've told you things I've never spoken about to anyone before. It's all about trust, isn't it?' I so want him to keep talking to me, to explain how he feels.

'We have a lot in common, Lexie, and I think we're both cautious people by nature. Or maybe it's because of our life experiences, who knows? I see that as a good thing because it rarely pays to rush into something. But getting into a proper relationship is a major upheaval. Your plans sound—'

He begins to reach out with his hand, when suddenly my phone kicks into life and I curse under my breath. Ronan immediately draws back, grabbing the carrier bag and easing himself up on his knees as I answer the call.

'Hey, Maisie,' I reply brightly as that familiar little voice fills my ear. The timing couldn't have been worse but it's not her fault. 'How are you, my darling girl? What are you doing home from school at this time of day?'

'Mummy picked me up early as I had to go to the dentist. It's raining and we got wet and now I don't feel very well, Auntie Lexie.'

She sounds upset, rather than ill, and I can hear Shellie in the background telling her she will be fine.

'You settle down on the sofa and I'll go and fetch your onesie from upstairs,' Shellie adds.

'That's what I do when I don't feel very well. I snuggle up on the sofa and watch a film, or something. Resting usually helps and before you know it, you're feeling much better,' I encourage her.

Maisie sniffs, sounding dejected.

'Ollie broke up with me today.' Her voice is low, almost a whisper.

'Broke up?'

'Katie gave him some sweets and she asked him to be her boyfriend. But he was my boyfriend, Auntie Lexie.'

Her voice sounds fractured, as if she's struggling to hold back a flood of tears. That welling-up feeling that takes one's breath away. I don't quite know what to say to her.

'Have you told Mummy?'

'No. Every time I try, I get this horrible pain... in my chest... and I can't... speak.' Her words come out haltingly. I screw up my eyes, wishing I could just wrap my arms around her.

'Oh, my darling girl. What exactly happened?'

Another sniff. 'He said he was breaking up with me because Katie was nicer to him.'

'What did you say to that?'

'I started crying and he said I was a baby.'

Ah, my heart is literally in pieces now as I hear the pain coming through so very clearly in her words.

'Maisie, you aren't a baby at all and it's fine to cry when you're feeling upset. One day, when you're all grown up, you will meet someone very special and he will be a keeper. Like your daddy. But until then boyfriends will come and go.'

'But I like Ollie, Auntie Lexie. He can run really fast and he's funny.'

'I'm sure he's amazing, darling. But you are even more amazing, believe me. For now, though, I think it's best if you just have lots of friends and lots of fun. But know that friends come and go. That's not a bad thing, but a good thing. A new friend could introduce you to a new hobby, for instance.'

'Have you made any new friends in France, Auntie Lexie?' Her voice at least sounds even, now.

'Yes, I have. Lots of new friends. And I've learnt so many new things and that has made me feel very happy. When I get home, I'm going to have so much to tell you and one day I know you'll want to visit Versailles too, when you hear all about it.'

There's a slight pause. 'It wasn't very nice when Ollie made fun of me,' she says. It sends a little stab of pain to my heart.

'I know and it was very wrong of him, Maisie. When someone is hurting, the kind thing to do is to try to make them feel better. That way, we feel good about ourselves, too. Make sure you remember what I said, Maisie – you are one amazing girl. You are strong, you are clever, and you can do anything you want to do and I'm so proud of you. Now, put a big smile on your face and think about what film you are going to watch to cheer you up.'

I have a lump in my throat the size of a golf ball as Shellie returns to the room.

'Here you go, Maisie. Let's get you out of that school uniform and make you more comfortable. Say goodbye to Auntie Lexie.'

I can imagine the doleful look on that angelic little face.

'I miss you,' Maisie croaks into the phone.

'Miss you, too, darling girl. Don't forget to wear that smile and I'll call you later to see how you're doing.'

Shellie's voice looms up again. 'Let's watch a little TV, then you can have a nice, relaxing bubble bath. What do you say?'

Maisie doesn't respond.

'I'll call you later when I'm home, I promise, and we can have a long chat.'

'You're coming home?' Maisie's voice sounds hopeful.

'Oh, no, I meant my home here in France. But I have lots to tell you, all about how they take little cuttings to make new plants. We could have a go at that when I get back.'

'Where are you now?' Maisie asks.

'I'm having a picnic with a friend.' I screw up my face, thinking that will pique Shellie's interest and I daren't look in Ronan's direction.

'I wish I was there, too,' Maisie replies.

'One day maybe we can all come here together for a little holiday. Now, get that onesie on and snuggle up. Love you!'

I jump up, slipping the phone into my bag, and Ronan and I scoop up the edges of the blanket, shaking off the crumbs and folding it into four.

'Sounds like someone's having a tough time. You're missed,' he comments.

'Yes. My niece Maisie is such a blessing, but it's tough not seeing her as she's such a big part of my life.'

'Sounds like she's in need of her auntie right now.' He grins. 'It must be nice having close family around you, though. Knowing that you make a difference to their lives.'

'I'm lucky,' I admit, trying not to sound homesick. 'But, getting back to business, I'll make sure you're paid promptly and I want you to know how grateful I am for what you're doing to help out.'

He looks a little embarrassed, chewing his lip before turning away to put the blanket in the boot of the car and slamming it shut.

'I wasn't, I mean, when I said about affording my lifestyle here it wasn't a hint. Please don't think that. I'm not desperate for money, but I am at that point where if I can't get any further with the third book that I'm working on then I have to make some tough decisions. I'm more than happy to help out until Elliot gets back, because chances are this is the line of work I'll be looking to get back into. So, it's good practice for me because it's either that or taking a job teaching French to foreign businessmen, by the look of it.'

I'm rather shocked he's that close to giving up on the final book in the series. That would be such a shame.

'I found one of my grandma's notebooks that has a little more information in it that might be of interest to you.'

That seems to get his attention.

'Really?'

'Yes. I tried to put them in some sort of chronological order, and I glanced over the first page of each one. Do you have time to head back with me and take a quick look?'

'You bet,' he says, sounding very keen indeed. 'But how about we take a little detour, first?'

Standing on the pavement outside the florist's shop, we tip our heads back and stare up at the tiny first-floor balcony. Whoever lives there now certainly loves their plants. The balcony is a riot of spring colour with baskets and tubs full of red and yellow tulips.

'Stay here,' Ronan says, looking at me rather pointedly. 'I won't be a moment.'

I continue to gaze upwards, ignoring the flow of people weaving around me. It's the address in the back of Grandma's notebook. Amazingly, it's less than a five minute walk away from where I'm staying. When I head up to the palace I'm literally following in her footsteps, and the thought of it sends a little quiver of excitement coursing through me. Taking a half-step backwards, I inadvertently bump into a pedestrian. Mumbling an apology in my best French accent, the man gives a courteous reply in return in English. I guess my accent isn't quite as liltingly French as I'd hoped.

The white and green awning over the shopfront adds to what is a very colourful picture. An abundance of shades of green, pink, purple, yellow, white, pale blue... and that smell. There is a heady mixture of perfumes and earthy notes from the woody bark of cut stems, mingling rather tantalisingly in the tightly packed space. Pots of fragrant spring bulbs, everything from grape hyacinths to crocuses, and buckets full of freesias and irises extend out, taking up half of the pavement. It's the perfect framing for a magnificent window display, which is burgeoning with a myriad of colours and textures.

While I love the more formal displays around the palace, this is a riotous, tumultuous display that delights the eye as it searches out hidden treasures. A trailing ivy hangs down over some clipped bay standards in elegant pots, which are covered in the start of the new season's growth. A bucket full of vibrant yellow daffodils partly obscures a common Buxus, shaped into a ball.

I'm so caught up with my thoughts that I don't notice that Ronan has returned, until a bunch of sweet-smelling narcissi is thrust under my nose.

'These are for you,' he says with a flourish. 'And I have a surprise. Come this way.'

He steps back inside the shop and I follow a pace or two behind him. He introduces me to the woman behind the counter, who gives me a big smile. I'm surprised to discover she isn't French, at all, but German, and she indicates for us to weave behind the point of sale and out through a door to the rear.

It's a large room with several tables, where they assemble the bouquets and prepare the flowers for display. An older Frenchwoman greets us, and Ronan enters into conversation with her. She pulls a bunch of keys from her pocket and leads us out through the exit and up a metal staircase. Inserting the key and swinging open the door, she indicates for us to go inside.

'Madame says before her family took this over the flat above the shop was rented out. Her granddaughter lives here now; she's a student.'

I nod in the direction of Madame, giving her an acknowledging smile as we look around.

'I told her that we believe your grandma stayed here back in the sixties.'

It's a small flat consisting of three rooms. The kitchen-cum-sitting-room isn't big enough to house a table, but instead there is a small breakfast bar. The bedroom is a reasonable size, although the bathroom is rather cosy. While the balcony to the front is bijou, the French doors leading out let in lots of light and it's big enough for two small wrought-iron bistro chairs. But it's the flower boxes and tubs that turn it into a garden.

I wonder if it was like this when Grandma was here.

'Has it always been a florist's shop, can you ask?'

Ronan turns to ask the question and I gaze around, taking in the rustic panelling above the small open fireplace. The walls are painted a very soft sandy yellow and are contrasted by the cornflower-blue covering on the sofa. It's charming and has a delightfully cosy feel. There are no ghosts of the past here, despite its age.

'Yes, she believes it has been a florist's shop for a long time. Maybe even back as far as the sixties.'

'Merci, Madame. C'est adorable.'

And it is.

We make our way back outside and I hold the little bunch of flowers Ronan gave me up to my nose, drawing in a deep breath.

'They're beautiful, Ronan.'

'I thought you'd like them,' he replies as I give him a grateful smile.

'I might as well leave the car here in case I can't get a space closer to the cottage.'

'Good idea.'

'It would be nice if we could really confirm this was where Grandma stayed, wouldn't it?'

Ronan steps back to let someone pass and then strides forward to walk alongside me.

'I haven't given up. Perhaps she'll mention it in one of the other notebooks. I can see why she'd have chosen that particular flat though. It couldn't have been more perfect and everything she would have needed is within easy walking distance.'

'It's funny, but I can't ever recall hearing her speak any French at all. I wonder how fluent she was. Oh, I have so many questions whirling around inside my head,' I reflect, as we enter the gates to the courtyard.

'Well, let's spend a couple hours researching and see if we can't gather a few more facts together. Darn it – I've left my notebook in the car. I'll just pop back and get it; I won't be long.'

'Okay.'

I turn around to see that Renée's front door is open and she appears, giving me a wave. I smile back at her before letting myself into number six. Leaving the door ajar for Ronan, I head upstairs to throw open the windows wide, then pop the flowers into a vase.

Life is so different here; even though there are a few things about which I could sit and worry, I'm feeling relaxed.

Is that the spell cast by Versailles, or because I feel so content?

My phone pings, and then pings again, and again. I grab it out of my bag and see that Ronan has taken some photos of the front of the little florist's shop. In between them is a photo from Shellie of Maisie in her onesie, snuggled up on the sofa.

✉ Thought you'd like these. I'm on my way back.

Ronan texts.

It's then that I notice I have a missed call. I don't recognise the number but it's local and I redial.

'Hello, this is Lexie Winters. I missed a call from you?'

'It's George, Lexie. Solange was kind enough to give me your number. I wondered if you were this way at any time, whether you'd like to call in. On your own, that is.'

I'm rather dumbstruck. This is the last thing I expected.

'Of course, I'd be delighted. When would suit you best, George?'

'Any evening from five o'clock onwards. You'll find me in the garden.'

It all goes quiet and I realise he's pressed end call. I have been summoned. The question is, should I tell Ronan?

When he returns, it occurs to me that George might simply be looking for a little company and I decide not to say anything. We spend half an hour sharing our notes and then Ronan grabs the next notebook in the new sequence.

It isn't long before he's reading out little bits to me.

'Now this is frustrating. Clearly, she's gone to dinner with someone, but she doesn't say with whom. Well, not a real name, or anything, but I think she did that on purpose.'

I look at him, rather mystified.

'Why?'

'Well, maybe in case she lost a notebook, and someone picked it up and read it. Have you come across any mention of "the Terrier"?'

'Terrier?'

'I think it's a nickname. She's mentioned it twice so far.'

'So, someone whose name began with T?'

'Maybe. I hope that will become clear at some point. She just says, "The Terrier is angry with himself, tonight" – would you say that about an angry dog?'

I shrug and we return to our reading material. Several hours pass and although I'm engrossed, I'm conscious that I promised Maisie I'd call her. As I make a move, Ronan says it's time he headed for home, anyway.

When I see him to the door, I step down into the tiny space rather than hanging back on the stairs. I look up at him and we very naturally find ourselves in each other's arms.

'It's been a lovely afternoon,' he whispers into my ear.

As our lips draw nearer, I close my eyes and suddenly my heart feels as if it's about to leap out of my chest. It's beating so fast that I fear Ronan will hear it, but I can tell he's feeling the same way. A kiss that starts off rather gingerly quickly increases in intensity and we sort of fall back against the wall with a gentle thump, as my arms go up around his neck, drawing him even closer.

I feel light-headed, relieved to give in to the desire that is flooding through me. As we draw back, the look on Ronan's face tells me everything I need to know.

'I think it's time to agree that we're fighting the impossible, Lexie. It might not be what either of us planned, so I want you to be sure before we take that next step. Sleep on it, lovely lady, because I don't want this to screw things up between us. All I can tell you is that whenever I'm around you I can't help the way I feel.'

He leans forward, resting his forehead against mine, and the temptation is to grab his hand and drag him back upstairs. But I love that he's thinking this through because it shows my opinion of him is correct. Ronan is a man whose feelings run deep and he's not a user. I'm safe when I'm with him and, while there are no guarantees in life, my mind is already made up.

'Thank you for the perfect end to a perfect day, Lexie – whatever you decide going forward. And enjoy your Skype session with your niece.'

My mind is racing after Ronan leaves, but I need to slow things down and focus, ready for my chat with Maisie. Afterwards, I decide to relax with a glass of wine, before tidying up. When I finally flop into bed, I can hardly keep my eyes open and it doesn't take long for me to fall into a dreamless sleep.

This morning I awake refreshed and full of energy. I end up running a little late, fussing over my hair and then laughing at myself as I realise it's nerves. Something I haven't felt over a man in a long time. I needn't have worried, because the moment I walk into the café Ronan puts down his coffee cup and stands to kiss me. Not quite as passionately as our kiss last night, but unashamedly on the lips. Regardless of who might be watching, he doesn't care, and when he pulls away, he gives me a beaming smile.

'How did you sleep?'

'Like the proverbial log. And you?'

Ronan pulls a face. 'I did a lot of thinking. Regrettably, some of it was about work.'

That makes me smile. 'It sounds like a heavy night.'

He shrugs his shoulders and I note the concern reflected in his body language. What's going on between us is one thing, work is another, and I admire him for that.

'You need to see this, Lexie – we can do better.'

As we go over yesterday's interview, he's right. I came across as a little stilted during the intro as I could tell Ronan was on edge and two of the shots where he panned around are a little shaky. In hindsight, we should have done a few practice runs, but the pressure was on to just get things rolling.

I check with Solange and she can't see a problem with us doing an adhoc bit of filming. She does warn me that it's very busy today, but we decide to go for it, anyway.

'It has to be a seamless transition between Elliot's filming and mine, Lexie. Anything less will be second-rate and I can't live with that.'

After a quick call to Cameron and a change of clothes, we head back to the gardens mid-afternoon to re-shoot the beginning. Once we find a quiet corner away from the crowds, it doesn't take long, but the sun isn't at a good angle and it's a bit stop-start at first. Unfortunately, Cameron finds it a bit of a struggle at times, competing with the level of background noise. Eventually, we're all happy.

Ronan is looking much more confident handling the kit and it has been worth redoing it, simply to boost his confidence. It's yet another cost to accommodate, but in terms of team building between the three of us, we're all feeling much more positive.

* * *

Thoughts of Ronan continue to fill my head on the way to see George. Not least, guilt over whether I should have come clean about the visit. But Ronan headed off on a high to research a new lead and I didn't want to spoil his mood.

'Hello, George,' I call out, announcing my arrival.

He turns in his seat and gives me a welcoming smile. 'You came, then.'

'Who wouldn't want to come and while away an hour in such a peaceful setting? Besides, it was an offer I couldn't refuse, and you knew that.'

He at least has the decency to give me a slightly sheepish look.

'Please, take a seat. Help yourself to a drink from the tray.'

There's a bottle of red wine and a jug of water. I opt for the water, pouring myself a large one to quench my thirst.

'I'm driving,' I say, raising my glass to him, and he lifts his own in return.

'It's true I don't get a lot of company. I've never been a very sociable man. People tend to annoy me very quickly. I like peace and quiet to think, but many gardeners are like that. We get used to our own company, you see. I never was a game player and I always said it as it was. Some folk think that's trite; I call it honesty.'

'Where are you from originally, George?' I enquire, unable to place his accent.

He laughs. 'The Lake District. I have fond memories, but it was a hard life in those days. My father was a sheep farmer.'

George lapses into silence and I'm content to sit here for a while with only my thoughts to keep me occupied.

'I've nothing against Ronan seeking answers,' George's voice suddenly booms out. The tone implies that might not be true, because he sounds angry to me. 'But I'm no fool.'

'I don't know what you think I know, George, but the reality is that I have no idea what you're talking about. I'm here with my business partner, Elliot, for three months to film an independently produced series about modern-day gardening at Versailles. My only interest in the past is a personal one.'

He stares at me for a moment and then grunts.

'He likes you,' he says.

'Who does?'

'Ronan. Do you trust him?'

What sort of a question is that?

'Of course. Why shouldn't I?'

'He thinks I had something to do with his grandfather's suicide.'

'Suicide?' My mouth goes dry.

'Ah, so he hasn't told you everything, then?' There's an element of satisfaction in his tone that makes it sound like some sort of accusation.

I put my glass down firmly on the table with a bit of a bang. If George wants to play games, then I'm done. Easing myself up off the seat, he then makes a motion with his hand for me to sit back down.

'I had to check. Whatever I tell him, which is nothing as yet, he wouldn't believe anyway. Fabien Arnoult was a troubled man in here.' He taps his forehead with his finger. 'It's not what Ronan wants to hear. He says this is my last chance to get some facts down in black and white, because he's adamant about publishing that third book. I'm not saying it's a personal witch hunt, because he is a historian and the truth matters to him, but he also wants closure. The two don't sit well together in this case, Lexie, believe me – but Ronan can't see that.'

'Closure?'

'He won't admit it, but I believe he feels his grandfather committed suicide because people turned against him. The project Fabien was in charge of was closed down due to lack of funds. He took it very personally and the truth is that everyone knew he had a point. It wasn't that the chief gardener – or any of his peers – disagreed, but his plan could never have been put into action. There was some convoluted idea about drilling holes and using nutrients to force the tree roots to grow downwards, instead of spreading out sideways. Oh, it all sounded plausible and I suppose it could have worked, but at what expense? The gardens have always been the paupers when it comes to distributing funds because there never is enough money to go around.

'If Fabien had been born in the 1600s, he would have emptied Louis' coffers quicker than any of the gardeners of that time. To Fabien it was a travesty not to be proactive. The truth is that the gardens of Versailles were doomed to change over time, regardless of what anyone did. Fabien couldn't bear that thought and refused to accept it was inevitable.'

My stomach begins to churn. So, it was Fabien's project – why didn't Ronan tell me? I wish I'd known earlier that his grandfather had committed suicide – for Ronan that must have been a particularly bitter blow, as his grandfather was the only male influence in his life. If he believes his grandfather was wronged, then how can he objectively listen to what George has to say?

'I'm prepared to talk candidly to you, Lexie. But only you. You can record the interview, but I don't want Ronan to be a part of it. The facts are what they are and I'm the only one left who knows what really happened.'

I don't quite know what to say and it takes me a moment to gather my thoughts.

'George, I... look, I think what you have to say is important and should go on record, even if it isn't a part of Ronan's research. However, it's going to have to wait until Elliot is back, if you want it to be documented but would prefer it wasn't Ronan doing the filming.'

I can see by the look on his face that his mood is changing towards me. I need to be very careful not to alienate him in any way.

'Of course, Ronan is looking for answers. I understand that and it's only natural given the circumstances. Please don't hold that against him. But you're right, it's too emotive for him to be involved directly. But at some point in the future he will need to face up to what happened, and I understand why this is important to you, as well. I want answers about my grandma, not to publish, but so that my family can understand the other side to the woman we knew. So, I doubt that Ronan is looking to blame anyone, he's just seeking the truth. Surely you can understand that?'

He narrows his eyes, turning to look at me.

'I knew her,' he declares. 'So did Fabien.'

George presses his lips together as he gazes out across the river. My heart sinks as the silence grows and it becomes clear he's not going to say any more.

How can I gain his trust?

'I would dearly love to learn a little more about her time here, George. Was she happy? Did she make friends with anyone in particular? Was she sad to leave?'

His look is almost a scowl as the memories come flooding back and a sense of anger takes over.

'You've grown close to Ronan. There's no point in trying to deny that you were defending him just then, when you don't even know the half of it. We're done. I can't trust him and now I can't trust you.'

I end up leaving with nothing else to go on, thanking him for his honesty, but worried sick about how I'm going to handle this new information. The reality is that I don't know much more than I did before the visit, although my suspicions have been confirmed. There's obviously a story to tell and George may well be the last surviving person who knows what happened. My instincts are telling me that we're not done here and I simply have to sit and wait for the next call. He wants to set the record straight and time is running out.

Only now, do I finally understand the dedication in Ronan's first book, to his grandfather *whose spirit lives on in the gardens he loved more than life itself.*

That's a tough legacy with which to come to terms for anyone. From a tender age, the men in his life, who should have been there to guide and support him, failed him – albeit in very different ways. Does he fear that those traits will eventually surface within him? That thought sends a chill to my stomach and my heart aches for him.

17

A CLOSER ASSOCIATION

'You look happy,' I remark, as I let Ronan in through the door. 'I'm guessing you had a good day.'

The last week has flown by and when we've not been working, we've been inseparable. It's the tonic I needed, as money is now really tight, so I've applied for a business loan. At the moment, no one – including Elliot – is aware of the situation. And I need to keep it that way until it's all sorted.

'I did, actually. Productive and, oh, I received some good news.'

'Come on up. Have you eaten? I was going to wait for you, but I was starving. I can rustle something up.'

'No. I'm good. I had a late lunch with Solange, which turned into a bit of a celebration. I assume she told you?'

'That Philippe has asked her to marry him? Yes. Is it still a secret?'

He nods, striding over to the sofa and gratefully easing himself down into it with a groan.

'So, come on, what have you been up to?' I enquire.

His smile is lighting up his face.

'Solange isn't the only one taking her relationship to the next level. My mother rang to break the news that she and Frank got married this week at the local registry office.'

I look at him, rather puzzled. 'And she didn't invite you?' I ask, hesitantly.

'She didn't invite anybody. They grabbed a couple of witnesses from the waiting room. That's just her style. She's not big on being the centre of attention and I'm only delighted Frank finally talked her into it. Anyway, they are heading off on a three-week tour of Europe. The second stop is Versailles.'

I sink down on the sofa opposite him.

'Is that wise? I mean... old memories and things.'

He sits up, resting his hands on his knees, and looks at me with a frown furrowing his brow. 'I thought the same thing at first, but she said it's time to put the past behind her. Revisiting my grandmother's house shows this isn't lip-service, and she really does mean to move on. She says that with Frank beside her she knows she can do it and it gives her a chance to check up on me.'

Now he grimaces. 'Which is why I'm here. I wanted to ask you a big favour.'

I look at him enquiringly. 'Of course. Anything.'

'They're arriving on Saturday and will stay at the house overnight. I don't really want to take them out to a restaurant, which isn't a problem as I can easily cook, but it would be a little easier if I had some help. Even if it's just to keep the conversation going while I'm in and out with the food. It's a lot to ask, I know, but—'

'Hey, it would be my pleasure. I'll help you get the house ready, too. This is a big deal for her, well, for them and for you. Consider me signed up.'

He looks relieved. 'Thanks, Lexie. That means more to me than you realise. And it deserves a hug.'

Ronan's words carry a sincerity that stops me in my tracks for a moment and as he walks around the coffee table I stand, relaxing into his arms as he folds himself around me. I think he's in need of a little reassurance and I can tell he has mixed emotions about the visit. After a few moments I look up at him and he takes the opportunity to kiss me softly on the lips. Kissing him back, this time he responds with vigour. This feels so good and so right. To know that he's turning to me for comfort is reassuring.

However, as I nestle into him again, I feel bad not saying anything about George. But last night in bed I mulled it over for a long time. Ronan is an experienced researcher and he knows the questions to ask, and where to go to find information. Maybe there's an element of self-preservation in the fact that he hasn't been able to get the answers he's looking for about his grandfather. He must have said something to alienate George at some point.

Obviously, Ronan's mother doesn't know any more than he does. George may be the last surviving person with any knowledge of what went on at that time, but I wonder how accurate even his account could be after all these years. Especially as it sounds as though he didn't get on particularly well with Fabien. Could there be an element of payback involved in this? I'd hate to think that George was a vindictive person, but how would I know whether or not that's the case?

I look up to see Ronan watching me with interest.

'You are sure about this, are you? Be warned – however I introduce you, my mother will know instantly that there's something going on between us.'

'I'd be disappointed if she didn't pick up on that.' I laugh.

Ronan's hands slide down to my waist and he lifts me off the floor quite effortlessly, until our eyes are on the same level.

'I can't get you out of my head, lady. You know what you're doing to me, don't you?' he groans. 'Whenever I'm around you I can't even think straight any more.'

When he lowers me back onto my feet, he grabs my hands in his and excitement bubbles up inside me. I look up at Ronan from beneath my eyelashes, flirtatiously.

'I'll take that as a good sign that we're moving in the right direction, then.'

His look is one of amusement, but I have to catch my breath as my eyes travel over his face. Ronan makes me want to ignore the voice in my head advising me to do the sensible thing and take this slowly, or risk being disappointed. That adrenaline high doesn't always last and the fall, afterwards, can leave you feeling hollow.

Whatever happens next, although I've only been living here for a few weeks, it's already beginning to feel like a lifetime. One I could never, ever have anticipated.

* * *

'I have another dog,' I announce, looking across at Ronan, and he immediately stops reading.

'The Bulldog, this time.'

'In what context?'

'Grandma was taking soil samples, she doesn't say who she was with, but she says, "The Bulldog appeared, even stopping to chat for a few moments. I was nervous in his presence, afraid I would say the wrong thing, but he wasn't checking up on what we were doing" and then she goes on to talk about an evening out. It was someone's birthday, but she doesn't give any details.'

'The Terrier and now the Bulldog. This notebook I'm reading is fascinating from a gardening point of view, but there isn't much else in here really. She mentions posting letters back home but, again, no names. I sort of sense she was a little homesick but then this was probably, what, towards the end of her first month here, I would think.'

I'm not sorry we haven't discovered anything revealing. Clearly, Grandma was aware of the personalities and friction involved, maybe even witnessed some of the arguments and that's why she exercised caution in her notes. For my purposes, I'm beginning to feel I'm journeying with her and I can't really ask for more than that. To Ronan I'm sure this is a growing disappointment. Another step towards giving up on his quest to discover the truth about his grandfather maybe.

'If this is getting too tedious, please say, Ronan. Eventually I'll work through them all but I don't think we're going to find anything to help your research.'

He leans his head back against the cushions, looking relaxed and mellow.

'I think you're right, but I'm enjoying reading about life here in the early sixties. Vivian talks about trees that are long gone and areas that are now so different even she wouldn't recognise them any more. It's fascinating reading.'

'I agree, but I think it's time we put this away. Let's do something else.'

He looks surprised. 'Okay. Let's head out and grab a drink. Somewhere with some noise and bustle. How does that sound?'

'Perfect.'

Ronan makes a neat little pile of some loose sheets of

paper he's been scribbling on, his A4 pad and Grandma's notebook, while I head upstairs to run a brush through my hair. I add a touch of lipstick and a squirt of perfume. The reflection looking back at me in the mirror is someone who is happy and content, because the smile comes from within.

* * *

As we head out through the gates, Ronan catches hold of my hand.

'Thanks for your support. You know, helping to keep my mother happy this coming weekend. I want her to head off on her little European tour without a care in the world. If she thinks she's leaving me in the hands of a warm-hearted, kind and intelligent woman, she'll be delighted.'

I burst out laughing. 'And I'm all of those things?'

'Yes, you are. And totally adorable. And sexy. And—' He pauses, mid-thought. 'And there are times when you drive me crazy. I don't mean in an annoying way, of course.'

I can feel the heat tingling in my cheeks and suddenly he spins me around, wrapping me up in his arms as we come to a standstill.

'I'm not sure that came out right, actually. But you know what I mean. Somehow, I'm a better person when I'm around you; more positive and life feels good. Now it's your turn. Did I make a good first impression?'

The answer isn't one I can voice. There was a vulnerability in him that was so tangible, it touched my heart – and that's what grabbed me from the start. Even when he was surrounded by people, there was a quality to him that screamed loneliness and an innate sadness, too. Now there is no comparison at all to the version of him I see before me now.

'I found you annoyingly interesting from day one, although you came across as a little offhand,' I admit, toying with him a little.

'Offhand?' he questions, indignantly. 'I was trying to impress you! That was me being cool... and enigmatic.'

'Then you were trying way too hard.' I retort.

Ronan tilts his chin, resting his forehead against the top of my head.

'I'm sorry about that. I'm out of practice and I never was a natural charmer.'

He kisses my cheek, working his way around to my mouth. My toes begin to tingle and I don't really want him to stop. When we eventually release each other, he catches my hand again as we resume walking.

'You mentioned it was a productive day?'

He nods his head, enthusiastically.

'It was. I've made some tough decisions about book three. I will finish it off, but the emphasis will change slightly. I've decided I have no choice but to work with the information I have. I'm done chasing the impossible and looking for answers that simply aren't there.'

It's a relief to hear him say that. I can fully appreciate how difficult it is to let go of something you've pursued with a passion. But the decision can only be his and it doesn't matter what anyone else thinks, so I simply squeeze his hand. Ronan sounds happier, as if at last he's free of a monumental task he never relished in the first place.

A suicide in the family is a traumatic thing to deal with for those left behind. How did it affect his grandmother, when her husband took his own life? I ask myself. And

Ronan's mother, losing her father in that way? Do the scars ever heal, and if they don't, for someone as sensitive as Ronan, that's a tough thing with which to make your peace. I really hope this decision doesn't feel like defeat to him, or that he's letting anyone down, but the decision of a man who has learnt that acceptance can sometimes bring inner peace.

I can empathise with that. For a long time after my father's death I blamed him for choosing a job that took him away from us. So far away that in his time of greatest need no one could help him. I believed there was a chance that his life might have been saved if he'd been at home with us. I felt angry with him for taking that risk, because our lives were suddenly filled with pain, sorrow and regret. Youth and inexperience are not good tools for handling the harsher side of life or having a balanced point of view.

'And what are your plans beyond book three?'

'I have two options. I've been offered a job as a *lecteur* in the languages department at the Versailles Saint-Quentin-en-Yvelines University. I'd have enough time to get this book finalised before the start of the new academic year. But I'm enjoying this little stint filming again. It's made me stop and think about the future in a slightly different way. A part of the reason why I walked away from my career was to spite my father. That might have been a big mistake in hindsight. So, I'm torn at the moment.' He turns to look at me, grinning. 'But I'm working on it,' he assures me.

There's a sparkle in his eyes that tells me he thinks his life is about to change in lots of ways. Could this spark between us turn into something more permanent? I miss my family so much but being here feels so natural. Maybe it's because spring is so invigorating, everything is going well despite the upset with Elliot and suddenly it feels as though fate is smiling on us all.

Is this the missing link I've been searching for all my life? A sense of belonging? I mistakenly linked home and family to that word in the past, because I didn't know any different. And yet, here I am with someone I've only known for a few weeks. But when I'm with Ronan I feel I belong... maybe not here specifically, but with him. He has turned my world upside down.

'Lexie,' Ronan's voice interrupts my thoughts. 'I've fallen in love with you and I have no idea how I'm going to handle this, because it's a first for me.'

'Bye, Auntie Lexie.' Maisie disappears as she hands the phone back to Shellie. But then I see her blowing an exaggerated kiss to me in the background and I blow one back.

'How I miss my little angel.' I sigh.

'Well, you're probably better off out of it at the moment, Lexie,' Shellie admits. 'With everything that's going on here we're all a little on edge, if I'm honest.'

'Gosh, that's not like you to sound so defeatist. Are you feeling okay?'

'Yes. My jelly belly is growing by the day and judging by the shape of me I think it might be a... *boy*.' She turned to check that Maisie was out of earshot before saying the final word. 'Boys are not the favourite choice right now,' she continues in a soft whisper. 'No, this is about Jake, really.'

I've been so caught up with what's happening here that it's easy to switch off and forget about the problems back in the UK. Especially now Mia is within a day or two of being able to leave hospital and Elliot is talking about flying back in about two weeks' time.

'Oh.'

'Mum has summoned us all to a family meal on Wednesday evening, so that Jake can meet Maisie for the first time. I'm fuming about it. I have to go along with it for Mum's sake, but this is all wrong. I swear if Jake fell out of a plane he'd land on his feet and walk away without breaking a sweat.'

Shellie is annoyed and I fully understand that.

Jake created a lot of havoc and family discord. After he sacked me, Shellie was the one who helped me keep it all together. She was my crutch at a time when my pride was in tatters; she refused to let me hide myself away and forced me to plaster on a smile. Because of her insistence, I quickly realised that one apparent failure didn't mean every door was shut to me. And I took the first job offer that came my way, albeit because I had no choice. But there was no time to wallow in self-pity.

It was only a few days later that Jake left for the States, with seemingly nothing rattling his conscience over the mess he was leaving behind.

It's only natural that Mum is going to welcome her only son back into the nest. I understand that and it's a maternal thing. But to try to force it on Shellie, well, that's not fair. If I were there would she be roping me into her little celebratory 'welcome home' dinner for him, ignoring the real damage he did?

'Just get through it as best you can and if you can't say anything nice, say nothing. Even if Mum doesn't rethink her decision, it doesn't mean you're obliged to have anything to do with him. In future, you could simply pick her up and take her out for the day. You sure as hell don't have to socialise with him if you don't want to.'

I can feel her sense of frustration. She doesn't want to hurt Mum, but, in all honesty, I don't think I could go and sit round a table with him as things stand. So, I know exactly how she's feeling.

'Of course, Maisie is excited to meet her uncle and I have to be so careful not to influence her unfairly. Oh, this is a nightmare, Lexie, and I so wish you were here. How am I going to get through the next seven weeks until you come home?'

My stomach does a little somersault. Shellie has no idea what's happening at my end. I can't simply blurt out the fact that Ronan has grabbed my heart in a very real way, and that on Saturday Ronan and I are spending time with his mother and her new husband, as a couple. She'll think I've lost my mind.

A warm glow makes me close my eyes for a brief second, realising that something deep inside me is saying Ronan is the one. Is this really how it happens, just like that? Quite how we'd make it work, I have no idea at all. But now is not the time to share this with Shellie and add to her worries. I feel bad that she can't just sit back and enjoy her pregnancy, but is dealing with the fallout of our latest family crisis.

'You can't tie yourself up in knots over it, Shellie. Plaster on a smile and be polite. Jake will, no doubt, commandeer the conversation anyway. You need to tell Drew how anxious you are about it all. He'll think of an excuse to make a quick exit if things start to get out of hand.'

She makes a sound that comes out like a disparaging snort.

'What is most upsetting is that Mum is so set on everyone

"making up", as she refers to it, as if we'd had some sort of childish squabble. If she sits at the table looking at Jake with adoring motherly eyes I will walk out, I swear. He did wrong and maybe we were wrong, too, for protecting her from the real impact of his actions.'

Shellie might well be right. If Mum had known how devastating and humiliating it was to have been sacked by my own brother, who'd announced quite publicly that I'd failed to meet expectations, it would have added to her misery. He'd already told her that he was being transferred to the States and she was mourning his loss even before he stepped on that plane. We skated over the hard facts and she thinks I left my job over a disagreement. And I don't want to be the one who shatters her illusions about who Jake is beneath the charming exterior.

'Stay strong, lovely. Think of you and the baby and focus on not getting stressed. Life has ticked over nicely without him in our lives, so just smile brightly and the least said, the better. And if you need to offload to someone afterwards, no matter how late it is, then just call.'

'I might take you up on that offer. If you pick up the phone to the sound of someone screaming their head off, you'll know it's me.'

PART II

APRIL 2018

18

THE FEMININE TOUCH

After a very successful day filming, Ronan and I are buzzing. We end up going back to his place and before we know it the big clean-up is in progress. With less than seventy-two hours until his mum arrives, I can tell he's excited but also quite nervous.

'I didn't realise just how dusty the place is,' he admits as he stretches to hit a cobweb. It's rather stubbornly resisting the long-handled feather duster and it's hard not to laugh at his flailing attempts to snag it.

'Well, in fairness it's a big house and I'm surprised you don't have someone helping you out.'

'Never thought about that. I don't make a lot of mess, anyway. I like things to be orderly.'

Scanning around, I will agree that he's right, but it's rather bare. I glance at him and see he's watching me.

'Okay. What am I doing wrong? It isn't just the dust, is it?'

His eyes are smiling, so I know it's a genuine question and he's looking for my input here.

'It needs softening,' I reply diplomatically. 'A few ornaments, maybe. We can get some fresh flowers on the day, too, as a nice welcome. It's going to be a big deal for your mother when she walks through that door.'

'Well, there's a whole load of stuff I boxed up and put in the attic when I renovated the place. Would you take a look around and maybe we can make it feel more lived-in?'

That raises a smile on both of our faces. I love feeling needed and he's making it very clear that he can't do this on his own.

It's all very practical and I love how he's decorated it in a way that allows the old pieces of furniture to exist alongside his vision to make it more contemporary country. But it just lacks cosiness.

'All that's missing is a little bit of texture and a pop of colour. I'm definitely from the less is more camp, too, but the table, for instance—'

We stand gazing along the full length of the beautifully polished table.

'It needs a centrepiece, not simply a stack of placemats.'

He nervously begins to chew his bottom lip. 'Ah, well, I will admit that is something I did intend to get around to at some point.'

'It's been, what did you say? Seven years?'

Ronan waggles his finger, pointing upwards. 'Come on. I'm sure there are treasures up there that I discarded in my haste to strip it all back.'

We traipse upstairs and I brave the substantial pull-down ladder because I'm excited about what I might find. Ronan is right, there are boxes everywhere and only a small overhead light with which to see.

As we forage through, I wonder if anything ever got thrown away in the history of this very traditional, old French house. There is an enormous amount of china, old chairs in desperate need of re-upholstering and stone pots whose plants have long since gone.

'I'm assuming you prefer a simpler style? I mean, this candelabrum is beautiful, but it's very ornate,' I remark, lifting it up and marvelling at how heavy it is. 'More Versailles than cosy country home.'

He raises an eyebrow, nodding his head in agreement. 'I like simple things; understated.'

After half an hour of searching we have a dozen items that between us we decide will add a little something. We make several trips, careful not to drop any of our newly redis-covered treasures.

The first is a very large, cut-glass punch bowl, which, after a good soaking in warm soapy water, is a wonderfully sparkly addition. It's very old lead crystal and screams quality. I sit it in the middle of the dining table, and it looks stunning.

'It needs a little colour,' I point out, standing back to admire the overall effect.

'Fruit?'

I shake my head. 'Um, no. Do you have any secateurs and a carrier bag?'

Ronan looks at me, his eyebrows raised. 'Yes. Why?'

'Grab them and join me in the garden.'

I head out through the glass doors in the kitchen and stroll down to the old stone wall to the rear, which is covered with rambling roses. A pale yellow intertwines with a ruby red. Both are very old stock, because they virtually cover the whole width of the wall and cascade down to floor level. It could do with a good pruning to my mind, but the prolific array of tight little buds preparing to open is simply a joy. Ronan sidles up next to me.

'Roses? The bowl is a bit wide to fill with water and stems. Should I see if there's a vase in the attic, as I'm sure I can find one if I keep looking?'

'No, what we're going to do is to give this all a bit of a trim and in the process cut off a pile of the rosebuds. Let me show you.'

He hands me the secateurs and I start cutting. Then I pick up the fallen branches and begin snipping, indicating for him to hold the carrier bag beneath. I don't want to strip it of colour, so randomly trawl across the entire length of the wall.

'Just the heads?' he queries.

'Yep. No water. Just a pile of colourful buds that will gradually dry out. I'm choosing the dark red ones as they tend to retain their colour well and will go a deep burgundy as the drying process continues. It's homemade potpourri.'

'But won't they simply rot?'

'No. Not if you turn them daily and if you start with dry blooms that haven't begun to deteriorate. The cut-glass crystal will reflect the colour, without making it too floral.'

'I would never have thought of that. What other tips do you have?'

'Well, we need to make a quick trip to the shops. A few scatter cushions for the sofa maybe, and some pretty curtains for the second bedroom. What do you think?'

He nods, seemingly on board with the idea.

I think we need to take this one step at a time, so I won't mention a new duvet cover and pillow slips, and maybe some new guest towels, yet. But they are on the shopping list.

'I knew this house needed something,' Ronan says, slipping his arm around my waist and squeezing, 'but I didn't realise what it needed was YOU.'

* * *

We had fun yesterday. There is this tantalising little buzz constantly going on between us and I find myself wanting to throw my arms around him for no reason at all, other than the fact that I'm so ecstatically happy.

Just being in his house and putting our heads together to brighten it up a little made us feel like a real couple. We laughed, we agreed and sometimes we disagreed over what looked best where, but happiness is infectious. Every little furtive glance, every little touch of hands... it's the small things, not just the sexual attraction simmering just below the surface, waiting to erupt. It's every second you spend together as you work towards the moment you cross a line. But we've both been there before and neither of us want to jump in until we're sure this is the right thing to do.

I'm home alone and waiting for Shellie's phone call, but it's hard to keep Ronan out of my thoughts. I keep remembering little things that instantly raise a smile, like when he threw me on the bed after we'd just put on the new bedding and I chastised him for putting creases in the freshly ironed duvet cover. My mobile kicks into life and I grab it, eagerly.

'You're not screaming,' I joke, as Shellie's voice filters through. 'You survived the ordeal, then.'

'It wasn't what I was expecting, at all,' she confirms, sounding a little stunned. Her voice is low, so I guess she waited for Drew to fall asleep before sneaking down to call me.

'How so?'

'Jake has a wife, Brooke, and twin boys. That's the real reason why Mum's going to live with him and his family. I felt a bit sorry for his wife, to be honest, as she's clearly sleep-deprived at the moment and missing her family. The boys are rather a handful and apparently they wake each other up at night.'

I'm dumbstruck. 'Twins? Married?'

'And they are only eighteen months old. Maisie was in her element, so Jake didn't have to win her over. He's invited us all over to his place at the weekend. All Maisie could talk about in the car on the way home was how excited she was to tell her friends at school tomorrow that she has twin cousins.'

This is so hard to take in.

'I can't believe he's married, let alone the fact that he has kids. Doesn't he feel bad that none of us knew what was going on with him? How long do you think Mum has known? For that matter, exactly how long has he been back?'

There's a pause. This is crazy and it doesn't seem real. I glance around the darkened room, feeling very cut off and, at this moment, very alone.

'I'm not sure. Maybe she's known for a while – longer than she indicated to you. It was difficult to ask any questions, but I'll find out more on Sunday. I got the impression it's long enough not just to get the house set up, but to organise some major renovation work. Brooke and the boys only flew in a week ago, but it took a lot of planning to get things ready for them.

'He's different, Lexie. It wasn't all about him; in fact, he was very hands-on with the boys and he encouraged Maisie to organise some games. He joined in, and at one point all three of the kids were bombarding him with little plastic balls and he was loving it. Brooke was very friendly and spent quite a bit of time in the kitchen with Mum, giving her a hand. I decided to leave them to it.'

'So, what's the story, then? Big house, big job, big plans? I hope it's worth him coming back for, because he's walked away from what many would think of as the ultimate dream.'

'None of that came up, as it was crazy with three kids running around. At one point, Jake disappeared and when he returned, I noticed him talking to Drew for a couple of minutes. I'll find out tomorrow what they were talking about. When Drew and I got back home, I think we were in shock and, after putting Maisie to bed, we sat down with a large G and T and feigned watching a film. Everything has happened so quickly, it's difficult to know quite what to think about it all.'

'It is a lot to take in, isn't it? I still think it's a huge mistake for Mum to sell up, though. Okay, I can understand she wants to help out, but even so... It's a cheek turning her into a live-in nanny, don't you think?'

There's a soft 'hmm' on the other end of the line.

'The trouble is, Lexie, she's more than willing. The boys are cute, and Brooke seems like a really nice person. I honestly don't feel that Jake is putting on a front – he really has changed.'

Throwing my head back against the cushions, I stare up at the ceiling.

'I wish I could believe that, Shellie.'

'I do know where you're coming from, but you had to be there to witness it for yourself to be able to understand. Anyway, I'll get my chance to quiz him on Sunday and I don't intend to go softly. Pity you can't pop back and join us for the weekend. Now there's a thought.'

Oh. I wonder if Mum put her up to this?

'I can't, I'm afraid. I have plans.'

'Plans? You aren't working?'

'No. Um... Ronan's mother and her new husband are here for the weekend and I've offered to help out.'

'Help out? Are you and Ronan—? Oh, my goodness, you ARE!'

I push away a tinge of guilt, knowing that I should have said something before now, but where do I start?

'It's early days, Shellie. Yes, we are involved but neither of us have any real idea where it's going. All I can say is that Ronan is an amazing guy and he makes me laugh.' I have my fingers crossed as I speak. Now is not the time to bare all to Shellie, not least because I don't want to jinx anything.

'Now you're trying to play it down – that means it's serious. Well, it's about time and it's good to hear you sounding so upbeat. Honestly, Lexie – is there anything else you haven't told me? Like Grandma Viv had a hunky French boyfriend who broke her heart?'

She's being sarcastic, of course, because she's annoyed with me. What is it with our family at the moment?

'Sorry, sis. It's been a bit of a whirlwind and I'm still trying to take it all in myself,' I reply, trying to impress upon her that there isn't a lot to say as yet. Ronan and I are moving forward but who knows for sure where we will end up? All I can do is keep to the facts. 'I can tell you that I think we've discovered the place where Grandma lived when she was here, though. It's a little flat above a florist's shop. I'm sure it will turn out that she lived her dream for a year, and, having got it out of her system, she came home to settle down and have a family. End of.'

'Well, I hope that proves to be the case. I don't think I could take any more startling announcements right now. Anyway, the good news is that Maisie is coming around to the idea of a little brother, thanks to the twins. That's something, I suppose.'

'You know for sure?'

'As good as. Mum did the pendulum test over my tummy with a crystal on a string. She says it's always been accurate. Besides, with Maisie I put on tons of weight all over and this one is like a neat little football. But the morning sickness continues, even though I'm past the three-month stage now.'

'Poor you, but how exciting – one of each!'

'Seeing the twins did make me quake a little. I hope that gene came from Brooke's side and not ours! Anyway, I'm off to bed. Take care, Lexie, and I'll call you on Sunday.'

I'm going to be an aunt to four kids. FOUR. Guess that really lets me off the hook with Mum now, as she's going to have her hands well and truly full.

19
_____

COMING TO THE RESCUE IN MORE WAYS THAN ONE

Ronan and I ended up going a little mad. With our arms full of shopping bags, we each had to do three trips to carry them in. Admittedly, some of it is food, as our last stop was a supermarket, but first we drove to a lovely shopping mall named Parly II. It's near to the Avenue Charles de Gaulle and had a wonderful range of shops.

We went to pick up a few things and then got carried away playing house.

'Did we overdo it?' I ask, as Ronan and I stand in the sitting room staring at the pile of bags.

'The house needs it, but I didn't really know what would look right. I'm excited. For me this is like having a makeover.'

'I could tell. I thought you'd never stop picking things up and shouting across at me, "What do you think of this?" and that's why I steered you to the checkout. If you want to take some of this stuff back, you know you can.'

I feel bad, as we only went to get some scatter cushions and a couple of things to brighten the second bedroom.

'No way. That's the longest I've ever spent shopping. I had no idea there was so much choice and I enjoyed it.'

I give him a look of disbelief as he throws out his arms, shrugging his shoulders. 'I mean it. Now let's get all of this unpacked and let the transformation begin.'

And what a transformation. Ronan isn't into twee little designs, but instead he loves colour, so we've gone bold. His sofas are quite a traditional style and have been re-upholstered in a dark grey linen. With deep buttoning and a roll-top back, they have period legs with castors. I begin pulling the cushions out of their plastic sleeves and throw them across to him. He places the first one at an angle, and as I keep them coming, he sets them up in a line.

He alternates the lime green, which has a skeleton leaf in a darker shade to add interest, with an equally vibrant fuchsia pink. I do love a man who isn't afraid to choose pink.

'Good choice. You learnt fast. I'm impressed.'

Ronan turns round to look at me.

'Hey, if you point me in the right direction then I can run with it, but I do have a tendency to overthink things. Then not a lot happens. This might sound a bit odd, but even when I was clearing out the house and doing it up, I felt my grandmother was standing by patiently waiting for the messy bits to be over. Since then I've been in limbo, I guess. Like I'm waiting for her to return to tell me what she wants me to do next. I've been living my life one day at a time for so long now that it's become second nature to me. I stopped noticing what was around me because without her here it feels like a shell.'

I walk across to him, raising my hand to touch his cheek, fondly.

'Aww... that makes me feel sad. It's your home now and life is all about change. Try to see that as a good thing and take comfort from the happy memories you have of the times you spent here with her. I bet the summer breaks were lovely.'

'They were. Life was a lot simpler then.'

My arms instinctively reach out and Ronan shuffles forward to close the gap between us.

'I've never had a reason to think about making long-term plans before. But you've changed everything, Lexie.'

'It's crazy, isn't it? I feel as if I'm standing on shifting sand and all I want to do is to go with the flow. That's not me. Well, not the me I recognise, but a different version of me.'

I lay my head against his chest, listening to the sound of his pounding heart. It's not just from the exertion of fetching and carrying; there's a vibrancy to him that he didn't have before. Before there was an *us*.

'Well, I like this different version of you, Lexie. Sometimes we all need to let go a little and learn to rely on other people. Some things can't be controlled, we simply have to allow them to happen.'

Ronan begins planting soft little kisses on my cheek, as he works his way across to my mouth. My body reacts before my brain can engage and I turn my face, my lips eager to show him that control is the last thing on my mind right now.

'Mia will probably leave hospital in about a week's time. It's going to take me a few days to get her all set up at home and I don't want to just rush off, if you can hang on a while longer. Her sister is going to come and stay for a week or two after I fly back to France. After that, her dad will come and collect her and she'll spend a little time with her parents, so it's all covered until we've finished filming.'

Elliot sounds as if he has it all sorted and it's good to hear him sounding so upbeat, at last.

'How is the budget going?' he asks and I hesitate for a moment.

'Okay. The good news is that we've kept up with the schedule and only had to change one of the slots. We did have to retake one of the intros, which was unfortunate, but we nailed it in a couple of hours.' It's time to change the subject slightly. 'Um, there is one thing that has come up and I sort of committed us to it when I should have checked with you first. It's not strictly business, more personal really.'

'Well, I owe you a huge favour for holding it all together in my absence, Lexie. So, I'm hardly likely to say no, am I? Give me a clue, as now I'm curious about what I've missed.'

I'm relieved to have diverted his attention away from talking about our financial issues.

'I'd like to film an interview at the home of one of the gardeners who was at Versailles in the sixties. Unfortunately, he had to take early retirement after being involved in a rather serious car accident. He's a bit of a prickly character, but he knew my grandma. He might be the only person still alive who came into contact with her while she was over here. George blows hot and cold, and our last little chat didn't end well. This isn't just about her, but a much bigger story. However, my gut instincts are telling me that the next time he calls he'll be ready to go on record. Whether it will throw up any material we can use, I have no idea, but it will be a one-off opportunity.'

'That's incredible, Lexie. I'm delighted to hear that because I know how much it means to you.'

'Me, too,' I reply enthusiastically.

'The budget is blown, isn't it?' Elliot blurts out, seeing through my little ruse. 'Otherwise you'd ask Ronan, because this would definitely be of interest to him. But you'd insist on paying him and that tells me everything.'

Awkward, because he's right about the budget and he has no idea what I'm about to do. And now I have to explain a little about the situation with Ronan. I'd sort of hoped that would go over his head.

'George and Ronan don't really get on,' I hedge.

'Come on, Lexie. I know you're holding back and as partners we need to be honest with each other.'

'I will admit that the contingency fund is looking sad; we both knew that would happen if we hit any snags. I have two credit cards with nothing on them and an eighteen-grand line of credit. I know you've incurred a lot of costs personally and lost time on your other job, so I don't want you to worry about it. I've applied for a business loan and we have at least another three weeks before the cash runs out. I thought I'd whack things on the cards and then pay them off as soon as the loan is approved.'

Elliot groans.

'Jeez. I left you with all this worry. Look, I'll phone around. We know there's interest, all we need is someone to commit and back it up with an advance. Maybe I need to approach an agent to tout it around and add that extra push. Don't sign on the dotted line until I've exhausted my enquiries. It will take me a day or two, to pull together a demo from what I've uploaded to our system, but it should swing it. Even unedited, I think it does the whole idea justice.'

'Seriously, though, it's not just the money, Elliot. George won't speak to Ronan directly, because whatever he has to say involves Ronan's grandfather, too.' As worried as I am about money, I need to share this with Elliot. 'Things have moved on and Ronan and I are involved personally, now. So, when the call eventually comes for this interview, it will have to be kept quiet. George might simply want to air old grievances, who knows? Oh, why do things have to be so complicated?'

'Ronan's a good guy, Lexie, and I'm not really surprised to hear the two of you have hit it off. I had noticed that little spark between you. Don't worry about the George thing – we'll get that done and think about the fallout afterwards. If necessary, we can file it away and forget about it. But, please, don't sign that loan agreement until I've exhausted the other options. Neither of us are in a position to add monthly repayments to our outgoings and this is down to me, anyway.'

* * *

When I arrive back at the cottage, Renée is sitting on her doorstep and she gives me a wave. Seconds later, Solange appears in the doorway behind her.

'Hi, Lexie,' Solange calls out and they both come hurrying over.

Renée looks excited and begins talking very fast at me. All I can do is smile politely and Solange starts laughing.

'It's official,' she says, holding up her left hand and waving around a beringed finger. 'What Philippe's grandmother is asking is whether you would mind if we had a little party in the courtyard the weekend after next. One of the other neighbours will be here and we're hoping you and Ronan will come, plus a few family members and friends, to help us celebrate our news.'

'Ah, that would be lovely! Of course, and if you need any

help with the preparation, I'm sure both Ronan and I can make ourselves available.'

Renée is beaming, and Solange looks at her and nods. She throws her hands up in the air and does a little jig.

'How are the preparations for the big visit coming along?' Solange asks, stepping forward.

'Good. Ronan is nervous, naturally.'

'I understand that. I know he speaks to his mum often and that it will be the first time she's been back to her old family home since her mother died. She found it hard to let go of him. The fact that she has finally found the man she's happy to spend the rest of her life with means Ronan did the right thing coming here. Ronan just needs to see that for himself.'

It's nice that Solange has been such a good friend to Ronan. We look at one another and I nod my head in agreement, thinking that every family has their problems, they're just all very different. It's how you resolve them that counts, and a tinge of guilt begins to gnaw away at me. Old hurts leave scars and I wonder if I will ever be strong enough to forgive my brother and give him a second chance.

'I'm sure it was a difficult decision for him at the time, but it sounds like they are both in a good place at the moment and he's so happy for her.'

'I think the visit will make her even happier,' Solange adds, giving me a pointed look. She thinks we're good together and that means a lot to me.

As I head back inside, I can't help thinking about the future; frequent weekend trips and holidays in France, maybe, in between long working days in the UK? Could Ronan and I make it work? Who knows what might happen?

I reflect. You grow comfortable in your own little routine and then suddenly something happens and everything changes.

All I know is that the thought of leaving Ronan behind and never seeing him again is unimaginable. Falling in love with someone is tough, I'm discovering; it's no longer about what you want, because suddenly there's another person to consider. When I fly back to the UK, Ronan is going to feel what – abandoned? I hope not. Hopefully we'll be impatiently counting down the days until we're together again.

'Why bring me to Versailles to fall in love, Grandma?' I appeal to the empty stairwell as I head upstairs. 'This could break both of our hearts if we can't find a way to make it work, and without making either of us miserable for what we're leaving behind.'

The silence in reply is deafening.

20

HAPPY FAMILIES

I was expecting a clingy, intense woman and instead Eve Arnoult – sorry, Eve Barrington, now – is nothing at all like I imagined her to be. Although she bursts into floods of tears the moment she steps through the door to throw her arms around Ronan, this diminutive lady is full of vibrant energy. She's a fighter, for sure, and a survivor.

Pulling herself together, she tilts her head around Ronan's arm to peer at me.

'Oh,' she says, stifling a sob, 'this must be Lexie. Sorry, my dear, but it's been a while since I've hugged this boy of mine and I'm having trouble letting go of him.'

I hold out my hand to Frank as he steps forward, but he ignores it and zooms in for a hug.

'We don't shake hands, lovely Lexie.' He has to stoop down to my level, as he's rather tall. 'We're not here for long, so we need to make the most of it.'

I'm a bit taken aback, but Frank is a hugger and I like that about him. He must be six foot six at least and Eve can't be more than five foot two.

'The missus has been unbearable the last few days and it's a relief to be here at last.' He grins, mischievously. Standing back, he watches as his new wife continues to hug her son with no sign whatsoever of letting go. Poor Ronan is looking rather uncomfortable.

'Ma, you have to let go. I can't breathe.' He groans.

'Yes, but it's been so long. And we're really here. I only agreed to get married because I knew Frank would let me choose where we went on our honeymoon,' she declares.

I look at Frank and he starts laughing.

'I'm fine with that, although I know I have no chance when it comes to the honour and obey bit in the vows. This woman is annoying, impossible and the love of my life.'

Turning to look at Ronan as he stares back at me over his mother's shoulder, I can't suppress a laugh. I wasn't expecting a couple whose banter was so amusing and light-hearted. And from what he'd told me about his mother I was expecting a rather staid, quiet lady – not someone with such a bubbly personality.

'Mum, seriously, let go!'

Reluctantly she steps back and then I'm next in line.

'Oh, my dear! It's wonderful to meet you. Ronan doesn't say much, of course, but he doesn't have to as I can hear the change in his voice. I've never known him to be so happy and that can only be down to you.'

'How about we stop with the embarrassing "the wayward son" thing and let's head into the kitchen? I'll put the kettle on,' Ronan says, turning and heading for the door. 'Although I might need something a little stronger than that,' he mutters to himself as he exits quickly.

Frank masks a little smile before heading back to the car to fetch the luggage. Eve links arms as if I'm her new best friend and she's not going to let go of me until she's good and ready. I love that soft little lilt in her voice – it softens everything she says and it's endearing. One tiny woman, one incredibly big heart. No wonder that falling in love at such a tender age and not having it returned hurt her so much.

'Let's leave Ronan to recover. Show me the house, Lexie. It's been so many years since I've been here and it looks a lot different now. Brighter, I'm delighted to see.'

It feels a little strange to be playing the hostess, but I can hear Ronan in the kitchen and the sound of china clanking and cupboard doors being opened and closed. He needs a few minutes to compose himself and I get that.

'Shall we start upstairs?'

Eve releases my arm, but only after giving it a gentle pat.

'You lead the way,' she insists, and I take a deep breath.

'Right, if I show you your room first, then Frank will know where to put your things. How was the journey?'

Eve chatters away as she takes her time, first walking over to gaze out of the window. She stands for a moment and I say nothing, allowing her to assimilate her surroundings. I'm sure the memories are now flooding back. Moving around the room, she takes in every little detail, rediscovering each piece of furniture.

'I remember this,' she murmurs, trailing her fingers over the top of an ebony chest of drawers. 'I had the small bedroom, of course. This was what Mum called the best bedroom; which meant it was for guests, even though it's the biggest. I remember family coming over from Ireland and the fuss she made, making sure everything was just so. Of course, there were a few of them, so we made up beds on the floor for the children. That was the norm back then.'

'It must be wonderful knowing that Ronan is living here, now.'

She turns to look at me.

'I'm not sentimental, well, not in that way. Life has taught me that money, possessions, buildings – none of them really mean anything at all. Like a wedding ceremony doesn't mean a thing,' she adds, without even attempting to lower her voice. I do a double take and she smiles at me.

'Oh, Frank knows that. I gave in because my therapist asked me a simple question. We were talking about it all a few months ago and he'd just asked me again for the gazillionth time. She said, "Why not say yes?" And I said, "Because I'm living with him, that should tell him everything he needs to know." And she said, "You might not need a little piece of paper, but maybe Frank does," and it made me stop and think. So here we are.'

Frank walks in and I'd be really surprised if he hadn't heard at least some of that conversation on his way upstairs. The poor guy has a case in each hand and a small, see-through plastic holdall containing a hairdryer tucked under his arm.

'I didn't tell her the licence doesn't have an end date,' he throws in, his voice sounding very droll until he throws a wink in my direction. 'Eve probably thinks it's like a driving licence – renewable.' He places his heavy load on the floor and walks back out, his shoulders shaking a little as he laughs.

'I keep telling him,' Eve says, her voice getting louder so he can hear every word as he heads down the stairs, 'you can only take a relationship one day at a time. If he behaves himself, I'll let him hang around for a bit longer.'

It's so hard not to start laughing, as the banter between them is hilarious.

'Actually,' she says, leaning in to me and finally lowering her voice, 'it's rather nice being Mrs Barrington. But aside from that, nothing has changed. We're still the same mad pair, but Ronan was right. I wasted so much of my life feeling I had something to prove and being scared to rely on anyone for fear they'd let me down. Now I know that Frank, bless him, would do anything for me. He was the one who suggested I get involved in this self-help group, run by the lady who is now my therapist, Jane. It has turned my life around and here we are!'

She turns to look at the freshly made-up bed.

'Everything is so crisp and lovely,' she remarks. 'These curtains are pretty. Did you choose them?'

'Well, I pointed them out, but Ronan knows what he likes, and the decision was all his.'

Eve continues to stare at them for a moment or two. 'I let go of this place a long time ago. I only hope that at some point Ronan can do that, too. I don't want him held back by anything from the past, as I was for so many years.'

'Are you ladies coming down? Because the tea is getting cold.' Ronan's voice filters up the stairs.

Her face immediately brightens. 'We'd better grace them with our presence. Besides, I can't wait to see the garden. I do hope some of the roses have survived the passage of time. My mother planted them in my father's memory. He might have been the gardener, but when he was at home it was my mother's domain. She grew vegetables and herbs mainly, but he loved his flowers and the two apple trees that are now long gone.'

She gazes out of the window rather wistfully, but it's a

fleeting moment and her smile when she turns back around is warm and engaging.

* * *

It turns out to be an enjoyable few hours. We go for a walk before dinner and Ronan's three-course meal is simple, but we all clear our plates. Soup, made with mushrooms one of his neighbours had picked, followed by a hearty rabbit stew and crème pâtissière tart. I can't take any credit for it at all, as my only contribution was to peel the vegetables and lay the table. Considering how tense Ronan has been in anticipation of this visit, it's good to see how relaxed he is now. Eve speaks her mind and that's great in one way, but I can see how difficult that would have been at times for Ronan. He's a little more reserved and I wonder if that's something he inherited from his father.

We end the evening sitting around with a glass of wine and chatting about all sorts of things. Sadly, Frank's first wife died in the mid-nineties. He's an interesting character, having owned a gym for more than twenty years, and he has us in fits of laughter over some of his boxing stories. As the evening wears on, he gazes across the table at Eve. 'Shall I tell Lexie how we met?'

She begins to laugh, nodding her head. I remember Ronan telling me they met at an art class, I think.

'Well, Eve here finally decided to get out and experience something new. So, she signed up for an art class held at a school nearby. It was a Tuesday evening – how long ago was it now, m'dear? Two years, three months, one week and a couple of days?'

Now she's giggling. 'If you say so.'

'There are eighteen in the group and most of them are regulars, so they know each other quite well. I'd been a few times off and on over the period of a couple of years. They're all sat around in front of the easels and in I walk. I saunter over to the chaise longue in the middle of the room and I drop my robe to pose. Poor Eve nearly fell off her stool. She didn't know where to look.'

I burst out laughing. 'It was a life drawing class?'

'It was. Only Eve didn't know that. Give the lady her due, she drew most of me, and afterwards, once I had my clothes on, I went over to her and began chatting. The next week I went along to do a bit of drawing myself and made sure that I grabbed the easel next to hers. One thing led to another and I managed to talk her into going for a drink.'

Eve is blushing and Ronan has gone very quiet indeed.

'That is hilarious!' I roar. 'Oh, Eve! I don't know what I would have done – probably walked out, I think.'

'I skipped all the other life drawing evenings and just went along for the still life. A bowl of fruit or a vase of flowers I could handle, but naked bodies – no.'

Ronan raises his eyebrows, trying hard not to laugh.

'You didn't know that, did you?' I ask, and he shakes his head emphatically.

'No. I didn't. Thank you for sharing that, Frank. Most interesting. Mum, I don't know what to say to that, as I was the one who talked you into signing up.'

Frank's face is somewhat apologetic. 'Sorry, Ronan. I assumed you knew. The guy who runs the class is an old friend and I step in from time to time. Or *stepped* in, as in the past tense, as Eve convinced me I should sit behind the easel, rather than in front of it.'

Maybe it's the wine and we're all getting a little giggly, but

Eve, Ronan and I find that extremely funny and, while Frank gazes at us quizzically, it takes a little while for the laughter to subside.

Eve might play it cool, but the way her eyes follow Frank I can see that he's the reason they have a little twinkle in them. Some people meet their soul mate early in life; others have to wait. In Eve and Frank's case, it's a lovely story and Eve is right, they are a mad pair, but it clearly works.

I fleetingly find myself thinking about Shellie and what tomorrow will bring when they visit Jake. Will it be all smiles and laughter as today has been for us?

'Are you staying overnight, Lexie?' Eve asks and I tune back in.

'Ah. No. I, um, need to get back, I'm afraid. I have an elderly neighbour I keep an eye on.'

Judging by the way Ronan is fighting to stifle a yawn, I feel it's time I made a move. He looks as if he's ready to drop into bed and it is getting late.

'I'll be back tomorrow morning though. Ronan thought we could tour the palace gardens.'

'Ooh, that's a lovely idea.' Eve's eyes light up.

'Can I propose a toast?' Frank interjects.

'Of course, you can, darling man,' she says adoringly.

'To life, love and laughter. May we all be blessed with all three.'

Amen to that.

* * *

'I've just put Maisie to bed. She was shattered after spending most of the afternoon either on the trampoline with the boys or chasing them around the garden. You were right. Big house. Big plans.'

She doesn't sound as irked as I thought she would.

'But it went all right? No problems, or outbursts?'

'No. It was fine. There were a few awkward silences, obviously, mainly when the kids were outside, and the adults were alone. We were shown around Mum's little two-bed house in the garden, which made it all a little too real for me. And there's a pool, of course. And a hot tub. And a kid's playground. Jake has done well for himself, but we knew that and all credit to him. He did what he had to do to get where he wanted to be and that's to have enough to set up his own business. And it's not a small affair, by the sound of it.

'He asked me about you, which was awkward. To avoid giving him any real info, I changed the subject and said you were spending some time tracking down the place where Grandma Viv stayed. He sounded interested, so I told him about the box Mum sent you. I hope that was all right, but I was really struggling at the time.'

She pauses, awaiting my reaction, but I understand she had to say something.

'Look, I don't think he's been trying to wheedle information out of Mum, really I don't,' she explains. 'I think she's just proud of you and he wanted to catch up with what was going on. There's nothing sinister here, Lexie, so please don't get wound up by it.'

I groan inwardly.

'Well, I'm doing just fine and if he asks again you can tell him that,' I reply, sounding a little more curt than I'd intended.

'As you're not here in person, it's difficult. If he didn't show any interest in how you are it would be odd, wouldn't it?'

Is she trying to be a peacemaker now?

'I knew you'd be upset, and I understand that,' she continues. 'But in fairness to him, he genuinely wanted to know. It might be his conscience pricking him at last.'

If I'm honest with myself, my real fear is that Mum knows Elliot and I are struggling financially and if she shared that fact with Jake, she has no idea how mortifying that would be for me.

'Thanks, I appreciate it, Shellie, and I'm sorry you were put on the spot. None of this is your fault. I'm glad it wasn't as stressful as you thought it was going to be. And as for Mum, you think she's making the right decision for the right reasons?'

That's all that matters to me in the grand scheme of things.

'Who knows? She seems happy around them all and Brooke is genuinely grateful for any help she can get. I think it's a done deal, to be honest with you. How did it go meeting Ronan's family for the first time?'

'It was very relaxed. I left them all at the palace, after spending the morning touring the gardens. They were going to have lunch before heading off to Paris for the next stop on their tour. It was time I gave this place a good clean anyway and I wanted them to have some time alone together.'

'It sounds like things are going really well between you both, then.'

I can hear the slight hesitation in her voice.

'Ronan was glad of the support. And I owe him. Look, I have to go, as I have prep to do for tomorrow. Thanks for having my back. I appreciate it. I'll speak to Mum maybe tomorrow. How's Maisie doing?'

There's a wry chuckle.

'She's fine, now. Thank you for having that little chat with her about Ollie. I knew something was up as soon as I picked her up from school to take her to the dentist. But Maisie insisted that she wasn't feeling very well, and I'd taken that at face value. I'd even given her some medicine. Whatever you said to her really helped and just before bed she told me all about it. Ah, I can't remember getting my heart broken at such a tender age, I must admit.'

'Me, neither. They grow up way too fast these days. And I'm telling you now, any boy who upsets my darling Maisie better look out when I get back. Boyfriend, indeed!'

21

'What's wrong?' I ask as Ronan lowers the camera mid-interview.

'I don't know. It suddenly powered down. Give me a minute.'

I turn to engage Claire, one of the students working in Le Potager du Roi – the King's Kitchen Garden – in conversation. Cameron heads straight across to Ronan and it isn't long before it's obvious there is a problem they can't fix.

'I'm sorry, ladies.' Ronan looks up with a frustrated frown on his face. 'It looks like one of the chips has failed, or something.'

I try not to groan at this setback and raise a smile, thanking Claire for her time and asking if we can reschedule. She's very understanding and rather enjoying the experience, it seems, telling us it's not a problem at all. When I walk over to the guys, I can see they are both as dispirited as I feel.

'It was going so well. Now this will put another dent in the schedule, as I'm going to have to take it somewhere to get it looked at. I have no idea what it's going to cost,' Ronan admits. 'I'll give Elliot a call, in case it's still under warranty. Sorry, Lexie.'

'Hey, it's not your fault, Ronan. Yesterday's filming went without a hitch, so I guess we were lucky as we could have had Yvette here, too.' I would have had to pay her even if filming had been brought to a sudden halt. But now I'm concerned about Friday's shoot, if we end up having to cancel that.

I know there's no point in asking how long it will take to sort the problem, because first of all Ronan has to find somewhere to take it and then it depends on their workload and what needs replacing, I presume.

Cameron pipes up, 'Look, Lexie. If you want to cancel me for Friday, then I can get a day's work elsewhere no problem at all. But I need to know today in order to arrange something. I'm just thinking about saving you a little money, although I appreciate that we'll have to make this up.'

It's a dilemma. What if this is a simple fix, and the day after tomorrow we're all ready to roll again? I look at Ronan, trying to gauge his reaction.

'I hate to say it, but I think that's a wise move. This is a specialist thing and I won't know until I speak to Elliot whether there's anyone close by who can look at it. I think it's a bit optimistic to think it will be sorted by Friday, to be honest with you.'

I feel my shoulders droop a little. 'I think you're right, Ronan. Thanks, Cameron, that's appreciated. Let's assume everything will be fine for next Tuesday then, shall we?'

Cameron reaches out to give my shoulder a reassuring squeeze. 'Anything to help, Lexie. Hopefully it won't be too expensive and we can get in at least one more session before Elliot returns next week.'

I nod, appreciative that Cameron understands the pressure. If it hadn't been for the way Cameron and Ronan have rallied around, Elliot's absence would have been a total disaster. There is no way we could have halted filming for several weeks. The fact that we will only have had to reschedule two interviews is little short of a miracle.

'Hey, guys, let's not lose sight of what we've achieved. This series is going to sell, and our names are going to be on it. I can't thank either of you enough and when we're finally done, we are going to have one hell of a party!'

* * *

The phone rings and I snatch it up; Ronan said he'd phone me as soon as he could to let me know what he's arranged.

'Okay, I have good news and bad news. Which do you want first?' Ronan's voice sounds quite upbeat and I guess that means he has some sort of solution in hand.

'Bad news first, please.'

'After a quick chat with Elliot I've spoken to a camera specialist on the outskirts of Paris and they will take a look at it tomorrow. It's about an hour's drive away though, but it could be worse. If they have the part in stock it will be a same-day fix; if they don't, then they will get it couriered overnight and I'll drive over on Friday to pick the camera up.'

Time to take it on the chin, but at least something is happening.

'That's the bad news? It's not quite as bad as I feared. What's the good news?'

'I think you need a change of scenery and you should come with me. I've found the perfect place to take you for an absolutely amazing lunch, as a thank you for putting up with my scandalous family. I had no idea about Frank and his nude modelling; if I had, I would most certainly have warned you!'

I think he's joking with me really, trying to lighten my mood as he senses the worry that never seems to leave me, these days. It's not solely about money, but Mum as well. I spoke to her earlier on and she's sold to cash purchasers. She's expecting to complete in around six weeks' time, so at least I'll get to look around the house one last time before she moves out, but it still doesn't feel right.

'Sorry, my mind wandered off there for a moment. I'd love a trip out tomorrow. That would be great, but lunch is definitely on me next time.'

'I'll pick you up at nine-thirty. I'm looking forward to spending some time together just relaxing for a change. And, Lexie, I'm here whenever you need me, you do know that, don't you? You're always in my thoughts.'

'I know. It's the same for me, Ronan. I'm getting used to having you around and when you aren't it feels as if something is missing in my life. See you tomorrow; sleep well.'

As I put the phone down, I stare at the coffee table, then reach forward to open the drawer. I threw everything back into Grandma's box the other day and it's all out of sequence again. Emptying it out, I begin sorting the notebooks into a semblance of chronological order. Jumping up, I grab the one from the kitchen table that I've almost finished reading and quickly settle back down.

This time I decide to number them on the reverse. Then I notice there is already something written on the back, but it's very faint on the coarse, buff cover. It's more like an imprint now, although it was originally written with an ink pen, by the look of it, which has since rubbed off from constant handling.

Holding it up to the light, I can see the indent of the word 'April'. Flipping them all over, it's easy to sort them out. I begin with June, the month Grandma arrived in Versailles and there are two for that month. Ronan and I took one each, so we've covered those. I'm working on the July one now. Ronan has already read through the August one and there are two for October, but there's nothing for September. Perhaps that's the one Ronan is reading right now. November also has two, then there's December and no January. I add March and April to the pile, only to discover there's no February and the final one is May.

How strange. I count them and there are only twelve, plus the one Ronan is reading. I'm sure there were fifteen, so two have gone astray. Glancing across at the stack of paperwork and files on the kitchen table, I wonder if they're buried amongst the piles there. On a few occasions both Ronan and I sat at the table while making notes.

After a quick tidy up I still can't find the missing notebooks and come to the conclusion that I miscounted and there were only thirteen to begin with. It just seems strange that Grandma skipped out two whole months. I will check with Ronan tomorrow. Maybe he put them to one side for some reason, and when I do a clean through, I'll find them in between a stack of invoices or something. He knows how precious the contents of this box are to me and he can only work with one notebook at a time anyway.

'Right, Grandma, let's finish off your July notebook and see what that throws up.'

After a couple of hours, it's all becoming a little clearer. We have the Bulldog, the Terrier and now, The Spaniel. But what we also have is a real sense of how immersed Grandma felt in her surroundings. Ronan read the first of the two June notebooks and it was full of intricate little drawings, but mostly it was about her daily routine here. But in the second one which I read, as the days went by there were more and more references to the internal wrangles and conflicting personalities around her. A month later and the tension had continued to build.

Another difficult and emotional day. The Bulldog has yet again upset things by bringing even more bad news. Today's committee meeting signalled the need to restrict spending further, due to emergency repairs to the roof of the palace. He had to beg for the basic things we need just to keep going, let alone looking to the future.
It's a tough time and the Terrier wanted to storm into the meeting at one point, eager to be heard before they made their final decision. It was all the Spaniel could do to hold him back. I feel the passion, the hurt deep inside of him. But it's an impossible situation. The Terrier simply will not listen, but what can be done? Public opinion, the committee said, is against major change to the gardens anyway, but the Terrier became angry. He said that if a replanting programme is not put in place soon, the future of the park is doomed.
The Spaniel said he's a fool and the cycle of nature is that the landscape will inevitably change over time. Trees will die and new trees will be replanted if and when money is conjured up. The argument was in French and I followed it as best I could. He said that money doesn't come out of thin air and rubbed his fingers together, thrusting them in the face of the Terrier. He was incensed and I had to step in between them.

How awful for her; she could see where it was all going and there was nothing anyone could do to change the outcome. When someone is fighting so fervently for what they truly believe is right, how can they simply give in and accept defeat? The atmosphere must have been unbearable at times.

I'm not surprised to discover that after work each day Grandma spent a little time in the gardens with her notepad, drawing. Perhaps that's how she relaxed and de-stressed after the battles that seemed to rage around her on a daily basis. The last page is entirely taken up with a sketch of Marie Antoinette's beloved Virginia tulip tree. It was planted in 1783 and uprooted in 1999, when storms devastated the park after 210 kilometres per hour winds tore through Versailles.

The trunk leant gracefully to the left and then forked as it rose, lofty limbs whose size I can't even imagine. It was summer and the canopy of leaves are merely strokes of the pencil, but so carefully applied that each line seems to graduate a little. Feathery wisps turn into dark smudges, as she pressed harder on the page to simulate the tight mass of leaves.

I wonder what she was thinking as she sat there drawing. My phone rings and I feel around, yanking it out from under the cushion next to me on the sofa. It's Mum.

'Hi, Mum, how are you doing?'

'Good, honey. I didn't want to disturb you, but I had a chat with Shellie, and she said I should be careful what I say to Jake about you. That means you've said something to her that you haven't shared with me. Talk to me, Lexie, let me know what's going on in that head of yours.'

I swallow hard. This is awkward.

'Look, Mum, please don't take this the wrong way, but I

don't want Jake poking around in my business affairs. When I get back, I'm sure we'll meet up at some point. But some of the information is, um, commercial in confidence. I hope you can understand that.'

That's stretching the truth a bit thin, but it might make Mum stop and think.

'Oh, of course, honey. I hadn't thought of that. He's just desperate to find out how you are, because you're not here and it's a real shame. The one missing link. Jake has learnt a lot about life and people – and family, in particular – while he's been away. You'll find him changed, Lexie, I promise you.'

'That's great, Mum. But it's going to have to wait until I get back. I'm fine. Things are fine and I'll be home before you know it.'

'As long as there's nothing you need. I mean, you would say, wouldn't you?'

'Yes, Mum, I'd say. And things are going marvellously, actually. We have an amazing team and they've all stepped up.'

Mum's intentions are good, I know that. What if she sees this as an opportunity for Jake to help me out? That thought is horrifying, given how things were left between us. Now Jake is back and encompassing everyone in his success. The fact that I'm trying to bridge a funding gap as the hole keeps getting bigger is something I don't want thrust under his nose. He's the last person I'd take help from, on principle. How do I tell her outright that I trusted him once, but I'll never trust him ever again?

I insist on driving. If Ronan is paying for lunch, then it's the least I can do.

Pushing back the passenger seat as far as it will go, he settles himself in and I suppress my laughter. He's rather broad-shouldered and has long legs, but once he gets comfortable, he seems fine. Our shoulders knock from time to time whenever I drive over a bump in the road, but I love these little cars.

'The steering wheel's a bit small. Not sure I'd get on too well with that, but it's zippy, I'll give it that,' Ronan comments.

'This is my dream car,' I reply. I've always longed to buy a cabriolet in two-tone, black on white; with the soft top rolled back it's utter heaven.

It's clear that Ronan is now the one who is struggling to keep a straight face. 'Your dream car? I'm impressed. There are women who spend more on a handbag than the cost of a car like this,' he jests.

'I like what I like. It doesn't have to cost the earth to make me happy. The one I drive at home isn't as new as this, but

Betty has seen me through a couple of good years. At some point I'm going to have to swap her in for a newer model, but she's always been reliable. We've had some great little trips out on a Sunday with Maisie, and on our once-a-month girls' day out.'

Even thinking about those jaunts puts the biggest smile on my face.

'I totally get it. Big isn't always best. Look at me, rattling around in that house all alone. It's a waste, really. Mum's trying to convince me to move back to the UK. She rang again last night for another of her little chats. She isn't about to give up.'

I'm stunned. I can feel him watching me, but the traffic is building up and I daren't take my eyes off the road. The satnav is heading towards an industrial zone and there are as many lorries as there are cars, all of them towering over us like hulking great metal monsters.

'How do you feel about that?' His voice looms up, sounding hesitant, and the tone tells me it's a serious question.

My heart skips a beat. Ronan's plans were firmly centred on Versailles and suddenly he really is contemplating a big upheaval. I gulp. Is he asking me what I think he's asking me?

'The question I want to ask is what do *you* think about it?' I decide to turn the tables on him.

'I think that I would miss Versailles and my grandmother's house, but it could be amazing.'

'Amazing,' I repeat. That was the last thing I was expecting him to say and I'm temporarily thrown.

'Like you think it would make my mother very happy?' Now he sounds disappointed.

'Yes, but it would make me very happy too, of course it

would.' My heart is literally leaping with joy at the thought and I say a silent *thank you* to Eve.

There's no point in pretending that with each passing day I'm not conscious it's one day closer to us having to say good-bye. But it's a topic we've been avoiding and we both know that, because there isn't a simple solution.

'You're serious about that? I mean, I've been worrying about how we were going to take this forward. And how I was going to cope on my own without you, after you fly back. Dreading it, actually.'

Damn it! That's our turning, by the look of it, and this is a conversation we so need to have, but without any distractions.

'What was the name of the place again?' I ask, slightly irked that the journey isn't a longer one.

Ronan pulls out his phone. 'Les Images. Unit 56. There's a big white roller shutter, which I assume is a loading bay, next to the service unit. There's a sign over the door but it's not huge.'

It's a massive complex and it isn't easy to cruise around slowly with a steady stream of lorries turning and exiting the various car-parking and delivery areas.

'Do you think we're in the right place?' I query, slowing the car as this is a dead end and I'm looking for somewhere to turn around. 'Oh, there it is!'

Tucked into the corner, the sign doesn't exactly jump out at you, but I guess they're unlikely to attract passing trade. This is for the specialist commercial market only. Annoyingly the car park is full and there are two vans queuing, totally blocking the entry.

'I'll grab the kit and jump out here. I can head inside and get the paperwork done while you try to find somewhere to park. It shouldn't take long, so don't worry too much if you can't find a spot. Hopefully we'll soon be able to escape the chaos.'

Ronan is right; I'm still cruising up and down the road when he appears, waving to attract my attention.

'What did they say?' I ask as he settles himself into the seat next to me.

'The guy fiddled with it and just said he'd be in touch later this morning. He knows Elliot, so that's good. I impressed upon him that it's rather urgent.'

'Thanks. Right, where's this wonderful place you've found?'

Ronan taps his phone.

'Okay. Retrace your steps and you have no choice but to turn left to get back out onto the main road. Then straight up to the roundabout and take the fourth exit. It's not far, but it's in the opposite direction.'

It's a relief to be driving away from the queues streaming into central Paris. Ronan continues to give me directions and eventually I pull into a car park in front of what looks like a modern version of an old wooden lodge. It stands on solid concrete pillars and its beautiful cladding helps it to blend in among the trees. As I follow the arrows and drive further into the sizeable grounds, there in front of us is a glorious old water mill.

'That's incredible,' I remark.

'I knew you'd like it.' Ronan looks pleased with himself.

'Why the frown?'

'It's lovely here. I just found myself thinking about my brother, for some obscure reason.'

Ronan looks at me quizzically.

'It's difficult.' I sigh.

'Well, we have at least an hour before lunch to walk and talk. You can tell me all about it. If I'm going to end up moving back to the UK, then you'll need to let me in on what happened, sooner rather than later.'

'There's not a lot to tell,' I reply as I manoeuvre the car into a parking bay.

There is no way I'm going to risk spoiling a relaxing day out by having this conversation and I'm pretty sure Ronan will pick that up from my tone of voice.

'I get the message. Come on, I don't want to put you in a bad mood.' His grin is a forgiving one.

We head towards the reception and Ronan confirms our lunch reservation. The woman behind the desk is very welcoming and hands us a map, leaning over it and talking very fast as she points out various landmarks. Ronan thanks her and checks his watch as he holds the door open for me.

'We'll take the river walk. It's the blue track here,' he adds, stabbing his finger on the map. 'We need to cross that bridge up ahead.'

Stepping off the gravelled path and onto the soft grass, it's satisfyingly springy beneath our feet. There's a gentle swoosh of cars driving at speed along the busy road, but the further we walk, the less noticeable it becomes. The sound of water flowing over rocks and the birdsong from the tall trees either side of the river ahead begin to take over.

I take in a deep breath, savouring the sweet air. After the unpleasant fumes from idling traffic, the contrast couldn't be greater. A huge swathe of beech hedging, sporting the tiny, fluttery bright foliage of a new year's growth, lines the approach to the hand-hewn wooden bridge. The span extends about forty feet, but it's only three feet wide. We stop in the middle of it to lean on the handrail.

'The river runs directly under the lodge,' Ronan points out.

The lodge is four storeys high, and every bedroom facing this way has a balcony overlooking the river. It's a huge building, easily spanning the width of the water and extending well beyond the edges of the banks.

'This is obviously a very popular place,' I reflect, noting how full the car park is from this viewpoint. It's only Thursday too, which is a good sign as it isn't just full of long-weekenders.

'I asked George to recommend somewhere a bit special.'

I turn to look at him.

'You've talked to George in the last couple of days?' I ask, rather nervously. I hope George hasn't mentioned that he's been in touch with me directly.

Ronan gives a wry smile. 'I ring him every now and again to remind him I'm around. I wanted him to know that I'm pressing ahead with the final book in the series. He didn't say anything, and I left it at that. He's had his chance and it's George's decision not to talk to me. But this restaurant was a good suggestion and I'm grateful to him.'

'Your research here is coming to an end, then?'

He nods. 'It is, I think. The first draft is almost done, but it needs a good tidy up as it's not going to be as anecdotal as the first two in the series. I found myself focusing on the effects of the two big storms in 1990 and 1999. It's an interesting story, because the first storm did a lot of damage, but the second storm was so devastating that it shut the park for a week. It was a battlefield of fallen trees, but it also left others unsafe. While the damage to the buildings was significant, having to close the park suddenly made everyone sit up. Once word got out about the full extent of the damage, everyone was in uproar. Making it safe was going to cost money, and a considerable amount.'

'But money has always been an issue, going way back. So, what changed?'

'When the first photographs began appearing in the papers they were received with shock and horror. The state had drafted in the military and the work began to make the park safe. Donations started to come in, not just from the established friends of Versailles and patrons, but from around the world. It was soon clear that it wasn't going to be enough. More men were needed, more equipment, and the costs were spiralling. So, the decision was made to let it go on record. Giving the press free access was an unprecedented step, but it worked.

'Continued coverage around the world attracted more wealthy patrons, people who are prepared to dig deep to support a cause they feel is worthy. For the first time in the history of the palace, I do believe the park and gardens became the focus of Versailles. And there ends my story.' He sounds content and I'm pleased for him.

'So, it is a cause for celebration, then.'

'I suppose it is, in a way. But today isn't about work, it's about us. The restaurant is located in the old mill. The first floor is a bar and café, the second floor is where we're going to eat. Stunning views, according to George.'

As we stand shoulder to shoulder, our gaze is drawn beyond the mill, towards the foamy white water heralding the point at which it flows beneath the huge waterwheel.

'This must have been amazing when it was working. What type of mill is it?'

Ronan indicates for us to begin walking again.

'Grain. According to the map most of the area over there,

extending for miles, is mainly farmland and pasture. There's a campsite here too, and individual log cabins in a forest.'

As we stroll along the riverbank together, I can't recall ever feeling as thrilled as I do right now about the future and what's to come.

'I'm so happy that Eve approves of *us*.'

Ronan draws to a halt, his eyes searching mine.

'She's relieved to think I'm in safe hands,' he declares. 'She took me to one side and told me how lucky I am and that I shouldn't drag my feet.'

He catches up my hands in his, lovingly, and I can see he's in a happy place. Gone is the edginess that was dampening his spirits a little and it's a release. He can stop worrying about her and focus on his own life.

'We both have loose ends to tie up before we can be together, don't we?' Ronan doesn't sound concerned, but accepting of the fact.

'Everything is going to be a first as we move forward. That's heady stuff but we'll work it out, somehow.' I stand on tiptoe to plant my lips on his and he lets out a soft groan.

My whole being is buzzing at the thought of having Ronan in my life permanently and what it will mean. Yes, it's a little scary stepping into the unknown, but it's also exciting.

With the warmth from the sun overhead taking the edge off the playful breeze, this is one of *those* moments in life. A memory I will recall and look back on fondly, knowing that the man in my life wants me as much as I want him.

'I wish I could fly back with you. I have no idea how long it will take to sort everything out. I'm a little nervous about meeting your family, to be honest.' His frown shows me he's serious.

'Hey, there's nothing to worry about. I've kept it simple,

but they know me so well and it's more about what I haven't told them, than what I have actually decided to share. I've told them you're special and you are. It will be easier when they can see us together and really get to know you.'

'I understand.' Ronan scoops me into his arms, giving me a lingering hug.

'Planning a new future takes time. I simply have to be patient, but it isn't going to be easy.' He gazes over my shoulder.

'Look, we have company!' Ronan releases me, pointing to a swan on the river in front of us. It glides easily, head erect and proud as it scans around attentively. 'See that little island in the middle of the river? Just to the right of that bush there's what looks like a pile of moss, old leaves and twigs. If you look closely, I think that's a nest. Yes, look, his partner is looking after their clutch of eggs. It won't be long before they have a bevy of cygnets.'

'That's so lovely to see. It's peaceful here; not too commercial considering it's also a campsite.'

'There's another bridge further down and what looks like an information board. Come on, let's wander down and take a peek.' Ronan yanks on my hand playfully. 'This is perfect, isn't it?'

'Simply perfect,' I repeat, but really what I'm thinking is that he's perfect.

I love his natural sense of curiosity and how inspired he is by the things around him.

'This looks interesting,' Ronan says as I try to slow the thoughts tumbling through my mind.

The river diverts to the other side of the mill, the main part heading off to the right and a smaller, shallower arm wending its way beneath a stone bridge. We stop to read the story and discover that a hefty grant a few years ago allowed the site to be developed in sympathy with the surroundings.

'It sort of restores your faith in human nature, doesn't it?'

'Money makes the world go around, I suppose, but it's wonderful when organisations can work together. This is a beautiful spot and it hasn't been spoilt.'

Ronan turns to look at me, leaning against the trunk of an old oak tree.

'France is in my blood; it always will be. But spending time with you has made me realise that the only thing that really matters is being together, Lexie.'

I had assumed he'd been walking along just taking in the view, but clearly his mind is still preoccupied too. The look on his face makes me draw closer to him and he throws open his arms, pulling me into a tight embrace.

My days here are numbered and now it's beginning to hang over us, ominously.

'I feel that way too, Ronan,' I half whisper. 'A part of me wants to stay here forever, even though I know that's not possible. No matter how hard it's going to be to leave you, I simply don't have a choice in the matter. Aside from my work commitments, I have to be close to my family as we've always been there for each other. Well, most of us have.'

'Come on, let's head inside for a pre-lunch drink and you can tell me the whole story. It's time I found out what I'm about to get myself into, don't you think?'

Although I was hoping to avoid this conversation today, I can't put it off any longer. Or pretend that what's in my past hasn't given rise to trust issues.

Ronan stoops, his lips softly touching mine, and I'm confident that we have a real shot at this. For two people with complicated lives and backgrounds, it's going to be a test.

And, yes, making a commitment is scary, admittedly, but this feels right and nothing is going to get in our way. As I told Maisie, one day someone will come along who will be a keeper, and now that time has come for me, at last!

* * *

I sip my half a glass of white wine slowly, in between downing probably the sweetest-tasting water that I've ever sampled, which is drawn from the local well.

'Is this amazing, or what?' Ronan enthuses.

We both plumped for the palourdes au gratin, which turns out to be baked clams in garlic butter and breadcrumbs.

'These are deliciously sweet, offset by the richness of the garlic.' I find myself reaching for my wine glass, then decide that I don't want to overpower the flavours in my mouth.

'Okay, time to tell me all about this brother of yours. You said he was successful?'

'Yes. If you think having lots of money in the bank, a huge house – which is now in the UK, I might add – an American wife and twin boys is the benchmark for having made it. I'd say Jake has ticked off most of his life goals. World domination next.'

The minute I stop speaking I realise how that sounds, but I wasn't being sarcastic. Not having met Jake, Ronan wouldn't understand that, of course. I wouldn't want Jake's lifestyle; it's simply not me.

'Sorry. Let me backtrack a little.'

I lean my knife and fork against the plate for a moment.

'Jake was a director of a big production company and he offered me a job as an assistant producer. I jumped at it, but then he knew I would, as that was my dream. I had a falling out with my boss, who spoke to Jake, and Jake fired me without even asking for my side of the story.'

I have no intention of letting this spoil my lunch, so I resume eating, waiting for Ronan's response. He finishes the last mouthful on his plate, wipes his mouth on the linen napkin and sits looking at me for a moment or two.

'Maybe there was more to it and it was a case of the politics behind it. Obviously, I don't know him, or the details, but you're his sister and the fact that he didn't listen to you seems a little bizarre.'

I nod, fearing that already this mouthful of delicious food has lost a little of its appeal.

'Business comes first over everything else in Jake's life. It wasn't solely about the fact he didn't talk to me, but about the announcement he made implying that I was being let go because I wasn't up to the job. It wasn't just humiliating, it shut down so many avenues for me. I had to take the first thing I was offered just to be able to continue paying my bills. It was yet another job as a presenter and for me that was going backwards. Overnight my dreams fell apart and it's taken five years of research, and every penny I have saved, to grab this opportunity. That's why the project with Elliot is so important.'

I can see that Ronan is a little shocked by my revelation.

'I knew this project was a big deal for both you and Elliot financially, but I hadn't realised quite how crucial. I can see now why you've been so worried. But you said your brother went to the States?'

'Yes, he'd already accepted a job and left for LA a week later. He was promoted to deputy CEO and put in charge of the American subsidiary of the company.'

Ronan frowns, raising the wine glass to his mouth and taking a sip. He glances at me over the top, looking distinctly uncomfortable as he can see how difficult it is for me, raking over old wounds. I put down my knife and fork, then take a sip of water. Talking about Jake is a mistake, but I've started, so I have to finish.

He looks at me pointedly, no doubt trying to piece together a motive. 'It wasn't down to something like a restructuring of the organisation, then?'

'No, that would at least have excused his behaviour. It was personal. My boss knew I could do his job better than he could do it and he had Jake's ear. He probably made up some stupid story about how I'd messed up and Jake was too busy to check it out. Jake didn't even take a moment to pause and think about the impact it would have on my life, or my future, because he was too busy organising his move.'

'What did the rest of your family say?'

I expel a rather lengthy sigh. 'Mum still doesn't know the full story. She thinks I just decided to move on. My sister knows the truth and we believe that's the real reason Jake made no attempt to make contact with any of us after he left: he felt guilty. But Shellie has seen him twice in this last week and says he's changed. Well, he has for sure, because he's returned with a wife and twin boys that we knew nothing at all about.'

'Wow.' Now Ronan is beginning to understand. 'Lexie, from what I've seen you're a fighter. And you're a very professional and capable person, so I'm sure it was obvious you could do the job justice. Why didn't you fight back and make your voice heard before he left?'

I try my best not to let my body language give away how

distressing I'm finding this and I straighten my spine, pushing back my shoulders.

'I made a big mistake. My boss, who was the CEO's nephew, invited me around to his house one night. I had no idea his wife wasn't going to be there, and it seemed genuine enough as I'd been there before. We had an important meeting coming up and we were going to pitch an idea for a new project.

'Something wasn't right, and I sensed that the moment I walked through the door. He didn't seem in a hurry to settle down to work and the longer he messed about sorting drinks and generally chatting, the more I realised he had another motive. Suddenly, he launched himself at me and in the ensuing tussle I ended up giving him a black eye. I couldn't get out of there quickly enough, because, if I hadn't fought back, I don't know how far he would have taken it.'

Ronan reaches out across the table, grabbing my hand. His face is ashen and, the way he's compressing his lips together, I can see how angry he is.

'No man should ever treat a woman that way. But you never told anyone? Why?'

'No. Until now. What was the point? It was my word against his and I know his wife. She's lovely. I don't think, I mean, I'm pretty sure it was a one-off. I went there of my own accord and how would it have looked, given that my own brother had immediately sacked me? No one would have believed my side of the story.'

Ronan shakes his head, a stony expression on his face.

'Once is one time too many, Lexie. That was a tough decision to make, but I understand why you didn't tell anyone. It's sickening that men like that can get away with it, though.'

Taking a moment to consider his words, I know he's right. I should have spoken up.

'Even the next day, I was still in shock, to be honest. At the time I had to focus on getting a job. If I'd kicked up a fuss, then I risked making myself unemployable. Everyone I knew professionally was talking about it and I decided, rightly or wrongly, to keep quiet.

'I didn't have the energy to face the fallout and I know that's an excuse, but it was a genuine concern for me at the time. I was scared that I'd start the process and not be able to see it through, which would have made it look even more like I wasn't telling the truth. The guy is still with his wife and I guess I've appeased my conscience by telling myself that alone justified my silence. Maybe he learnt his lesson.'

Having never told anyone about the attack, even Shellie, now I hear my own words I shudder, wondering how I could have been so stupid. The guy made me a victim and that wasn't fair. It left me doubting my own judgement of other people, because it hadn't even occurred to me that I wasn't safe around him.

'These things happen all the time, sadly, because life isn't always fair. Only those close to me would have known I would never make a false accusation. But those who only knew of me, or saw me from a distance – well, people are left wondering, aren't they? And that's the injustice of finding yourself in a situation like that.'

Ronan squeezes my hand, withdrawing it as the waiter approaches to take our plates.

'I'm glad you told me, and I didn't mean to make you feel bad, I just wanted to understand. You can't change the past, but you should tell your brother the truth now he's back. He made a horrible mistake and it's come between you both for the wrong reason. He'd have to be a very hard person indeed to know the whole story and not regret his part in it.'

Desperate to change the subject, I move on to talk to Ronan about Mum and the new plans for the move, then about Shellie and her amazing little family. I want him to understand why my life in the UK means so much to me. I don't want him to feel that he's relegated to last place, but some choices are tough. Even though I know I'm hopelessly in love with Ronan, I can't walk away from my old life.

As the waiter reappears, my appetite is back and the aiguillettes de boeuf aux girolles – or slices of lean, moist roast beef served with wild chanterelle mushrooms – is truly divine. I savour every little mouthful as I refuse to dwell upon old wounds.

While we await the crème brûlée flavoured with pungent Kafir lime, Ronan tells me a little more about his father and the time he spent working for him. He sounds like a man who has to control everything in his life and his aim was to distance Ronan from his mother. His father wanted him to leave that side of his past firmly behind him, asking Ronan to change his name one last time. But it's clear he didn't know his son at all. How could he expect Ronan to do that? The lure was the promise of an inheritance, which has since been withdrawn.

When the phone call comes, confirming that the camera won't be ready until tomorrow, we don't rush back. Instead, we linger on the terrace outside with coffee, overlooking the river; it's relaxing to simply sit and chat for a while. Then we take another stroll through the grounds and on into the forest.

It's weird how fate engineered this today, off the back of what I thought of at first as a nightmare situation. We badly needed this time away from everything, with no distractions and no threat of being interrupted.

Eventually, it's time to head back to Versailles and we both take it for granted that Ronan will stay over for the night. We've reached the point where any lingering doubts about our future together have dissolved.

Wrapped in his arms, I have never felt as safe, or as protected, and it's a feeling that makes my heart soar. Now we have bared our souls to each other, even our respective hang-ups that won't quite go away don't seem quite so draining, or problematic.

Dating can be fun, but it can also be a temporary lift and then a gutting realisation it's time to move on. That feeling of loneliness remains and it can be isolating, making you feel vulnerable. But until you're really *with* someone – that special someone – you have no idea what's missing from your life, you are simply searching for something to fill the emptiness inside you. I had no idea how uplifting and complete it makes you feel to be loved and to love in return.

It's all about trust. I never thought I'd share with anyone a scene I'd pushed way back into the attic of my mind. And now I've shared my worst experience, something that scarred me, with Ronan. In the intervening years I chose only to remember the satisfying moment when my fist hit the target and my assailant crumpled to the floor. I like to think that the shock of my instant reaction taught him a lesson he's never forgotten.

23

THE BEST-LAID PLANS

Even after Ronan reluctantly heads off home, the joy of a blissful night together leaves me wrapped in my own little bubble of happiness. Everything looks different – brighter, more vibrant – and I feel alive in a way I never have before. I catch myself singing out loud as I get ready to face a new day and I can't remember the last time I did that.

I promised I would help Solange with the preparations for tomorrow's party, but this morning it hasn't stopped raining. Even the weather can't dampen my positivity and I look up at the sky, willing those clouds to move on. As I stare across at number one, she waves across at me from Renée's sitting room. Swinging open the window a few inches, I do the same.

'It's beginning to brighten up,' I call out, optimistically. 'Fancy a cup of coffee?'

She puts up her thumb and disappears. I head downstairs to let her in, as she runs across the courtyard holding one of Renée's black cardigans over her hair.

'Thanks, Lexie. Renée is working on the surprise engagement cake, so I'm not allowed in the kitchen.' She literally jumps in over the doorstep as I make way for her.

'The kettle is boiled. White, black, sugar, no sugar?'

'Black, one sugar, please.'

'Come on up and take a seat on the sofa. I reckon another hour and it's going to ease off. At least everything will be nice and fresh. And the forecast for tomorrow is a little cloud, but mainly sunshine!'

She folds Renée's cardigan up very carefully and I point to the corner.

'There's a clothes rack. Might as well hang that up and it will be dry by the time you head back. What's the plan of action?'

I fill the mugs and carry them across to the sofa. Solange joins me, tucking her hair behind her ears as she flops down onto the soft cushions.

'Well, the food is covered. In fact, we have way too much. Philippe is sorting out the drinks and he has two cocktails on the menu. One is non-alcoholic. A friend is going to drop off a delivery of metal tables and chairs in a little while. When it dries up—' she holds up crossed fingers and grimaces '— perhaps you could help me set them up?'

'Of course. How about tomorrow? Anything specific I can help with?'

She leans back, her body sagging, and smiles at me.

'I had no idea planning a little party took so much energy. Imagine when we get married! I think I will employ one of those wedding planners, because it's all too much for me.' She feigns wiping her forehead with the back of her hand, and it makes me smile.

'Says the woman who expertly organises large press conferences and promotional events,' I comment.

'Yes, but this is not easy. It started small and it's growing. How can I say no when everyone keeps adding names? If they all turn up it will be madness,' she declares.

'Okay – let's plan for the worst-case scenario. Instead of a long row of tables in the centre of the courtyard, let's put them around the outside edge. No one will mind and then if it gets crowded there will be a large area for people to stand and mingle.'

Solange nods her head, her face brightening considerably.

'Good idea. Perhaps to put the food table in front of Renée's cottage and it will be easy to go in and out of the kitchen to replenish the platters.'

'How about I open up the garage door in the morning and we put the bar up in front of it? Philippe can store everything safely inside and we can use my fridge if we need to keep anything chilled. How does that sound?'

She picks up her mug and holds it aloft.

'To a wonderful friend in my time of need,' she says, and we chink.

'So, what else does that leave?'

'Well, we have lots of flowers coming tomorrow to decorate the tables. They will need trimming and placing into jam jars as table centres. We also have some bunting to string between the trees. And I thought we were keeping it simple, but I have been overruled because Philippe says we must have a fountain. A fountain!' She shrugs her shoulders, but I can see she's excited by the thought.

'Look, the rain has already eased off,' I point out. We head over to the window and stare up at the clouds as they continue to part and a watery sun peeks through at last. 'And there's a rainbow. Oh, my, and Renée's cottage is directly beneath it.'

Solange's face is a picture of happiness. It won't be long before we can make a start, and whatever we get done today makes tomorrow's workload lighter. A vehicle pulls up at the gate and as it swings open Solange's face pales.

'What's wrong?' I ask, assuming this is the neighbour in the corner, the one Renée said will be here for the party.

'That's my papa. We knew Maman was coming, but he refused.' She takes a step back away from the window.

'But this is good news, isn't it?'

Solange is clearly flustered.

'He has never met Philippe and Papa is not a timid man. He will say exactly how he feels. This could ruin everything tomorrow if he decides to be difficult.'

I thought she'd be eager to go and greet them, but instead she heads straight back to collapse down on the sofa.

'Maman booked a hotel, so hopefully they are only coming to pay their respects to Renée. Can I stay here until they leave?'

'Of course, you can.'

There's a lull in our conversation and I don't quite know what to say. I can see how unsettled she is now. Solange gazes down, idly, at the items on the coffee table.

'Is this your work?' she asks, pointing to the little stacks of notebooks.

'No. I use the table as my office. These belong to my grandma. Ronan and I have been working through them to piece together her year at Versailles.'

'But that's amazing. I knew Ronan was throwing himself into something new as I hardly see him these days unless it's with you, filming. How exciting.'

Something new? I don't think he's spending that much time on it. But maybe she isn't aware he's putting the finishing touches to the last book in his series.

'It's mostly drawings and the sort of things you'd expect a horticultural student to record.'

The sound of a car door slamming has Solange up out of her seat again, to peer very gingerly out of the window.

'That was a quick visit. As I would expect. Papa will, no doubt, feel awkward and Maman, too, if he is not talkative. Oh, why did he change his mind?' She slips into her native tongue and speaks so fast I only catch a few words of every sentence. Her eyes are blazing, and she sounds angry, almost bitter.

When it's obvious I'm a little taken aback, she immediately halts and raises one hand by way of apology. 'I'm sorry. I want tomorrow to be a happy memory with no upsets and now I cannot guarantee that will be the case. He has had a year to make amends, so I fear his intention is to find fault with my plans for a life here.'

I see her to the door and reflect on the fact that family members are so often the cause of our problems. But I know only too well that it's hard to walk away from them, even when their actions cause nothing but pain.

'Let me know when the tables and chairs arrive, and I'll come straight out and give you a hand. Remember, there will be a lot of people here tomorrow, by the sound of it, and help will be at hand if needed. It's your special day and I'm sure he will respect that. You are his daughter, and he loves you – that's why it's hard for him to accept your new life here in Versailles. When he sees how happy you are it will change everything.'

She looks at me, putting on a brave face, but I can see she

isn't convinced. 'I hope you are right, Lexie. I can't thank you enough for your support; it means so much to me.'

'Just in time,' I call out, as Ronan steps in through the gates.

He hurries over, leaning in for a kiss as he gives me one of his wicked smiles. The look we exchange is an intimate one, as his hands slide around my waist. I kiss him back, closing my eyes for one brief moment and remembering last night.

'Hmm. Right. What can I do to help?'

'We have to clear this mountain of flowers. They weren't due to be delivered until tomorrow morning, but at least they're here. These big branches of cherry blossom need to be trimmed into stems of about ten inches. The jars are in that box and the bucket of water is under this table. If you can give a hand with that, I can start cutting the burlap into narrow strips to tie in bows to pretty them up.'

Ronan rolls up the sleeves of his pale blue cotton shirt. He looks rather smart today, but then he did have that trip to Paris.

'Is the camera good to go?'

'Yep. The bank transfer went through immediately, thanks, and I didn't have to wait around. So, I'm just using these and cutting about here?' He checks, picking up the secateurs and a three-foot-long branch, moving them down one of the stems covered in glorious blossom.

'That's fine. No longer than that though, or the jam jars could topple over as they'll be top heavy with the weight of the blossoms. Two or three stems per jar. You are my hero!'

'Hi, Ronan, thanks for helping out.' Solange appears with a pile of bunting, a hammer and some tacks and he stops to kiss her on each cheek. 'I'll give you a hand with the burlap, Lexie, as it will need two people to put these up. One to hold the ladder as it's going to be a bit wobbly on the cobbles.'

We form a production line and, once the jars are done, we put some gorgeous white lilies into tall metal containers and fill them with water.

'We'll put these out tomorrow, but for now they can be placed under the tables. We don't want anything blowing over if the wind picks up during the night,' Solange says. But looking up at the red-streaked sky as the sun begins to dip, I think it bodes well.

'Red sky at night, shepherd's delight is what they say, so fingers crossed. And there's hardly a breeze at the moment, too. But doesn't everything smell wonderful? Fresh, clean and sparkly,' I remark, gazing around. The timing of the rain couldn't have been better.

Just then, a handsome guy with dark hair and a bushy beard appears and hurries towards Solange, wrapping her in his arms. He kisses her on the mouth, and she squeals. Pulling back, I notice that she has no intention of letting him go and she turns towards me, her face beaming.

'Lexie, this is my Philippe.'

He eases himself away from her, then steps forward to kiss me on alternate cheeks.

'I 'ave heard so much about you, Lexie. Thank you for 'elping with the water leak and now... our party!'

'My pleasure, Philippe, and it's lovely to finally meet you.'

He immediately turns to Ronan and they shake hands.

'What can I do to 'elp?' Philippe asks enthusiastically.

Solange takes him off to sort out the bunting, leaving Ronan and I to finish off, then begin assembling the small tables and chairs ready to set them out.

'How was your day? It all went smoothly?' I turn to look at Ronan, who breaks out into a sardonic smile.

'Yes. But it wasn't any fun hanging around on my own. I did get some work done this afternoon, though.'

'Oh, that reminds me. How many of the notebooks do you have? I thought there were fifteen, but I can only find twelve.'

He wrinkles his brow. 'I'll check. I must admit I haven't had much spare time, but I know I'm still only part way through September. Sorry I've been so slow.'

Obviously, Ronan is now intent on wrapping up his own work so he can begin making plans. It's time-consuming reading Grandma's notes and maybe it's something I'm best doing on my own anyway. But it did achieve one thing and that's to bring Ronan and me together. Funny how things work out, isn't it?

Renée appears with a tray of cold drinks and some little apricot tarts. We quickly assemble two of the tables and five chairs, then sit around for a while enjoying the ambience of a fine evening. Life couldn't be more thrilling than it is right now, with so much to look forward to, and Ronan isn't the only one desperate for everything to fall into place as quickly as possible.

24

When I awaken, Ronan isn't lying next to me, but I can hear the sound of china chinking downstairs and several minutes later he appears with a breakfast tray.

'Croissant and coffee for the love of my life.'

I push back the thin cotton sheet and pull myself up into a sitting position so he can place the tray on my lap. As he does so he stoops to steal a kiss, hovering for a few seconds and making me laugh.

'Stop – we're going to tip the tray over! What have I done to deserve breakfast in bed?'

'Well, you've turned my life upside down, for one. I've been mulling over what to do about the house and I don't think it's the right decision to sell it. Not because I have any doubts at all about moving back to the UK, but—'

'I'm relieved to hear you say that, Ronan. The house isn't just bricks and mortar to you – it holds so many memories. It's been in your family for too long to cut all ties with it just like that.'

He gingerly slides onto the bed next to me, resting one

hand against my thigh. Leaning over to grab a croissant, he bites off the end, thinking as he chews.

'The problem is that I need the money to tide me over when I move back to the UK. I don't know how long it will take me to get a job. I suppose I could get an agent to list the house as a holiday let, but I don't want you to feel that I'm not ready to make a firm commitment. I want us to be in a position to start afresh in a new place, together.'

I raise my hand to run it down the side of his stubbly cheek and he leans in to kiss me, this time more passionately. Sitting back, I don't take my eyes off him.

'I'm actually relieved you're really taking time to think this through. What's important is that you don't make rash decisions you'll regret at a later stage. Your dilemma, like mine, doesn't change how we feel for each other. But we're a couple now so you'll move in with me, obviously, and we'll manage until you're settled workwise. Two can live as cheaply as one. Then we can look at getting a place together that we can afford maybe, so that you can keep the house here, too. That works for me, how about you?'

'If you're happy with that, then great. But I want us to have the best start, Lexie, and it's important to me that you understand that I need you, more than I need the house.'

He replaces the croissant on the tray, and I grab his hand before he can retract it.

'If you let it out, then it's a place we can return to as a couple for holidays ourselves and where better? Who knows what the future might bring, anyway? For now, take the only decision you can that makes any sense at all.'

He closes his eyes for a moment, moved by my words.

'Let's do this. I know the moment you're gone I'm going to be desperate to join you, so I'll start the ball rolling straight away. I know it's quick, but I've never been more sure of anything in my life than I am about you.' He leans in to seal the deal with a lingering kiss and before pulling away trails his fingers down over my shoulder. My skin tingles at his touch, as I imagine what it will be like waking up next to him every single day of my life.

'Me, neither. Now get into party mode. Everyone is arriving at noon and it's going to be a full-on day.'

There are going to be some surprised faces on my return, when I break the news. If only we were flying back together it wouldn't feel quite so daunting. I know that once they get to know him, they'll see what a wonderful man Ronan is and why he captured my heart. But the parting isn't going to be easy and that weighs heavily upon us both.

There are few clouds in the sky today, and it's a brilliant blue – the sort of colour that is mesmerising and when it catches your attention you can't help but gaze upwards. It's one of those days when your heart soars because you feel so happy to be alive and spring is a reminder that summer is coming.

With two hours to go, Philippe and a group of guys are all still working on the fountain. It's a clever, romantic and slightly crazy idea, but who doesn't love the sound of water in the background? Although so far, it's more of a dribble than a cascade.

Philippe has set it up in the middle of the courtyard and an electrical wire runs into Renée's house. It's all been taped securely to the cobbled floor and we rearranged the tables so there's no fear of anyone tripping over it.

With my car parked out on the street first thing this

morning, Ronan and I had a tidy up and were able to set the long trestle table up inside the opening to the garage, creating a little more space in the courtyard. Moving the ladders to the rear, we stacked the boxes of beer, wine and water to obscure the general garage muddles. There was even some bunting left over and Ronan managed to hang it from the wooden beam above the opening.

There's a huge half-barrel of ice now, too, after a delivery van turned up and several of the guys helped to carry in the heavy plastic bags. I'm buffing glasses, as Ronan finishes off lining everything up. He's waiting for Philippe to come and instruct him on how to make up the cocktails and we have two of the largest silver punch bowls I've ever seen, ready and waiting.

There's a loud gasp and finally the little drizzle from the fountain has turned into an enormous shower, raining down on the guys who have been trying to figure out what was blocking the flow of water. There's a little raucous laughter and I guess that whatever was causing the problem has now been flushed through.

Well, a party in Versailles wouldn't be quite the same without a fountain, now would it? After a little adjustment to the flow, there's a big round of applause and Solange appears, the rowdy celebration having filtered through into Renée's kitchen.

'Magnifique!' she declares, her hands flying up to her face, which sports a look of pure joy. Behind her Renée's face is a picture, too.

I stop buffing for a moment and gaze around. This is the embodiment of quintessentially French chic, and it couldn't be more romantic because of that. The tables and chairs are weathered and charming; the floral displays add a glorious

profusion of colour in alternating pink and white. The
bunting is delightful, fluttering in the breeze like gossamer
wings, and frames the courtyard as it hangs from the trees.
The long buffet table is covered in beautiful white antique
lace tablecloths, ready and waiting to display a homemade
feast.

The front of number six now has its own pop-up garden,
with an array of silver pots full of gorgeous white lilies and
tall, leafy stems of various types of greenery. Two of Solange's
friends arrived with their arms full, first thing this morning.
Already I can breathe in and capture the pungent eucalyptus,
sweet bay, vibrant rosemary and wisps of ivy.

'You're loving this, aren't you?' Ronan sidles up to me,
interrupting my little moment of sheer bliss.

'This is idyllic.'

And it really is. My time here in France may be limited,
but I'll always have my memories of this most perfect springtime at Versailles. And when I do have to leave, Ronan will
join me as soon as he can. To have both of our families
around us will be a blessing and the best start we could have
asked for.

He leans in to kiss me and whispers, 'I promise you one
thing – I'm going to make sure you get the party of your
dreams when it's our turn, my darling.'

I grin, shaking my head and laughing. 'Flowers, French
delicacies and fountains... hmm. I think maybe Prosecco,
pizza and posh raincoats – it is the UK we're talking about,
after all.'

He leans back. 'There's a true romantic in here, you know,
and I'm going to embrace it,' he says, tapping his chest with
his hand. 'Who says we can't bring a little Versailles magic to
wherever we end up living together?'

At this moment the sky couldn't be any bluer and the birds couldn't sing any louder. As I stare deep into Ronan's eyes my heart soars. He loves me every bit as I've come to love him. What more could any woman ask for to make her life complete?

* * *

When Solange started to panic about the numbers yesterday, she was right. On the stroke of noon, a steady stream of party-goers makes its way into the courtyard. The guys have only just finished stringing lights in the trees, as this party promises to stretch way into the evening.

Solange is visibly nervous awaiting the arrival of her parents, but I'm caught up helping Ronan behind the bar and it's probably an hour later before I catch sight of her talking to her father.

'Ronan, do you think Solange is okay?' I nod in her direction and he cranes his neck to see what's going on.

'I can't tell from here. Should I wander across?'

'Would you mind? He doesn't have a drink. Maybe use that as an excuse and bring him over here to distract him?'

I watch as Ronan interrupts them, and he boldly offers Solange's father his hand. They shake and all seems well, but Solange turns to glance in my direction. I can tell from her expression that she needs rescuing. Thankfully, the two men turn and walk towards me, engaged in conversation.

Ronan introduces me as his girlfriend and Monsieur Forand shakes my hand rather formally. There's an awkward silence and I decide that, rather than struggling to string together some suitable words, I'll ask Ronan to interpret for me.

'Ronan, can you tell Monsieur Forand that I am very pleased to meet him? Solange has become a very good friend and I know he and his wife must be very proud of their daughter. She is such a hard worker and her love for the Palace of Versailles is a credit to her. Solange and Philippe have spent hours pulling everything together to make this such a special day to share with their family and friends. It couldn't be more perfect, and I'm honoured to be a part of it.'

Ronan crooks an eyebrow at me, but he does as I ask. The reaction is the same dour look that Monsieur Forand seems to wear quite naturally. After a rather awkward few seconds, I pour a large glass of red wine and he inclines his head a little, wearing what I assume is his version of a smile. Raising the glass up to me, he takes a sip and nods his head briefly, giving his seal of approval. I may just have made a new friend.

As he walks away, I let out a sigh of relief.

'Do you think he took the hint?'

'I hope so. But I'll keep an eye out in case anything untoward develops. Any other worries?'

I shake my head. 'It's all good. And the happy couple are both glowing.'

'Let me take over here and you can go and grab something to eat from the buffet. Did I tell you how lovely you look in that dress you're wearing?' His arm wraps around my waist as he stoops to steal a quick kiss. But I don't let him off that easily and one kiss turns into two, then three.

'I'm glad you approve of my outfit,' I half whisper, pulling away from him with great reluctance.

It's something I picked up when we were shopping for Ronan's house and I saw it in the window of a little boutique. An impulse purchase, really, as it's not a style of dress I'd normally choose. *Floaty* is a perfect description for it. It's comprised of several fine layers of silk organza, large roses printed in very soft pinks and mauves making it floral without being overtly so. The result is a shimmer of colour; old-style romantic chic, I'd call it. With long sleeves and a slim navy-blue belt at the waist, it drapes beautifully. It has the sort of skirt you want to swish, and I feel elegant today.

Ronan continues to gaze at me, dropping his arms and grabbing my hands quite intently as if he's about to say something important.

I hear my name, but it isn't Ronan speaking and reluctantly I drag my gaze away from his face.

We both turn and my hands fall from Ronan's grasp.

'Jake, what on earth are you doing here?' I almost hiss at my brother as he approaches, his arms filled with a ridiculously large bouquet of flowers.

I rush up to him and lean in, seeing that several people are already looking our way, having noticed the new, and unexpected, arrival.

'This is an engagement party. What were you thinking, turning up like this? Our hostess, Solange, is coming this way. Pretend the flowers are for her and say congratulations.'

I pull away from him and decide it will look odd if I don't kiss his cheek, so reluctantly I play the adoring sister. It's hard to relax my face as I do so, then turn back around to face the smiling Solange.

'Surprise,' I say, trying my best to make it sound genuine. 'Solange, this is my brother, Jake. I hope you don't mind him gatecrashing the party.'

She immediately looks across at him as he proffers the flowers, bending to kiss her on both cheeks. It's so typical of him. There isn't even a hint of embarrassment or awkwardness in his demeanour.

'Hearty congratulations on your engagement, Solange, and it's lovely to meet you. My sister said it was going to be a wonderful party. The decorations are fabulous, by the way – you did a great job.'

What a cheek he has! For starters he wasn't invited and what the heck is he doing here, anyway?

She lowers her head to sniff the fragrant assortment of very expensive flowers and proceeds to thank Jake profusely, much to my embarrassment.

'I'm going to whisk him away for a quick chat, but, at some point, we'll seek out Philippe and I'll make sure they are introduced. Ronan is running out of lemons and limes, I think – are there any in the kitchen?'

Solange nods. 'Yes, you go off for your chat and I'll sort Ronan out. I had no idea you had a brother, Lexie, and a very handsome one at that,' she throws over her shoulder, as she heads off to Renée's clutching the bouquet in both hands.

My stomach is churning as I yank at Jake's arm to drag him in the direction of number six. He follows me inside and up the stairs in total silence. When I turn round to look at him, I'm lost for words. He doesn't seem fazed at all; he takes his time to gaze around the room.

'It's bijou, but very you,' he comments.

What on earth does that mean? Is he trying to put me down because I'm not staying in some big, fancy apartment?

'Is Solange a new friend?' he enquires, not at all concerned that he's disrupted a very special occasion, one I was enjoying until I set eyes on him.

I flop down on the sofa opposite him and he follows suit; we sit eyeing each other, uncomfortably.

'She's a friend who works at Versailles. Why are you here?'

He looks at me, rather shocked at the tenseness in my tone.

'I felt bad, being back in the UK and meeting up with everyone, when you weren't there. Lexie, I didn't want you to feel left out and that's the truth. Clearly my turning up here unannounced has upset you and I'm sorry. That wasn't my intention at all. I thought it might be a rather nice surprise, but if you don't tell people you even have a brother, then obviously I'm out of order.'

My mind is in a whirl, then I realise his eyes are now scanning over the mess of items strewn across the coffee table in between us. I sit up, quickly scooping the contents back into Grandma's box and shoving it back into the drawer. Although I know Shellie mentioned the box Mum discovered, he has no idea what exactly it contains. I don't want him picking something up out of mere curiosity and then quizzing me about what I've discovered. I certainly don't intend sharing anything with him before I've spoken to Shellie and Mum.

'What did you expect, given what happened and the lack of contact ever since?'

That refocuses his attention. Now he's ill at ease, shifting position, and his body language tells me that my reaction really has come as a complete shock to him.

'I'm a workaholic, you know that. The minute the plane landed it was all go and I knew it was a golden opportunity. I would have been a fool not to have run with it, but I've never worked so hard. Networking isn't easy when you are starting from scratch and there were times that I felt so isolated, but it was my choice to go and I had to get on with it.'

That's so Jake. Black and white. He had a job to do and nothing was going to stop him.

'It didn't occur to you that we'd be worried about you? And you weren't at all concerned about your family, or what you had left behind?'

He squints, staring at me as if he simply can't comprehend my animosity.

'I knew you'd all look after each other. You aren't trying to say that anyone really missed me, or my input, surely? And I'd heard you were offered a job, so damage limitation there as I'd ensured Mason didn't press charges. Which was what he'd made very clear he intended to do, at first. What else could I have done?'

He shrugs his shoulders, implying he can't see what all the fuss is about. I'm so angry that I don't know where to begin.

'Well, first of all you have a niece you knew nothing about. Secondly, you have a wife and two young boys that none of us knew anything about. And as for Mason, if I'd known he'd made that threat it would have changed everything. I might have hit him, but it was in self-defence.'

Jake looks at me, his jaw dropping ever so slightly before he has time to compose himself.

'What do you mean?' His brow knits together, and I can see a moment of doubt flash over his face.

'Mason lured me to his house under false pretences and then tried to force himself on me. You didn't even ask for my side of the story and I regret panicking now and not making it clear what really happened. But the way you sacked me so publicly and the statement that was issued the following day... you must have known my life would unravel.'

He sits forward on the edge of the sofa, looking visibly shaken.

'I had no idea. Mason said there was an argument and

you lashed out. He was the CEO's nephew, for goodness' sake. When I received the call from the top it was clear, either I handled it as instructed, or you were going to be charged with assault. I thought I was saving your future after you'd made a stupid mistake, not simply looking out for my own career.'

'But you didn't think to check with me, first?'

'I was moving abroad, managing the sale of my house and getting the last of my things put into storage. There was a handover to be done and suddenly I had a big mess to sort out. Lexie, please tell me you haven't spent the last six years thinking the worst of me? Do you really think that I have no conscience at all, or that I'd let anyone treat my own sister in that disgusting way?'

I look past Jake to see Ronan hovering in the doorway, not sure quite what to do. How long he's been standing there, I have no idea, but I beckon him in. Trying desperately to swallow and force down the lump in my throat, I stand.

'Sorry, Ronan, I didn't introduce you. This, as you've no doubt gathered, is my brother, Jake.'

Ronan steps forward, holding out his hand, but his eyes are steely. Jake immediately jumps up, walking towards Ronan, and I can see the handshake is a firm one. The contact between them is cagey, very alpha male.

'I'm Lexie's boyfriend,' Ronan says rather gruffly.

'Oh. I see. Well, nice to meet you, Ronan, and I'm sorry, as I seem to have caused offence by not informing Lexie I was coming. It was a spur-of-the-moment thing. Please, you two, don't let me keep you from the celebration. This was a bad idea and—'

He sounds genuinely regretful and I wish instead he'd

just lost his cool and stormed off. Now I have to handle this somehow.

'Have you eaten?' I ask, floundering to find something to say. Jake turns back to look at me. Over his shoulder Ronan is making faces and it's obvious he wants me to send Jake away.

'No. I dropped my stuff off at the hotel and had the taxi bring me to the address I'd been given. Only Brooke, my wife, knows I'm here. I wish now I'd spoken to Mum, or Shellie, first. They thought I was just going to send you a card.'

'Look, I don't want there to be any animosity today, as that wouldn't be fair on Solange and her fiancé. Ronan, would you mind introducing Jake to Renée and Philippe, then take him over to the buffet? It will look odd now if he just disappears. I need a moment or two to touch up my make-up and then I'll join you.'

Both men stare at me and I can't look them in the face. A few seconds later I'm alone and I collapse down onto the sofa.

'Why today of all days?' I murmur between gritted teeth.

The thing I really can't get over is that, as far as I can tell, he has nothing to gain from his rash decision to come and see me. Did he really come all this way expecting me to what... burst into tears and hug him like a dutiful sister?

There are always two sides to every story. Obviously, Jake's version is very different from the one I've been stewing over. Now I find myself wondering if he wasn't quite the villain I thought he was. Nothing could have prepared me for that; nothing.

25

A TWILIGHT CONFESSION

At the height of the party there must be nearly fifty people milling around, lots of comings and goings, as some head for home and others arrive. The buffet table is cleared and early evening a guy arrives with a huge frying pan, the biggest I've ever seen. It takes two of them to set everything up and light a fire in a huge metal cage. Once the coals are hot, the oil in the pan starts to sizzle and it's quickly filled with wild boar and apple sausages, spicy Andouillettes and the moist, distinctive boudins blancs.

The buffet table is filled with baskets of sliced baguette and condiments. There are bowls of several different types of mustard, some very peppery and spicy; and some milder sauces similar to a classic béarnaise, the latter made from scratch by Renée.

As the light begins to fade the ambience is more intimate and people are happier sitting now, some wonderful French songs wafting out from number one. Slowly people start drifting home or settling in groups, and eventually I can no longer avoid my brother.

Ronan steers us to a table in the far corner, which looks directly across at the gorgeous water display. This was supposed to be such a perfect day and it has been for everyone, thank goodness, but not for me, or Jake, or Ronan, for that matter.

Ronan has continued to grit his teeth and introduce Jake to keep him circulating. It took Jake a while to get over the shock of my initial reaction, but he's a sociable person by nature. Put him in amongst a group of people and he'll find something to talk about. In fairness, his French is pretty good, because when he was fifteen, he took part in one of those school foreign-exchange programmes. He spent a month living with a French family, near Toulouse, and a young man named Luc took his place at home with us. As the youngest, I can't really remember much about it, only that I felt we had the best deal.

Have I always resented my brother just a tad? I wonder. The fact he was older and had more freedom, more ability? That need, as the youngest of three, to be heard, even though you don't really have much to say that hasn't already been said.

'Are we going to sit here eating in total silence the entire time?' Ronan enquires, sitting between us as we stab at the delicious food on our plates, rather than making eye contact.

'You're right. This is ridiculous. Look, Jake, I don't want to talk about the past tonight. You're here now, so you might as well bring me up to date on your news. It was a shock to hear that Mum had sold the house and I am a little worried about that, to be honest.'

Jake has hardly touched his food yet, I notice, but he picks up a chunk of crunchy baguette, opening it up to manoeuvre slices of sausages inside. It does smell delicious and, after having skipped lunch, I follow suit, because my stomach is beginning to complain.

'You can't repeat this,' he says, pausing for a second as he chews, 'but she's tired of worrying about the maintenance of the old house. It's too big for her and, as much as it's full of memories, the last handyman she had has now retired. Mum said that she phones a plumber and he doesn't turn up, so she rings again, and they promise they'll call round to price up the job, but they don't. The same with the garden. It's too much for her and she's had a succession of people in to cut the grass and trim the bushes and hedges she can't reach. She'll find someone good and then after a while they either say the job is too small, or they suddenly stop calling in.'

Guilt begins to wash over me and I'm wondering why this has come as such a shock. 'Mum never said anything.'

'She didn't want to worry anyone. Both you and Shellie have your own lives to lead and it's not in Mum's nature to ask for help, is it?'

'But she told you the minute you arrived back?'

I can't help a little note of suspicion creeping in, as it's so convenient for Mum to live in and help with Jake's family. Isn't that just a little bit too much of a coincidence?

'No, actually she didn't say anything. I paid her a couple of visits, as obviously there was a lot to tell her and I've been a bad son. A bad brother, too, I know that – now. I noticed some damp around the kitchen window and some of the tiles were loose. When I mentioned it, she said, "Oh, I have a list of little things as long as my arm, but I've given up looking for a man who can. Seems there aren't many of them about these days, unless you want to have an extension built, or all of the windows in your house replaced." And I realised she's been struggling for a while.'

'But you encouraged her to sell the house?'

Ronan is tucking into his food, but he's listening to every single word. There is an edge between Jake and me as we talk, and I'm having to try very hard not to sound accusatory.

'No. Of course not. It's been her home for a very long time, but have you taken a good look at it lately? I suggested that she move in to Betterwood Farm for a few months while we get the builders in. It needs a new kitchen, upgraded bathrooms, maybe even new electrics.'

I study his face and scan his eyes, looking for anything that might indicate he's lying to me.

'And now she's sold up, thanks to you.' I throw the words at him because I don't want to leave him in any doubt at all that I think he's manipulating her.

Suddenly he pushes his plate away and sits back in his seat, staring across at me.

'The decision to put it on the market was all hers, I simply contacted an agent who had someone on their books looking for a fixer-upper. The truth is that the place Mum's moving into has everything she needs. Privacy, as it's detached and has its own little garden, and it was fully renovated only eighteen months ago. She's excited about it as there will be no more worries about who cuts the grass, or if a tile gets blown off the roof.'

It's as if he's appealing to me, begging me to understand.

'Because you'll sort everything?'

'When you say it like that it sounds all wrong. I'm not trying to take over her life, quite the reverse. I want to make it easier. This isn't about using Mum, Lexie, why would you think that? Mum offered to help out as Brooke and the kids get settled in. Admittedly, at the moment that's precisely what we need, as I'm busy getting the business off the ground. But Mum will still have her own life and go off with her friends and do the things she enjoys doing. It's not like she's going to be an unpaid servant.'

He seems rather horrified that's what I assumed.

'Your problem, Jake,' I reply, talking very slowly and in the most even tone I can muster, 'is that you don't communicate. You just do things. Did it never occur to you for a moment to at least let Shellie and me know what was going on? It's like history repeating itself.'

'How?' He is genuinely struggling to see what he's done wrong.

'When you flew off, you left behind total chaos. You fly back as if you haven't been gone for six whole years and the chaos instantly returns. Like turning up today. Oh, in your head, and the way it probably sounded to Brooke, it was a great idea. Find your baby sister and catch up, so that everything is fine on her return to the UK. Another annoying little thing ticked off the list.'

Jake sucks in a deep breath at my harsh words, taking a moment to look around the courtyard. It's buzzing with chatter and laughter, the bunting and the twinkling lights adding a delightful ambience to an already beautiful setting. And yet, here we are, sitting here all tense and angry. When he starts speaking, he can't even look at me.

'I jumped in with both feet without thinking and it was wrong of me. I couldn't wait for you to get back, because everything else is coming together nicely. Even Shellie has forgiven me for my absence and lack of contact; she hasn't said as much, but I can tell. I know I did wrong. I didn't mean to hurt you, Lexie, and I'm truly sorry about that. I'd have punched Mason myself if I'd known the truth. I'm shocked he would do that to you. If only you had told me, I wouldn't have hesitated, believe me.'

I shake my head, sadly.

'You don't always make time to listen, Jake. You get so caught up in pushing forward and getting things done that you don't see people backing away from you. I just don't want Mum getting caught up in that way and ending up regretting her decision, that's all.'

Even Ronan has stopped eating now, as the words being exchanged take a sudden turn. The anger has subsided, but the hurt remains.

'I didn't know you felt that way, Lexie. But I have changed in many ways. Brooke slows me down and having the boys, well, it wasn't planned, but it's the best thing that ever happened to me. It's why I've come home, because it reminded me that what was missing from my life was family. Everything I had was centred around work; it filled every waking hour. Every *friend* I had wanted something from me, and I guess I wanted something from them. Brooke saw another side of me and overnight everything changed. She sacrificed a lot so we could settle in the UK because she knew it would change me for the better.'

And Ronan is doing the same thing for me. At least Jake realises what she's giving up in order to make him happy.

Was I wrong to assume his motive in coming here was to interfere in my life? It's strange to hear him talking like this about his feelings.

'Look, guys, it's almost nine p.m. and people will begin heading for home soon.' Ronan places his hand on my arm, giving it a squeeze. 'You were up early, Lexie, and you're bound to be tired. I'll hang around and help clear up.

Perhaps Jake will give a hand too, if you want to call it a day and get some rest.'

'Great idea,' Jake jumps in. 'Maybe we can all meet up for breakfast tomorrow, as I fly back in the afternoon. I have some photos to show you of Brooke and the kids, and Mum's place, as I wanted you to feel a part of it. What do you think?'

Ronan is right. I'm done for today and there's so much whirling around inside my head that I need time alone to process it all.

I stand, allowing Jake to come around the table to give me a lingering hug. When he steps away, Ronan places his arm around my shoulders, steering me in the direction of the door to number six.

'I'll be in as soon as I can. Don't worry about anything, just try to unwind and jump into bed.'

I'm overtired and a little overwhelmed, so many conflicting emotions flooding through me that I don't even try to answer him as his lips brush my cheek. Did my brother abandon me, or did I abandon my brother?

* * *

Sitting up in bed nursing cups of strong black coffee, Ronan and I watch the dawn breaking. As the sky takes on that surreal, early-morning opaque quality and the birdsong heralds the beginning of a new day, I'm feeling surprisingly upbeat.

'Tell me, honestly, what you thought about the conversation last night. Was I wrong?'

He expels a cursory 'hmm' and then pauses for a second. 'Honestly? I'm an only child, Lexie, and it's hard for me to imagine what it's like to have one sibling, let alone two. From what you've told me, it's obvious you are very close to Shellie. You two are very different, though, but it's abundantly clear that Maisie has enriched your life and brought you even closer together. That's wonderful.'

Ronan stares down into the coffee mug, nestled between his hands.

'But your relationship with Jake is more complex, as there are some qualities you share which seem to rub you both up the wrong way. The age gap between you both is bigger, so his relationship with Shellie will be completely different anyway. And, as the youngest of three, you were the baby of the family growing up. You're a strong person, Lexie, and I can imagine that was probably a cause of some frustration for you at times. And Jake is undoubtedly an over-achiever. But you do have similar personality traits whether you like that or not. It's just that you have a totally different approach to life.'

I can see he's trying to be both diplomatic and fair.

'You think this is about sibling rivalry? That I'm jealous of him?' The words sound stark in the gloom of the early-morning light.

'No. That's too simplistic and it isn't true. You simply strive to achieve your full potential; I believe that Jake is more aggressive in his approach and he definitely measures success in a different way. Clearly, that seems to be changing a little now he's a family man, if I understood him correctly.'

'That's a kind way of saying my brother is materialistic,' I point out.

'You asked for the truth. I think that what hurt you most was the fact that you felt he sold you out. But after hearing what he said, I think he genuinely believed he'd made the right decision. It was a bad situation, but it could have had an even more negative impact on you. He made his decision based upon the facts as they were presented to him. You can't blame him for what he didn't know, can you?'

There's something about an injection of strong caffeine on an empty stomach. It's sobering.

'So, you'd have reacted in the same way?'

'No, because I'm a very different person from him. As a researcher, I tend to over-analyse everything, but it's not always easy for me to keep my emotions out of it. Jake keeps business strictly separate and that's a trait found in many entrepreneurs. I think that you're convinced he took the easy way out for fear of upsetting his own boss and losing his precious new appointment.'

My chest suddenly feels heavy. I guess Ronan is right. I felt used and betrayed by my own flesh and blood, so what was the point of speaking up? My brother was lost to me and that hurt more than the gossip, if I'm being honest with myself. It felt as if he didn't need any of us.

Ronan turns to look at me in the gloom and I nod my head in reluctant agreement.

'He'll always be the man he is, but I believe he has genuine regrets for some of the things that happened in the past. And I'm sure you do, too. But people mellow with age and experience; it's never too late to change, Lexie, and you have to allow him that prerogative.'

Draining my mug, I put it down on the bedside table, then snuggle into Ronan's shoulder.

'I never wanted to be my brother, but I did want him to be proud of me. I guess that, after my father died, it was only Jake who really understood how hard I worked to get where I was; I suppose in offering me a job he was acknowledging that. Oh, what a waste of... all those years, when I could have – should have – reached out to him.'

'Hey.' Ronan shifts position, wrapping his arm around my shoulders to snuggle me even closer. 'He wasn't ready, and neither were you. Lessons have been learnt, but it takes a while for old wounds to heal. All I'm saying is that I believe the process began last night. Why not simply take it from there, and see what happens?'·

'I love you,' I say, a little tearfully. 'I love that you understand me even when I'm feeling confused and not thinking straight. You've made me see that it's time to admit I made some mistakes, too.'

He tilts my chin to look at me directly. 'I just want you to be happy going forward and I know that making up with Jake is a part of that. He didn't mean to hurt you, Lexie. Love has the capacity to heal everything and forgiveness will set you free.'

26

LIFE IS GOOD, WHAT CAN POSSIBLY GO WRONG?

Over breakfast at the cottage, Jake shows us several folders full of photos that Brooke put together for him on his iPad. It is rather touching. It captures their journey together up to the present day. From two people who were tentatively getting to know each other, to photos of the proud parents running after two boisterous toddlers.

I realise that the person staring back at me from those pictures is a very different Jake from the one who had originally flown off to the States. He smiles a lot more and, even before the boys arrived, Brooke certainly made sure his life wasn't all about work. Just seeing him casually dressed in T-shirt and jeans, being a tourist, is a shock.

Jake admits that he spent much of his time pre-Brooke in limousines, hotels and conference rooms, rather than exploring the wonders of the USA. They met by chance and went on to have a wonderful year of discovery together, before Brooke found out she was pregnant. They were thrilled and the wedding was simply a formality because the panic was on to prepare themselves mentally and physically for the arrival of the twins. And he admits that he was scared. He tells me that for the first time he felt his life had meaning but he thinks he was being taught a valuable lesson. Success isn't measured by the amount of money you have in the bank, or your job title.

When we say goodbye, it is a little awkward, still. Ronan is right, we are at the very start of rebuilding our relationship and that takes time. But I'm excited now at the thought of seeing what happens when I go home, although I wish Ronan could be with me from day one. It's becoming clear that it will probably be several weeks before he can join me and that makes everything bitter-sweet.

Shortly afterwards, Ronan heads for home, too. He has a busy week ahead of him and a little thrill courses through me as I realise that he's doing this for us. Every loose end he ties up brings us one step closer to starting a new life together.

As I wave him off, I step out into the courtyard. The bunting and the lights are still up in the trees, but the trestle tables are gone, and the metal tables and chairs have been stacked ready for collection. The jam jars full of flowers have been neatly lined up on the wall around one of the raised flower beds and in the warm afternoon sun the perfumed notes tickle my nose.

'Hey, stranger,' a voice calls out from behind me. Glancing around, I see Elliot hurrying towards me.

I fling my arms round him; he lifts me up off the ground for a moment before lowering me back down.

'I'm back. Mia is on the mend and I'm ready to work. I owe you big time, Lexie.'

'Mia must be doing well – you're a day early. Come on in. A lot has happened while you've been away. Are you thirsty, hungry?'

'Starving. I had a snack on the plane, but my stomach is grumbling quite loudly now, so apologies if you can hear it. But I just wanted to get here and reassure you how grateful I am for what you've done for me, and for Mia.'

The day just seems to be getting better and better.

Elliot follows me inside and I immediately start raiding the fridge, handing him a bottle of water.

'Here you go. Right, Mia first. Was it tough leaving her?'

He grimaces. 'Yes and no. She says I fuss too much and now she's starting to regain a little of her strength, she almost forced me out the door. She has lost a lot of weight and her appetite isn't fully back yet, but the doctor says that's only natural given how ill she's been.

'The best thing I can do now is focus on work and making some money. Talking of which, I have some cash to transfer into the account. It's a temporary fix, I know, but I'll bring you up to speed on where we're at with regard to a very promising first meeting. There's been an unexpected development, but I need to sit down quietly with you to go through it in detail. My mouth is watering at the smell of that ham,' he admits as I slide the plate towards him.

'Sorry about the mess of paperwork on the table, but it's my office now. Let's go and sit somewhere more comfortable.'

'Mostly time sheets and bills, by the look of it.' He grimaces as he carries his plate across to the sofa.

Just then, my phone kicks into life.

'Hello?'

'Lexie, it's George. If you want to hear what I've got to say then this is your chance, before it's too late. The choice is yours, but I'm here and I'm ready to talk now.'

The line suddenly goes dead. I find myself staring at the phone, frowning.

'What's wrong?' Elliot asks, putting his hand in front of his mouth, as it's rather full.

'That was George. He says he's ready to talk. Like, right now.'

Elliot raises his shoulders as he swallows. 'That's good news, isn't it?'

'Well, yes. But he said, "before it's too late", whatever that means. Ronan has the camera and, oh, why today?'

I feel exasperated and a little annoyed that George thinks he can just summon me at a moment's notice. Why the urgency?

'Don't stress. I have the old camera in the boot of the car. We can head off this minute if you don't mind driving, as I really do need to eat this baguette, and do you have any fruit?'

I head back to the kitchen area and find a plastic lunch box, handing it to Elliot. Grabbing some apples and apricots, I search around for my bag and throw in a few things. A couple of pens, a small pad, the file in which I'm now keeping my own notes and Grandma's photo.

'Okay. I'm ready. Anything else you need?' I ask Elliot, who is devouring everything as quickly as he can.

'No. I'm good to go. Let's get this done.'

* * *

'We called her *the Rose*,' George says, staring down at the photograph of Grandma Viv. '*Vivian Rose Hanley*. She was one of a kind, that lady. She's the reason we all survived that summer of... discord, when everything seemed to come to a head.'

Elliot is sitting to the side of us, as I face George across the dining table. The room is stuffy, and I wish I'd thought to ask if we could open the window a little, before we began. But I don't want to distract him now, because it's obvious that he has a set agenda today.

'I want to make things clear,' George states rather sternly, 'because I know he's working on that last book and he needs to be told the truth.'

'Ronan, you mean?'

I'm treating this like a formal interview, although I have no idea whether anyone will ever see this, aside from Elliot and me. It could turn out to be the rantings of a man with a grudge to bear, so maybe this is a way for George to get everything off his chest once and for all.

'Yes. We all know why Ronan wants to believe that Fabien Arnoult took his own life because he was bullied. It's the easiest way out.'

Why hasn't Ronan talked to me in detail about this? I knew there was disagreement, but bullying? He can't surely think they were ganging up on Fabien? It wasn't personal. And if George knew about *the Rose*, then I find it puzzling that Ronan hadn't heard mention of her, too.

'He won't publish what I know, because it isn't what he wants to hear,' George continues. 'That's why I continue to refuse to answer his questions. But he told me he's going ahead, and he will publish the last book anyway. The account will, no doubt, neatly gloss over the truth.'

It's obvious they've spoken fairly recently and that's what has triggered today's impulsive phone call. Why didn't Ronan mention it? I have no idea if George knows Ronan will be leaving Versailles but now I feel that I have to be very careful what I say.

'I gather Ronan's intention is to bring the story up to the

current day,' I point out. I wonder why George would even feel what happened to Fabien all those years ago should feature in the final book.

'He knows what people want to read and what will catch their interest. That's what sells books, right? But without knowing what happened, it will be a biased account. The devastation resulting from the storms in 1990 and 1999 will, in his eyes, validate his grandfather's prediction. Fabien was a passionate man to whom the trees and the plants were fundamentally living things, more important even than the people around him. In fact, he could be heard muttering away as he worked, nurturing and encouraging as he tended to his beloved plants and trees, as if they were his alone. He saw everyone else as out for themselves, or corrupt. He ranted constantly about money being thrown at the fabric of the buildings and very little being spent on the gardens and the park.'

George pauses and I can see that the memories are painful.

'Do the nicknames the Bulldog, the Terrier and the Spaniel mean anything to you?' I'm just throwing it out there, but I am curious still about why Grandma didn't use their names.

George begins to laugh, easing himself up out of his seat and approaching a large wooden cabinet on the other side of the room. Elliot pans around, following his every move with the camera.

Opening a drawer, George rifles among some papers and pulls something out, walking back to the table and placing it in front of me. It's a colour photo, but faded as if it has been hung on a wall in the sunlight for a very long time. I peer down at it as George points his finger, stabbing at one of the three men standing in a row and smiling rather awkwardly back at the camera.

'The Bulldog is Maurice Perrin, the chief gardener. In the middle is Fabien, the Terrier, as the Rose used to refer to him. And last, this is me – the Spaniel. She said that Maurice had to demonstrate his strength to keep us in order, because the Terrier was constantly yapping and me, the Spaniel – well, spaniels tend to use their heads,' he adds, tapping the side of his temple. 'Hunters rely upon them to flush out the birds and that requires patience and a practical nature. I didn't always like, or agree with, some of the decisions made at Versailles, but I wasn't a dreamer. I kept it real.'

That stops me in my tracks. This isn't some little code in my grandma's notebooks and I find it hard to believe that Ronan hadn't even heard a whisper about this from his interviews, or from his extensive research.

I even remember him asking if I'd come across the nicknames and I thought he was talking about the notebook I was reading at the time. But did he know all along and he was simply checking, in case there was anything I knew that I hadn't already mentioned?

'And Fabien was, what exactly?'

George makes a deprecating sound.

'He accused everyone of taking the easy route, rather than fighting for the cause. He could be quite offensive at times, calling us cowards. "The trees will die and the landscape will be laid bare," he'd rant. "You will be sorry you weren't man enough to rise up and let your voices be heard," and that's what he did, constantly. But people stopped listening, tired of his continual doom-mongering and moaning. Where did he think the money would come from, when even the project to identify the trees most at risk ran out of funds? He took it personally, of course, because that's the sort of man he was, too intense for his own good.'

George's voice softens a little, much to my surprise.

'And eventually it became too much?' I probe, gently.

'We all knew it wouldn't end well and the Rose, well, she tried so hard to stop him dwelling over what he couldn't change and encouraged him to throw his energies into what he could. Today, of course, a doctor would probably say he was suffering from manic depression and, in the later stages of his illness, total paranoia.

'When the Rose returned to the UK, he lost the only person who seemed able to lift him out of the black moods into which he often descended. It was a bleak time. The stark truth is that no one bullied him, but it's hard not to avoid or argue with someone who is constantly angry with the world and overtly aggressive towards everyone around them. Ronan will find that hard to accept, I know, because his grandfather wasn't a bad man, but he wasn't stable mentally.'

'And yet Fabien went on to marry and had Ronan's mother, so his life must have improved as he did move.on.'

George stares off into the distance for a moment, memories clearly flooding back, and his face pales.

'I can understand why you think that was the case, but it wasn't as simple as that. It was such a difficult time,' he reflects, sadly. 'You and Ronan have more in common than you think,' he adds, looking at me and narrowing his eyes.

I feel my own body language changing as I shift in my seat, straightening my back and easing down my shoulders.

'Fabien was in love with the Rose,' George continues. 'She cried the day she said goodbye to us all, even though it was clear to me she had made the right decision.'

'Decision?' I don't understand.

'He wanted her to stay. He begged her to marry him. Not once, but repeatedly. She saw the difference it made in him whenever she was around because no one else could talk him down when his anger went through the roof. Eventually, one day, she agreed and he was ecstatic. Even before it was common knowledge, we knew she'd given in – and the reason why. He was becoming a danger to himself, picking needless arguments, and if he continued in the same vein, they would have no choice but to let him go. And what would he do then?'

I feel as if I've been punched in the stomach and had the wind knocked out of me. How do I know he's telling the truth? Does Ronan know this? Did he know this all along?

'Another thing you didn't know. I'm sorry, Lexie. It wasn't a secret; everyone felt he would go downhill fast if he was sacked but no one talked about it. The Rose, well, she was all heart. And hers was breaking. Can you imagine what it was like for her? Fabien loved the Rose as fiercely as he loved Versailles. She cared for him and worried about his increasingly erratic behaviour, but they were never lovers as far as I was aware. As time passed, she felt a sense of responsibility for him, which saddened us all but what could anyone do? She would have been living a lie and we knew the truth would come out.'

I try to speak, but on my first attempt my voice breaks up and I stop to take a few deep breaths to calm myself.

'But when she decided to return to the UK to marry my grandfather, Fabien accepted her decision. It was several years later that he committed suicide.'

George is leaning forward, but he instantly looks up.

'Fabien met his wife, Colleen, in London. Think about it. This is a man suffering from severe depression, who leaves his beloved Versailles to fly to the UK for a holiday? No, he went to meet up with the Rose one last time, after she'd asked him to stop writing to her, because it was too late. She was married by then. When he returned, he never referred to what happened, but letters started coming through and at first we assumed they were from the Rose.'

I'm aghast. None of us could have guessed what Grandma was going through. No wonder she couldn't bring herself to talk about her time in Versailles. I wonder if she felt a sense of guilt, or worse – torn between two men, even after she had married.

'When, eventually, he let slip that Rose was married and he had, in fact, met someone else, everyone was in shock. He seemed to get over his disappointment too easily. However, Colleen was good for him. She took charge. Bubbly, capable and caring, she began as his wife and his lover, but before long she became his nurse and his crutch, trying to salvage his sanity. Sadly, the demons in his head eventually won. He was a heartbroken man, who believed he was standing alone, fighting a battle no one else had the courage to defend.

'He was only thirty-two years old when he took an overdose of prescription pills. Leaving behind a distraught widow with a three-year-old child. It shook us all. Everyone who knew him probably felt a sense of guilt in some small way. But what could any of us have possibly done to change a tragic end, to a tragic life? Fabien and I didn't always see eye-to-eye, but he didn't deserve a life of torment. Intelligence and passion are heavyweight companions that can be as much of a curse as a blessing. He ended up locked inside his own little world and it bore no resemblance to reality.'

I feel drained emotionally, unable to comprehend the full horror of this story. Is it really possible that Ronan didn't know about the real connection with my grandma? I suppose it would have been hard for his grandmother to tell the story of her husband's love for another woman – I get that – but Ronan has interviewed so many people. Did they all keep silent, as George had, out of respect for Fabien's memory?

'George, I can understand why you didn't want to sit down and have this conversation with Ronan. And I'm grateful for your honesty in telling me what you know about the Rose.' I pause; the cold feeling in the pit of my stomach feels like a stone, weighing me down. 'But this wouldn't factor in Ronan's wrapping-up of the series, as it hardly impacts upon the story of Versailles. It's too personal, for one thing.'

He looks at me without blinking while I'm desperately trying to put my thoughts into some semblance of order.

'Because he'll present Fabien Arnoult as a visionary who was proven right, when that wasn't the case. A book is either fact, or fiction, even when it's based on stories handed down over the years. Fabien was a good gardener, he will rightly point out, but his was a story of one man's personal battle and that was all in his head.

'Maurice was the one who ensured what little money came our way was spent in the best manner, so he was the true hero. He did a lot with a little and without his sound rationale to keep things ticking over, the gardens would have suffered. The Rose called him the Bulldog for a reason. My concern is that Ronan mistakenly blames three people for his grandfather's untimely death, because he's not in possession of all the facts. The Rose, Maurice and me.'

His words make me feel sick to my stomach.

27

COMING CLEAN

As I drive back to the cottage, I'm tearful as I admit to Elliot that I have no idea how to broach this with Ronan. Or how totally and utterly devastated I am that he hasn't been totally honest with me from day one. Elliot says I have two choices – one of them is to forget the interview ever took place.

'I can't do that,' I admit, with great sadness in my heart. 'Even though I need some proof before I'll believe it myself. I'm not saying that I think George is twisting things, but it's still only his version of what happened. How did he know what was going on between Fabien and my grandma? The trip to London was maybe too much of a coincidence to misinterpret, and I grant that it's likely he went there for one reason only. Grandma certainly wouldn't have wanted to have upset my granddad in any way, so a meet-up in London makes perfect sense. But I can't help wondering if George's version contains some major assumptions, too. Fabien might have told everyone she'd agreed to marry him, but what if that wasn't true?'

Elliot is clearly a bit fazed by all of this and I can't blame him. When he left, everything was very different; Ronan and I were colleagues, not lovers.

'I need proof,' I mutter, almost to myself. I'm distraught and I'm not sure what to do next.

Elliot's eyes are watching me intently, but it's taking all my resolve to focus on the road ahead and I daren't turn to look at him.

'Lexie, you need to tread carefully here. I had no idea what to expect going in, but this is a shock.' He hesitates for a split second. 'Can I ask you a rather delicate question?'

I nod.

'You were the one who picked Ronan from the list of interpreters. Why him?'

I swallow hard.

'Because in general conversation when I was given the list, the connection between his grandfather and Versailles was mentioned. I researched him a little and found out that his grandfather was there in the sixties. I just thought... well, maybe their paths had crossed, briefly. That's all. It didn't seem like a big deal. But thinking back, the woman I spoke to laboured the point and, oh, please – I hope this isn't true. Do you think Ronan put her up to it?'

Elliot has gone very quiet. He clears his throat, ominously.

'I might... no, I did – I mentioned it to my contact that your grandmother was at Versailles. I used it as a bit of a hook, you know, the personal angle, and I remember that now. Look, I'm sorry, Lexie, I had no idea what impact that would have.'

Tears are now coursing down my face.

'I'm in love with Ronan, and I thought I could trust him

with anything and everything. And now I find I don't know him at all.'

We lapse into silence, trying to process what's happened. Can any good come out of a relationship that began with a lie?

Can I forgive Ronan for what he knowingly chose to hold back?

'Are we heading back to your place?' Elliot asks.

'Yes. Why?'

'I think it would be wise to go straight to Ronan with this now. But first, pull over Lexie, because you're in no fit state to drive.'

As we swap places, I let his words sink in. If I delay for a day, or two, I might be able to disprove some of what George said, or at least see if it's motivated by jealousy or revenge. Maybe George was in love with my grandma, too – who knows? If I go through her notebooks there has to be a clue in there somewhere, surely? But how long will that take? What are the chances of stumbling upon the answers I'm seeking as I skim through? This is like a living nightmare and I can't believe it's real.

'You're right. There's no point in delaying the inevitable. It is what it is but I can only hope and pray I'm wrong.'

'I suggest we simply let Ronan watch the recording. But be prepared, because witnessing your reaction was hard for me and there's no way of knowing what exactly Ronan knows, or whether he's able to discredit anything George said. Just take some deep breaths and we'll get to the bottom of this, I promise.'

'I'm so glad you're here, Elliot. I couldn't face this on my own.'

* * *

'You filmed this behind my back?'

My face drops as Ronan's first words aren't to dispute the content but to challenge me.

Elliot and I are sitting at the long, polished table in Ronan's dining room and the interview with George has just come to an end.

I look up at Ronan, horrified, as he stands, striding purposefully out of the room. Elliot and I sit in silence, listening to his footsteps as he climbs the stairs and then returns a couple of minutes later with a whole sheaf of papers.

I stare in disbelief; it appears to be photocopies of pages from Grandma Viv's notebooks.

Ronan rummages through, looking for one particular piece of paper, and waves it in front of me, before proceeding to read from it.

In desperation I had a session with a psychic medium today. She came highly recommended and, as my days here are drawing to a close, I needed someone to tell me it was the right thing to do to leave. She told me: "The lines on your hand show two loves. One will bring you lasting happiness, the other has a link to your soul you cannot deny, but the end is not a good one. The choice is yours."

She was wrong. I have no choice in the matter. I cannot ruin the lives of two good men, when I know that one is beyond saving and given that I now fully understand that my heart has always belonged to Thomas. It always has – but how could I know that for sure, until Versailles tested me?

That doesn't mean my heart doesn't bleed for Fabien. A soul mate

on another level, but it isn't this earthly one. I weep tears of frus-
tration and despair for what I cannot fix. And for what I cannot
heal.

'The Rose accepted his offer of marriage and then she changed her mind.' He throws the photocopy down on the table, angrily. 'Can you imagine how I felt when I found that half-written note tucked into one of the notebooks? But because I love you, I decided to let it go. We aren't responsible for the past and yet you're sitting here, angry with me.'

My eyes fill with tears and I'm unable to speak. Did Grandma intend to send this to someone close to her, feeling isolated and in need of some advice? But who could she ask who would understand what she was going through?

'She knew that leaving my grandfather would break his heart,' Ronan continues, his own voice overcome with emotion as he hands the photocopy to me. 'He obviously tried hard to move on. But the harsh truth is that five years later even the love of my grandmother and his young daughter weren't enough for him.'

I shake my head to clear my thoughts. He's sweeping aside the other issues surrounding a man who was clearly troubled on many levels. If he stopped to think this through, I'm sure he'd see that no one had any way of knowing how fragile Fabien truly was.

'When did you find this? What were you going to do with it?'

Ronan slumps down in his chair.

'This afternoon.' He pauses, his head tilting back and his eyes staring upwards into nothingness. 'I needed to know for sure, before I wrote "The End", that I hadn't missed anything.

If I'd known that George was in contact with you, I wouldn't have needed—'

'To take the notebooks without telling me? And to photo-copy them without my permission?'

A horrifying thought begins to worm its way into my head – did Ronan share so much of his backstory with me solely to gain my trust? Was he simply gathering as much information as he could with one aim in mind?

'But I never left you alone with the box.'

My eyes don't move from his and he realises I want the truth.

'The day that Renée knocked on the door to give you the plant, after the water leak, I slipped a couple into my pocket without really thinking about it. It was easy enough to pop them back on my next visit. The box was usually on the coffee table and then I found myself taking another, and another. I didn't have time to go through them, as by then we were filming and spending so much time together. I know it was wrong, but I had to know what really happened. It doesn't change how I feel about you.'

Elliot shifts awkwardly in his seat, as he proceeds to put the camera back into its case.

'But you lied from the start,' I say bitterly.

'This has been my life for nearly seven years, Lexie. Not just since you've been here. I'm a historian and I wouldn't be very good at my job if I ignored a significant piece of informa-tion, just because it didn't suit me. But can I ask you why you didn't tell me George had made contact with you? I was the one who introduced you to him in the first place, so you owed me something, surely.'

My head is spinning. How can I be sure of Ronan's motives any more? I feel that he's trying to counteract my accusations by turning this around and questioning my part in it. Which sure as hell was nowhere near as devious as he appears to have been.

'What exactly are you accusing me of doing, Ronan?' I ask, trying not to sound as cross as I feel by this conversation.

'Withholding information that is rightfully mine.'

That stops me in my tracks and my frown deepens.

'Ronan, I was doing what I thought was in everyone's best interest. If I'd insisted you were there, George wouldn't have spoken to me. And I'm here, now.'

'You did what you thought was best.' He shakes his head, grimly. 'As your brother did for you and look how that ended!'

'That's unfair and you know it,' I yell at him.

'Why do you get to be the judge of what I should and shouldn't be told, Lexie?'

I look at him, shocked by the spiralling anger he's trying so hard to suppress. And this is the man who claims he's in love with me. I'm speechless with anger and indignation.

'You think you can come here for a couple of months and take the lid off something that has repercussions way beyond your understanding. You knowingly kept me out of the loop on this. Is that because you're disappointed your beloved grandma turned her back on a man she knew couldn't live without her? For all I know, you might have been fully aware of that fact from the start, but you desperately needed confirmation that she hadn't had an affair. Well, my grandfather wasn't like that.'

I shake my head in disbelief at what I'm hearing. He's blaming the Rose for the death of his grandfather and keen to let me know that Fabien never took advantage of her.

'I realised this would upset you; it's upset me, too. It's a truly horrible situation, Ronan, but I had no idea what George was going to reveal. You can't seriously blame my grandma; in her heart the choice had already been made and that was her fate. Staying wouldn't have changed anything, because she loved someone else. She wanted to save Fabien from himself, but that would have meant living a lie. It wasn't meant to be, Ronan, and she knew that.'

Elliot steps in.

'Look, guys, you both need to calm down a little. Lexie went into this with no prior knowledge of what was going to happen. I can vouch for that, Ronan. I don't want either of you to do anything you will regret. Take a little time to think this through, guys.'

Elliot's words make me see red.

'You don't need to make excuses to Ronan on my behalf, Elliot. I'm not the one who has done anything wrong. He took photocopies of personal documents without my permission. He's not the only one whose family is involved here, and he's just levelled an accusation at my grandma, as if she was solely to blame for a terrible tragedy. I'm sorry, but I'm done here,' I declare vehemently as I push back on my chair and stand. 'None of this is relevant to the history of the gardens, it's about one man fighting his own demons and a woman whose heart was torn because she knew no one could save him. If you include this in the book, then you're obviously not the man I thought you were, Ronan.'

He jumps up out of his chair but I literally run out of the house, leaving Elliot to restrain him. Ronan hasn't only shattered my trust in him, but also my heart.

PART III

JUNE 2018

28

ALL WORK, NO PLAY

'Today on the Morning Sunshine show it's time to hit the shops. As summer kicks off with record temperatures, we're looking at the latest fashion trends and zooming in on the must-have items you need to add to your wardrobe. We'll also be talking about what not to buy, because trends aren't always a great investment.

'This season it's all about the vintage look and the fifties are definitely in vogue. Colour is key and it's a softer, prettier feel, full of the promise of summertime romance.'

My smile for the sake of the camera is as fake as the skip in my voice.

'Sasha Regan, you've been touring the various shops to pick out the very best of those seasonal bargains for our lovely viewers. So, it's over to you.'

I shuffle my notes, preparing to sum up Sasha's report after the hand-back, when my earpiece kicks into life.

'Nice intro, Lexie. Smooth. There's a bit of forehead shine going on – Make-Up is on their way over.'

Another day, another dollar, as they say. Only one hour and fifty-eight minutes to go.

Jake's offices sound impressive, but then that's his style. Before, it would have been London, not Oxford, but it demonstrates his brand-new approach to life. He's living in Stow-on-the-Wold; his main priority was that it had to be within an hour's drive of the new house. Work, it seems, no longer comes first above all else. If I needed further convincing that he is a changed man, this is it.

It wasn't until I returned home though, that I realised how close Jake's new property is to both Shellie and me, being less than a ten-minute drive from Bourton-on-the-Water.

As Elliot negotiates the lunchtime traffic, I reflect upon the fact that you never know from one day to the next what life will throw at you.

I lost a boyfriend but gained a brother.

'You are fine with this, aren't you?' Elliot asks, checking for the umpteenth time.

'Yes. What impressed me was that Jake hasn't waded in throwing money at us and trying to take over. He's brokered a deal and it works all round.'

'It's such a relief to hear you say that, Lexie. After the turmoil of the last couple of months it's going to be nice to pay ourselves back and get those credit cards cleared at last. And to know that we have some good pay days coming our way. *The Gardeners of Versailles – a Modern-Day Legacy* is going to be a big success, I know it, and this is just the beginning for us.'

It's true enough, everything is looking good, but for me the world is tarnished, because my heart is in tatters.

Right now, all I have is work to keep me going.

I'll survive because life goes on and I'm back spending lots of time with Maisie and contemplating the arrival of little Arlan, Harry, or Thomas – whichever name ends up being chosen. Then there are Jacob and Reece, two live wires who tire me out after just an afternoon, so I have no idea how Brooke and Mum cope. But they do. So, I'm counting the blessings I do have and trying not to dwell upon this enormous sense of loss that is constantly hovering around me like a cloak.

After cutting all contact with Ronan the day of that fateful visit, filming wasn't quite the same for the rest of our stay. Yvette stood in for him and Ronan refused the ex gratia payment Elliot offered by way of compensation for the cancelled sessions.

I had no involvement with it whatsoever and was surprised when I received a recorded delivery from Ronan with the three missing notebooks inside. Clearly, he'd finished with them and I didn't even have the heart to see for myself what he had discovered. I felt that my grandma's memory had been betrayed by a man I'd trusted implicitly. Not just with her things but with my heart. I slipped them back into the box and sealed it this time, ready for the journey home.

Look ahead, Lexie, I keep reminding myself. Look ahead.

'This is it,' Elliot confirms, pulling up at a barrier and punching in the code Jake texted him. The car park is small and there are only two free visitors' spaces left, marked up 'Betterwood Productions'.

'Nice,' I comment, thinking the old Jake would have said

anything outside London was a huge mistake. But he lived his life out of hotels, as we both did, Monday to Friday, in those days. Getting home each night wasn't a priority for either of us.

By contrast this high quality, period building on Woodstock Road is a prime city-centre location, refurbished to a very high spec indeed.

'Ready for this?' Elliot asks and I nod as we make our way to the rear reception door.

We aren't kept waiting for long and Jake himself appears as the lift doors open.

'Welcome to Betterwood Productions,' Jake says, stepping forward with a big smile on his face. He shakes Elliot's hand enthusiastically and throws his arms around me in a brotherly hug.

'I hope the traffic wasn't too bad,' he adds.

'Pretty good, actually. This is very smart. It's a beautiful building, Jake.'

He nods. 'A lucky find. Right, follow me and we'll organise some coffees.'

There are three floors, and he whisks us straight up to the top and into a ridiculously large conference room. It has the most enormous table I've ever seen.

'It came with the building,' Jake informs us. 'It's growing on me. As you can see, we don't use this room for meetings, it's my office by default. The acoustics aren't good because of the high ceilings and how often do you have this many people in one meeting? So, I work my way around it.'

That's obvious from the various folders that are stacked in neat little piles at regular intervals.

'Looks like business is brisk,' Elliot remarks.

'I'm not complaining, and the interest in your series has

been beneficial all round. Please take a seat. Let's use this end of the boat, as I call it.'

It does look rather like a boat, oval and shiny. But it's a beautiful room with tall, very elegant sash windows and reclaimed wooden shutters pulled back to let the light flood in.

That's yet another surprise I never expected, to be doing ongoing business with my brother.

It seems everyone is happy these days. Well, almost everyone.

* * *

'I'm a little early, Mum,' I say, as she answers the door. She leans in to give me a hug, before I even have chance to place a foot over the threshold.

Stepping inside, I still find it strange walking into this compact little house she seems to love so much.

'Time for a cup of tea, then, Lexie, before we head off. It's so nice to be able to pop into town for lunch together like this. I'm glad things are working out so well for you and Elliot.'

Life is less pressured when you have a little money in the bank and another project lined up ready to go. Once my contract ends as a presenter for *Morning Sunshine*, I've already told them I won't be available and that this will be my last job as a presenter.

'Life is a lot easier these days, thankfully. How are the boys?'

Mum turns to look at me, kettle in hand.

'Poor Brooke. She tried them in separate bedrooms, then felt guilty for splitting them up. They are happier together, but they wake each other up. It's very weird. It's like they sleep in turns. And they are all *Mumma* again, at the moment; which is upsetting Jake, of course, because only a couple of weeks ago they were shrieking and clinging to his leg as he tried to leave for work in the mornings. But that's how it is with kids.'

As I look around, virtually every single thing I see is new, just the odd item Mum would never part with. None of them have any value. I thought she might feel sad getting rid of the accumulation of almost thirty years of stuff in the old house, but quite the reverse. She said it was cathartic, although she did shed a tear as I stood next to her when she turned the key in the door of the family home for the very last time.

But Jake was right. When I arrived back from France and visited the house for what was to be the penultimate time, I saw it with fresh eyes. Why hadn't I noticed how tired it was looking and how many things needed attention? I guess when you know and love a place, you don't see it afresh every time you're there; it's imprinted on your memory. I felt sad, but also glad that she was moving on then, because finally I knew that it was the right thing for her to do.

'I'm glad you came early, because we need to have a talk. A serious one.'

I pinch a biscuit off the plate she carries across to the table and add half a spoonful of sugar to my Earl Grey tea before sitting down.

'Serious? That's sound ominous,' I joke.

'It is,' she sighs. Mum sets herself down opposite me rather heavily, as if she isn't relishing the thought of what she's about to say.

'I had a phone call from Ronan. I have no idea what went wrong between the two of you, but he was very emotional. He asked if he could send something through to me in the post. It's a book, and he really wants you to read it.'

'He rang *you*?' My voice instantly ratchets up a level.

'Yes. He said that if he sent it to you, he was worried you would destroy it. And there was something in his voice... well, I felt sorry for him, Lexie. It wasn't so much what he said, but the way he said it, and he was so apologetic. And earnest. And regretful. And sad.' The way she's labouring this doesn't bode well and her voice is unusually firm.

'Was he, now? Manipulative is another word for it,' I retort, barely able to keep the bitterness out of my voice. There was no way I could tell Mum what happened.

She leans across the table, placing her hand on my arm to grab my attention.

'My gut feeling is telling me that if you don't read it, it's a decision you might regret forever. I have no idea why, but I can't shake it off and it's worrying me. So, no *ifs*, no *buts*, please, honey, just do as I ask as a favour to your old mum. It's only a collection of words strung together, after all. What harm can it do? Humour me, because, whatever he's done, he feels this is meaningful to you. And to him.'

Withdrawing my arm, I prise off the parcel tape securing the flap of the padded envelope and reach inside, sliding out a hardback book. Turning it over and glancing at the cover, I look across at Mum and see that her eyes are sparkling.

'*A Year at Versailles* by Ronan O'Byrne. Oh, my! It's not what I think it is... is it? I mean, I know he was helping you with your research, but you said it didn't really go anywhere. I will admit I was more than a little disappointed. I felt the time had come and I'm curious to know what happened.'

I open my mouth to speak, but nothing comes out as a crushing feeling wells up in my chest. He published it even though I had hoped he'd respect me enough to avoid putting me and my family through this.

'Oh, and Ronan asked me to make sure you read the inscription first,' she adds, insistently.

With trembling fingers, I turn over the first two or three pages until I spot a hand-written note. It's penned in ink and signed by the author, as if it's an official copy from a book signing.

'What does it say, Lexie?'

I read the words out aloud in a faltering voice.

'From Ronan to Lexie.
Copyright Alexandra Winters 2018.
All rights reserved. No part of this publication may be reproduced,
stored in a retrieval system, or transmitted in any form, or by any
means electronic, mechanical, photocopied, recorded or otherwise,
without the prior consent of Alexandra Winters.

Copy #1 of a print run of one.
The author holds no rights whatsoever to the content contained
within.'

'Oh, that's not really an inscription at all, is it? Don't they usually print the copyright details as standard?'

I gaze across at Mum, my eyes smarting as I hold back the tears. I feel a mix of anger, loss, self-pity even, and most of all regret for my part in this. And now he's dragged Mum into it without understanding how it might change the way she remembers her mother. Mum's hopes are up and now she's intrigued.

'One copy, Lexie, that's all that exists,' she utters excitedly. 'He's written this just for you, honey.'

'And you believe him when he says that there's only one copy of it?' I scowl, holding it up and staring at it as if it's some sort of booby trap.

'I do. Why would he have any reason to say that if it wasn't true? Now I understand why he rang to enlist my help. You aren't speaking to him any more, are you?'

Mum is looking at me and trying to work out why I'm being so negative.

'No, I'm not, and he can't earn any money from a print run of one, can he? So that makes no sense at all. Have you considered that there might be information in here that isn't true, or was never meant to be shared?'

The look Mum gives me makes me cringe. Her frown tells me I can't wriggle out of this. She's known from the moment I returned that I was keeping something from her.

'Ronan said that once you've read it, he hoped you would allow me to read it too, so I doubt that's the case. Obviously, he doesn't want to upset you, but if you destroy it then it's lost to us all, forever. He's taken the trouble to write an entire book just for you – that thought rather takes my breath away.

'Look, Lexie, I don't know what caused you to fall out, but this means a lot to him and I think you should do as he asks. Can't you do this one little thing for me? If you don't like or agree with what he's written, you can burn it. But a man who goes to this much trouble deserves to be given the benefit of the doubt. If only once.'

What has he done? Now he has Mum on his side, and she'll think less of me if I totally ignore her advice. Guilt tugs at me as I can't ignore her right to read this for herself, because everything in that box belongs to her, first and foremost.

'How did he get your number?'

'Now don't be cross. People do things for all sorts of reasons and someone close to me gave it to him. I don't want to tell you who that was, until you've read the book. I'm not going to say another word, but when you've read it, I hope you will at least share your thoughts with me.

'Now, drink your tea and let's enjoy a wonderful lunch. I want to ask your opinion about something, just in case you think what I'm planning is a little... silly.'

Mechanically, I stir the tea and then sip it as if what I've just learnt isn't in the least bit upsetting. Mum knows what she's doing, and she won't let up until I've read the darn book.

Annoyingly, my eyes keep straying to it on the table next to me. The cover is a photo of the florist's shop where we eventually discovered Grandma had stayed when she was in Versailles. It's one of the photos Ronan took and texted me when he popped back to his car that day.

'Right. I'm ready to go whenever you are,' I inform Mum in the brightest voice I can muster.

Casually sliding the book back into the padded bag, I pop it into my handbag, knowing that I'm going to need nerves of steel before I can begin turning those pages.

29

A RIVER OF TEARS

Oh, how I cry. Throughout virtually the whole one hundred and eighty-three pages. I read through the night and don't finish until other people are getting up and thinking about breakfast.

I retired to bed early, armed with a fluorescent-pink high-lighter pen, more than ready to challenge every single assumption and accusation. Instead, I spend much of the time wiping off the tears I miss that end up plopping down onto the pages, for fear they will leave a stain.

I cry for Versailles, for the trees, for Fabien the Terrier, for my grandma – the Rose – and for the Bulldog too. Even the Spaniel, George, brings a tear to my eye as I realise, as brusque a manner as he has, he tried his best to be a peace-maker and calm the often- troubled waters.

When I read the final page, I sit and sob my heart out. Instead of the recriminations I expected to find, Ronan pays tribute to each of the characters who were involved in my grandma's year at Versailles.

The verdict? Ronan finished by making a statement so

profound that I feel ashamed I have ever doubted him for even a second.

My dearest Lexie, my love

I cannot take any credit for writing this story. I was merely the scribe. It was not an easy tale to research, or to recount, but I truly hope I have done it justice in your eyes.

What leaps off the page, now it is done, is the compassion that was extended to a troubled man who loved the gardens of Versailles more than he loved life itself. Something that you know I always suspected was the case but struggled to accept in my heart. And I hope you can understand and forgive me for that, because coming to terms with it was a truly painful process.

I've learnt that the nature of life is that everyone's journey is different and, therefore, no one should ever stand in judgement of another. Not least because they have not travelled that same road. Instead, it's wise to feel grateful if one's own road is less arduous, or one is simply better equipped to deal with the harsher realities of life.

The truth is that for me this turned out to be a humbling journey of my own. One that would allow me to cross paths with the woman I believe I was destined to be with forever.

Lexie, I've waited all my life for you without even knowing it and I messed up. I'm sorry for that; sorrier than I could ever express to you in words. As I pulled together the final strands of this story, I realised that if your grandma had not spent that year in Versailles, our paths might never have crossed. You were drawn here because your curiosity sparked an even greater interest in the uniqueness of a place of wonder.

And, poignantly, if my grandfather had not taken his own life,

then maybe I would not have become obsessed with unravelling
the mysteries of the past, while researching the history of it.

I found myself wondering, though, if that had not been the
case, might we have both visited Versailles at some point in our
lives and passed each other by as strangers, as we strolled through
the gardens? And that, I knew, would have been another tragedy.

So, when I say that we have the Rose and the Terrier to thank
for bringing us together, I do not say that lightly, for I believe it to
be true.

This story is their legacy to us and it's the reason we found
ourselves together for our own springtime adventure in Versailles.
Every breath I've taken, every single little thing I've done so far, led
me to this one defining moment when I wrote THE END.

Finally, I have become the man I was supposed to be, and you
helped to give me the strength I needed to accept a very painful
truth.

So, my darling Lexie, this book is my gift to you and along
with it goes my heart, forever.

* * *

'Lexie... it's Mum,' her voice croaks down the line. 'Oh,
honey... I... can't stop crying!'

She sobs intermittently and I wait patiently while she
blows her nose and sniffles.

'I'm brokenhearted, I really am. I knew she loved my
father, but I had no idea just how much, or what she'd been
through. And that poor man, Fabien. Such suffering, such
intensity it literally tears at one's heart and soul.'

'I know. It left me with such an overwhelming sense of
admiration for a woman whose strength and compassion

went way beyond anything I could ever have imagined. She will always be my inspiration.'

'She'd be so proud of you, Lexie. And how beautifully Ronan told the story. Moments of anguish, pain and tenderness literally jump off the page. The words will stay with me forever.'

I sigh. There is only one thing left to tell her.

'On my return I combed through everything in Grandma's box and found a note she'd written to Fabien, shortly before she returned to the UK. Whether she ever intended him to see it, we'll never know. Perhaps she realised after it was done that sometimes it isn't about the words we use, it's about what we do. I'd like to read it to you, though, if you don't mind. It begins:

"Dearest Fabien,

Parting is hard; harder than I thought it would be, even. And yet the day is almost here, and I know this is how it's meant to be. You have taught me so much and my life is richer for having known you.

I have never met a man whose passion consumes him so completely. You opened my eyes to see nature in a way I never had before.

You took me out into the great park and made me listen to its beating heart and I felt at one with it. You taught me that it nurtures us and if we fail to nurture it, then we are lesser beings and the worse for it.

Planting, watering and creating bounty teaches us to respect, to love and to be grateful. You made me understand that we are all a part of creation and yet we are all creators in our own right. And that is the true gift of life.

It is with great sadness in my heart that I leave both you and Versailles, but feeling blessed for the knowledge I now carry with me. I hope in some small way to pass that on to willing ears. In doing so, I will be honouring you until the day I die. You will never be alone. Rose."

Sorry, Mum, I need a moment here.'

Struggling to control my emotions, I take a few deep breaths until I'm feeling calmer and a sense of peace is instilled within me. Folding the note, I slip it back inside the box, knowing that it's time to put it away. I now understand why it was so important for Grandma to share the lessons life had taught her. She was upholding a promise and the pupil became the teacher.

Gathering my resolve, I push my shoulders back, sitting straighter in the chair.

'It's a poignant, yet humbling declaration, isn't it, Mum?'

'It is, Lexie, my darling. But it sums up the very essence of your grandma and for me this has been an unexpected gift and that's down to you. And Ronan. How is he?'

I wait while she blows her nose again.

'He's good – we're good, and I'm waiting for his call now, Mum. Ronan is right, Grandma's notebooks succeeded in bringing us both together, but it was the way she lived her life that was the true adventure. We just didn't understand that until now.'

30

ACCEPTANCE AND FORGIVENESS GO HAND IN HAND

'What a mess we made of it, Ronan, didn't we? I'm sorry for turning my back on you, thinking the worst and not giving you a chance to talk about it.'

'You have nothing to be sorry about, Lexie. This was all my fault. I couldn't handle it, pure and simple. George was upset to think he'd come between us, as that was never his intention, either. We finally sat down together, putting old grievances aside to talk openly for the first time. I've made my peace with it now, and with him. Explaining it all to my mother was tough, I will admit. But the funny thing is that she simply said she was glad I was finally able to let it go. She'd accepted what happened to her father wasn't anyone's fault. Not even his. He was ill, but he didn't know that.'

That doesn't surprise me. Eve is a strong woman who had to stand up for herself and her son from the very start. Learning to accept the things you can't influence is a big part of that. It's the only way to survive.

'What did she say when she read the book? My mum cried copiously, as I did.'

'There is only one copy, Lexie. It's yours to do with as you wish.'

I'm stunned. I thought he'd at least share this with his mother too.

'But it's a part of Eve's history, Ronan.'

'That's as maybe, but I wrote this for you.'

'So, there is no official third book?'

'No. Oh, it began that way, but to put a very personal story into context I had to merge the two. Neither part is complete unless it's whole.'

I gasp. 'You can't leave the series unfinished.'

'I can, because I now understand that there are things which are much more important to me. It's a story that promises to be never-ending, if you really can forgive me, because we'll be carrying it on.'

What is it about this man that keeps making me want to cry?

'You've done a beautiful thing, Ronan. And all I need to know is where do we go from here?'

He laughs, softly. 'I thought you'd never ask. Well, the house is already being marketed as a holiday rental, and it won't be long before I have to hand over the keys. You are sure about this, are you? I'm not exactly penniless, but with no more paid work in the pipeline I'm a bit of a risk, aren't I?'

I groan. 'Don't worry, I know exactly what I'm getting myself into and it's a risk worth taking.'

* * *

'When is Ronan coming?' Maisie asks, dipping her cookie into the glass of milk in front of her.

'Soon. He has to do the packing all by himself and he lives in quite a big house.'

'As big as Uncle Jake's?'

Shellie smiles across at me.

'Not quite, but it's full of beautiful old things and some of them have to be put into storage in case they get damaged. They belonged to his grandmother.'

Maisie's brain ticks over as she continues dipping her biscuit.

'So, when you get married,' she says with a serious look on her face, 'can I be a bridesmaid?'

I stifle a laugh and I can see Shellie has to turn away for a brief moment.

'Well, I'm not exactly sure when that will be, but yes, of course. If I get married, you can most certainly be a bridesmaid.'

'And will you be having kids, too?'

Eek! I need rescuing.

'That's enough questions for now, Maisie. Finish up, as it's time to tidy the toys that are covering the whole of your bedroom floor. I need to have a quiet chat with Auntie Lexie.'

As soon as Maisie is out of earshot, we burst out laughing.

'I'm astounded by what goes on inside a five-year-old's head these days. Seriously, they are hard work to be around even when they're past the troublesome toddler stage.'

Shellie pats her stomach, affectionately.

'Thanks sis, for reminding me about what's to come.'

I grin. 'Sorry. Everything passes with time. Besides, I know you love every single moment of it.'

'Yes, but Maisie was a good sleeper and they do say that you never get two the same. I could end up like Brooke; some days she's a walking zombie.'

'I'm full of admiration for you both,' I acknowledge. 'It all seems rather scary to me.'

Shellie eases herself onto the tall stool next to me.

'It's all about routine, to-do lists and organising your brood. They'll always put a smile on your face and the cuddles alone make it all worthwhile. But hey, following on from Maisie's question – there will be a wedding, won't there?'

I shrug. 'Ronan and I talk all the time, but it won't seem real until he's actually here. He's so busy sorting everything out, although Solange and Philippe have been wonderful. I know Ronan is nervous handing the house over to a management company, but it's the easiest option for the time being. One day I hope we will be able to afford for him not to have to let it out but keep it just for family use only. You should all go and experience it for yourselves and I know he'd love that. It might take a year or two before we're in that position, though.'

'Gosh, that would be wonderful. I'd love to follow in Grandma's footsteps, and it would really bring Ronan's book to life for me.'

As the book does the rounds of the family, even Jake admits he shed a few tears.

'So, Mum's all caught up in this party of hers that she's calling a house-warming. The fact it's being held in the Forest View room at the local arboretum seemed a little bizarre at first, but the new house is very compact, and it would be a squash. I bet Jake's a bit miffed she's not holding it at the farmhouse, but I think she's sending a clear message to us all.' Mum is certainly a lot more lively these days and that's undeniable.

'Well, it's her party and she's never keen to accept our

help, is she? I'm sure she's enlisted someone to organise it for her and I think we should just back off and leave her to it,' Shellie replies, obviously feeling confident Mum isn't stressing over anything.

'Are we taking gifts on Saturday?' I ask, wondering what on earth Mum would possibly want.

'No. I don't think so. The new house is all set up and you know what she's like. If she needs something, she buys it. I thought we could order her a really nice bouquet of flowers a few days after the party, when she has time to enjoy them, and pick her up a nice potted bay tree for the garden. What do you think?'

'That's a great idea. I'm up for it.'

When Mum asked me if I thought the idea of a party was a bit 'silly', I simply said that everyone loves a party. But I thought she meant like a little tea party at her house.

'I suspect the truth is that she just wants to get everyone under one roof to celebrate being the matriarch. I don't think any one of us thought we'd all be together like this ever again and there's a lot to celebrate!'

PART IV

AUGUST 2018

31

A TRULY GLORIOUS EVENING

I've never been inside the Forest View room before, although I often come to stroll around the arboretum, revelling in the seasonal changes. There's something about the sense of peace that descends when nature so completely shuts out any sign of the outside world from view, and all you can see is a myriad of different shades of green.

As we stand on the large decked area with the wall of bifold doors open and the rolling lawns extending way into the distance, the sound of a gentle breeze amongst the leafy trees is wonderful. That intermittent little rushing, whooshing sound as a light summer breeze sends the birds fluttering away. And then they settle, squabbling over their preferred spot on a branch.

'Mum, this is utterly gorgeous and the perfect location. Everything looks amazing.' Gazing around, I take in the huge amount of effort she's put into turning this room into an indoor garden. There's still plenty of room for people to circulate and the kids to run around inside, or out.

'Oh, it was really only a few phone calls,' she leans in

conspiratorially to whisper. 'I can't take the credit for this, although the instructions were rather explicit.'

'Instructions? What did you say? "Empty the contents of the garden centre and bring it indoors, then turn the outside into a beautifully manicured setting for a garden party?" Which, give them their due, is exactly what they've done!'

Originally, I assumed it was going to be a rather more intimate party, but our extended family, friends and neighbours are still filtering in. There are three large circular buffet tables and tall metal planters filled with flowers everywhere you look.

Outside, just beyond the decking area, small bistro tables and chairs are set out within a large rectangular area, bordered by a line of potted bay trees. There is a central island with a collection of hollies, a multitude of shaped Buxus, neatly pruned fir trees and tall rosemary bushes; the smell is wonderful. They must have emptied the greenhouses and the nursery to turn a bland, although beautiful, expanse of grass into a classical little garden setting.

Behind me, the groaning buffet tables are covered in the most delightful array of canapés and the biggest cheeseboard I have ever seen. In the centre of each is a large, tiered, Perspex cake stand in the shape of a tree. It's so cleverly designed and on each tier is an assortment of little cupcakes, tarts and choux buns. Pretty, tempting and utterly gorgeous.

'I love the bunting and the bows. And the twinkly little—'

I stop talking and realise Mum hasn't moved a muscle. She's staring at me rather awkwardly.

'You were only passing on the instructions, weren't you?' I mutter, my heart fluttering in my chest.

'Yes,' the solitary word comes from behind me, and I don't give Ronan a chance to utter another syllable before I spin around and launch myself into his arms. My lips hungrily seek out his as I hug him fiercely to me. I can hardly believe he's finally here and the waiting is over.

'You... you... argh! I can't believe you did this and kept it all quiet!'

I gaze around at everyone and you could literally hear a pin drop. I always thought that was such a stupid expression, but it's true. Everyone was in on this, except me, and they're all nervously awaiting my reaction.

'You wonderful... family, you!' I shriek – hardly the most eloquent of acknowledgements, but they have all taken my breath away.

Suddenly everyone is talking at the same time, but Ronan and I are just hugging each other, and we don't want to let go. I'm speechless and so is he.

After a couple of minutes, Maisie rushes over, tugging at my sparkly new dress. The one I hesitated over buying that day Mum and I went to lunch but am so glad now that I did.

'Auntie Lexie, is this Ronan?'

'Yes, it is, my darling Maisie.'

Ronan has no choice but to pull away and he bends, putting out his hand to Maisie, who shakes it rather solemnly.

'I'm going to be a bridesmaid,' she announces. I burst out laughing, both mortified and charmed at the same time.

'Um, that wasn't quite what I said, Maisie, but—'

Ronan puts up his hand to stop me. 'I have this, Lexie,' he says, as he rests one knee on the oak floor so he can talk to Maisie on her level.

'That's a rather exciting thought, Maisie,' he says, giving her a wink. 'Could you do me a huge favour?'

We're all listening intently, and I think it's so cute that he's humouring her.

'You see the table over there and the big silver box? Could you bring it to me?'

She runs off, eager to please.

'It isn't as heavy as it looks,' she whispers to him as she hands it over. 'Mind you don't drop it.'

He passes the box to me. I look at him, rather quizzically.

'Just something I thought you might like. A little memento of our time at Versailles,' he says, looking a little bashful as all eyes are firmly focused on us.

Opening it, all I can see is a mass of pale-pink, shredded tissue paper. Maisie stands on tiptoe and I lower it so she can look inside. Soon Jacob and Reece run over to join in the fun, not wanting to be left out. The circle of people around us begins to draw closer, as everyone is now curious.

'What do you think it can be?' I ask, as intrigued as the kids.

As little hands begin to tease out the wriggly strands of tissue paper, nestling at the very bottom is a little box and I gaze at Ronan, who is still crouched on one knee. He raises his eyebrows.

'You need to open it,' he declares.

I pass Maisie the big box and flip open the small lid to expose the most beautiful white gold ring, set with a square diamond.

'Lexie Winters, will you do me the great honour of being my wife?'

As we both stand to hug and Ronan slips the ring on my finger, there isn't a dry eye wherever I look.

'I promised you a party full of love and romance; well, this is without doubt a room full of love and I have your wonderful mum to thank for delivering on what was a very detailed list of requirements. As long as we're together we can always surround ourselves with beauty, and Versailles will always be there to remind us of our beginning.'

I take one step back and wipe away my tears. 'It's perfect. You're perfect and thank you, everyone, for being a part of one of the best evenings of my life.'

* * *

It's a crazy night. Noisy, filled with introductions, laughter, and a real sense of new beginnings.

'Eve and Frank couldn't make it?' I ask, when eventually we try discreetly to slip outside into the dusky night together. As we step into the shadows, gazing back at the Forest Room, the proliferation of flickering candles lends that perfect, romantic touch.

'That's entirely my fault, I'm afraid,' he admits as we stroll hand in hand. 'They're in Portugal celebrating Frank's sixtieth birthday and I'd totally forgotten about it. My mother was cross with me, but they are due back in a week's time and are going to drive down to spend the weekend with us. Elliot has been taking copious amounts of photos, because I promised her that she wouldn't miss out on a thing. She berated me because I changed the date suddenly at the last minute, but I couldn't wait any longer. Did I do the right thing? You don't feel I overstepped the mark by surprising you? I did ask your mum whether she thought you'd prefer to plan the party yourself if we had it a little later on.'

'What did she say to that, out of interest?'

Ronan steers me over towards a wooden bench sheltered in the nook between a group of tall oak trees, part way between the decking and the old pond. Far enough away that we can hear the faint sounds of laughter and chatter on the breeze, but we can also savour the quiet of a summer's evening in the semi-gloom.

'She said that every woman secretly longs to be swept off her feet and I should go ahead and do whatever I thought was right. Mind you, she might have paled a little when I emailed her the vision. I went online to find the venue and it was perfect, but it really was teamwork. We had great fun and she sent me daily updates on how the arrangements were progressing. Lots of photos of plants and bunting and cakes—'

He sounds so happy and so relaxed.

'And... close your eyes.'

I stare at him. 'Why?'

'Just close them. I'll count down from five and when I get to one you can open them.'

I do as he asks, and he lifts my hands up to my face, wanting me to cover my eyes in case I get tempted. As the numbers decrease, I feel a little movement next to me on the bench. I have no idea what he's doing.

'Five... four... three... two... one!'

When I withdraw my hands, the lights in the grounds have been turned on and in the distance the pond that I've often stopped to admire has a cascade of water shooting up into the air in a flurry. The uplighters surrounding it create the most glorious chandelier-effect, as the droplets turn into little silver shards of light, glinting as they fall.

'I had no idea the fountain even worked!' I exclaim.

'It didn't. But it does now.' Ronan reaches out for my hand and our fingers entwine.

Lapsing into silence for a short while, I just savour the

moment. When I look back at the partygoers, everyone is gazing out across the grounds in awe.

'No regrets, then,' Ronan eventually murmurs. 'And you approve of the ring?' His voice is low, hesitant, and I can tell he wasn't sure until he saw my reaction for himself.

'I love the ring. I love you. I suppose my only regret is that I so wish the story had a happier ending for your grandfather, Ronan. It's clear my grandma struggled to accept what I think she later saw as the inevitable outcome. I'm sure she carried a sense of guilt for that, throughout her entire life, and that's why she could never bring herself to talk about it. She wasn't one to give up on people and it would have hurt her so much to think of his suffering.'

Ronan extends his arm to draw me even closer and I shuffle up on the bench alongside him.

'She did what she could and, most importantly, she cared. No wonder they all admired the Rose, and it's those same qualities that made me fall in love with you, Lexie.'

I lean my head against Ronan's shoulder.

He turns to place a soft kiss on my cheek, lingering for a moment before pulling away.

'Versailles has always touched people's hearts,' he half whispers. 'I keep remembering something I found amongst my grandfather's personal effects. He wrote that "*Nature is a reminder of the fundamental principles that are the fabric of life and sustainability. Cherish the habitat around you, for it is a healer for all.*" I think what he meant wasn't necessarily linked in with the effects of modern-day living, but he was talking about people's mental well-being. He found his peace when he was alone, tending the plants; it was the only time he was able to truly relax – a little respite from the thoughts and fears that haunted him.'

I turn, touching Ronan's cheek as our eyes meet.

'We don't live in a perfect world and that will always cause those who are visionaries to suffer. But without people like that, people who care so much that it becomes their reason for being, so much could be lost. Plants, trees, animals… you name it. People like your grandfather make us all stop and think, and ultimately that's a good thing, Ronan.'

'I know, but I'm done with the past. Now it's all about us and the future.'

He adjusts his position to throw his arm around my shoulders and we both feel the promise of what's to come.

Ronan leans in to kiss me so softly that when I close my eyes the touch tingles, like a spark of electricity arcing.

Staring down at my hand, I touch the shiny stone that glints back at me, reflecting shards of light from the floodlight situated behind the bench.

'But Versailles will always be in our hearts, for good reason,' Ronan continues. 'And one day, we might even be whisking our child – children, even – off to show them where we met and fell in love.'

The legacy doesn't end with the story contained within a poignant and beautifully written hardback book. It's time for Ronan and I to begin the next part of the journey. I can't wait to discover what the first chapter will hold, but I know the perfect man to help write the story, at some point in the future.

The story of us.

ACKNOWLEDGMENTS

I'd like to give a virtual hug to my amazing editor and publishing director, Sarah Ritherdon, who is truly a real pleasure to work with. You are an inspiration, lady!

And to the wider Boldwood team – a truly awesome group of inspiring women I can't thank enough for their amazing support and encouragement.

There are so many friends who are there for me through thick and thin. They suffer periods of silence when I'm head down, writing. I hide myself away to spend my days with characters who become very real to me and I'm sad when a story draws to a close. But when I pop my head back up it's like I've never been away and no–one refers to the fact that I'm such an erratic friend!

A very special mention to Maisie Rothman, the granddaughter of a dear friend, Sarah. She was my inspiration for the cameo role of five-year-old Maisie in the story. The real-life Maisie is a little girl who always puts a smile on everyone's face, including mine.

As usual, no book is ever launched without there being

an even longer list of people to thank for publicising it. The amazing kindness of my lovely author friends, readers and reviewers is truly humbling. You continue to delight, amaze and astound me with your generosity and support.

Without your kindness in spreading the word about my latest release and your wonderful reviews to entice people to click and download, I wouldn't be able to indulge myself in my guilty pleasure... writing.

Feeling blessed and sending much love to you all for your treasured support and friendship.

Linn x

MORE FROM LUCY COLEMAN

We hope you enjoyed reading *A Springtime To Remember*. If you did, please leave a review.

If you'd like to gift a copy, this book is also available as a ebook, digital audio download and audiobook CD.

Sign up to Lucy Coleman's mailing list for news, competitions and updates on future books:

http://bit.ly/LucyColemanNewsletter

ABOUT THE AUTHOR

Lucy Coleman is a #1 bestselling romance writer, whose recent novels include *Snowflakes over Holly Cove*. She also writes under the name Linn B. Halton. She won the 2013 UK Festival of Romance: Innovation in Romantic Fiction award and lives in the Welsh Valleys.

Visit Lucy's website: www.lucycolemanromance.com

Follow Lucy on social media:

facebook.com/LucyColemanAuthor

twitter.com/LucyColemanAuth

instagram.com/lucycolemanauthor

ABOUT BOLDWOOD BOOKS

Boldwood Books is a fiction publishing company seeking out the best stories from around the world.

Find out more at www.boldwoodbooks.com

Sign up to the Book and Tonic newsletter for news, offers and competitions from Boldwood Books!

http://www.bit.ly/bookandtonic

We'd love to hear from you, follow us on social media:

 facebook.com/BookandTonic

 twitter.com/BoldwoodBooks

 instagram.com/BookandTonic

Made in the USA
Las Vegas, NV
25 May 2022

49359648R00192